The Long Road From There to Here

Foundations of American Education

Edited by

Frank Guldbrandsen

University of Minnesota—Duluth

Kendall Hunt
publishing company

Kendall Hunt
publishing company

www.kendallhunt.com
Send all inquiries to:
4050 Westmark Drive
Dubuque, IA 52004-1840

Contents

Introduction to The Long Road from There to Here: Foundations of American Education

Welcome, dear reader, to **The Long Road From There To Here**. It is my wish to be your guide through this text with the goal of reaching a greater understanding of how schools in America have come to be what they are.

First, you will learn a bit about the various branches of philosophy so that you will better understand some basic approaches to answering such questions as: What is real? How can I know? What is the nature of the good, the true, and the beautiful? What are the principles of right reasoning? It is in the answering of these questions that wise people through the ages have crafted courses of study, curricula for teaching, and learning.

Second. we will examine several of the major philosophies of education, distinguishing one from another. Each educational philosophy is accompanied with a primary source reading, so that rather than having me tell you what these thinkers had to say, you will be able to read their thoughts for yourselves.

Next, we will travel through the history of American education from colonial times to present. There have been a number of major events that have shaped our schools to look as they do, and I plan to highlight many of them. Again, you will have the opportunity to read what famous educators and politicians, as well as some less famous ones, wrote at that time as they cobbled together a system of education from disparate parts.

From the history of American education we will then examine the sociology of education. Under this umbrella we will find topics that aid our understanding of social class, race and ethnicity, gender differences, and others. We will gain insight into how the schools have been a major tool of Americanization and have made true the phrase, Out of the many, one.

In addition to the philosophy, history, and sociology of education, we will next explore some fundamentals of the psychology of education. Within this section we will read a bit about views on how we learn, what is human development, moral reasoning, motivation, and how we are intelligent.

Our last section will include some contemporary issues of education early in the twenty-first century. Issues of equity, assessment, and transformation, among others, are topics guiding our views as to how we shape U.S. schools as we go forward.

If we hope to understand with any insight as to how the schools of the United States got to be what they are today, we need to know the foundation upon which they have been built. That is the purpose of my putting together this volume. Let us begin.

Part 1

Philosophy of Education

Introduction to Philosophy of Education

With a clearer understanding of the divisions of philosophy—namely, metaphysics, epistemology, axiology, and logic—our next task is to look at some of the major philosophies of education and attempt to distinguish one from another.

PERENNIALISM

The first philosophy of education we examine is known as *perennialism*. Perennialists have very clear answers when they ask themselves the foundational question, What knowledge is of most worth? Because students cannot learn everything and because the curriculum of study must by necessity be limited, the perennialist strongly believes that works, writings, findings, and truths that have stood the test of time take first priority. There are principles so central, so important to the development of a culture, that they cannot be ignored. For the perennialist, there is a universality of Truth. It is Truth with a capital T. It is an absolute absolute; all people should be taught this Truth, and they should learn it. Rationality takes precedence. Humans are born with the power of reason, and reason, above all else, is what should be cultivated.

For the perennialist, education is about the shared body of knowledge that has accumulated over the millennia. It can be found in a core curriculum of literature, mathematics, science, languages, social sciences, and the arts. These subjects are valuable in and of themselves, they hold intrinsic value, and they should be studied for their own sake. It is through their study that a student learns his or her identity, learns what is of value and to value what is of value, and learns the inner workings of the universe.

An informed and knowledgeable teacher who knows the classics deeply and broadly, in addition to the particular subject field he or she is teaching, anchors the perennialist philosophy of education. Whenever that teacher enters a classroom, he or she always does so within a context of the history of insight over centuries of what the very brightest people have thought and written.

ESSENTIALISM

Essentialism shares many common characteristics with perennialism but also contains some unique differences. For the essentialist, the common core of study is based on what one needs for successful living in the real world. The essentialist believes in the philosophy of realism, discussed in the last section. The real world is "out there" and makes demands on one, and an essentialist curriculum allows the prepared student to answer those demands. The perennialist, in contrast, might well be an idealist and be more focused on the inner world, the world of thoughts and ideas.

The essentialist curriculum addresses today's needs in society and the world of work. For the essentialist, education is preparation for taking one's place in adult society as a contributing member. There is a clear bottom line for the essentialist, and accountability is critical in the teaching/learning process. Much of the focus of America's public schools for the past generation has been on assessing student and teacher performance, a key essentialist idea.

For the essentialist, there is a core curriculum that looks very much like the curriculum of the perennialist, but with some notable exceptions. The essentialist is concerned with students learning the basics, as is the perennialist. The basics of mathematics, literature, science, languages, social sciences, and perhaps the arts are shared. In addition, for the essentialist there is a need to learn information technology to be prepared to be successful in twenty-first-century postindustrial society. The essentialist might pare back on the arts when monies are tight in order to ensure that students are learning the other core subjects at world-class standard in order for students to be competitive in the global marketplace.

BEHAVIORISM

A third philosophy of education—namely, behaviorism—is grounded in twentieth-century psychology. For the behaviorist, human behavior can be shaped and molded into any form whatsoever if enough of the variables can be controlled. Humans are born neither good nor evil but are remediable to reward/punishment schedules and can learn to behave usefully. Along the continuum of nature at one end and nurture at the other end, the behaviorist sees human beings as natureless and nurturefull.

In countless classrooms, there is a focus on motivating students to do the desired work. When they do it, they are often rewarded by pizza parties, happy smiling faces, more time at recess, sweet treats, or "good job" comments on papers with gold stars. The behaviorist believes that students need outside, extrinsic motivation to do the preferred thing, and it is up to the teacher to decide what that preferred thing is.

One basis for behaviorism can be traced back to the seventeenth-century British empiricist, John Locke. Locke is perhaps most famous for coining the phrase *tabula rasa*, Latin for blank slate. He argued that all humans are born ready for life's experiences to be inscribed upon them, and it is these experiences that make up the nature of each person. Empiricism is a philosophical viewpoint that is Realist in focus. It is the world out there that matters most, and when the world impinges on an individual, then the individual is influenced and changed by it. It is a rather small step then for the behaviorist to take this viewpoint and understand that it is critically important who is doing the writing and what the writing is on that blank slate.

ROMANTIC NATURALISM

Romantic naturalism is a result of nineteenth-century optimism about the perfectibility of the human spirit. Thinkers such as Rousseau, Froebel, Peabody, and, later, Montessori drew on the works of Erasmus and Comenius to focus on common sense, benevolent treatment of kids, and confidence in the good nature of children. Their ideas reflected on the belief that human nature is basically good and that corruption comes from outside influences and urban growth. Rousseau had great influence on American leaders and thinkers during the Revolutionary War period and the founding of the new country. His *Emile* was read by many and set the tone for the education of young men. His views of young women as the helpmates and passive male pleasers lacked feminist sensibilities that would come from others. The German philosopher Froebel popularized the idea of early childhood education with the kindergarten, a place where children could blossom naturally under the tutelage of loving caregivers. Montessori, Italy's first female physician, saw play as children's work that could be structured for self-directed learning as each unique child's development unfolded naturally.

PROGRESSIVISM

Progressivism in early twentieth-century America was spearheaded by John Dewey. Rooted in Pragmatism, Dewey saw education and schooling not as preparation for life, but life itself. Knowledge was to be constructed through experience, through the interaction of the person with her environment. A major goal of education was to spread democracy by living democratically. Science and the arts produce enlightened citizens, people who could solve problems through the scientific method of analysis and evaluation leading to new syntheses, formulations and creations. Out of progressivism grew **reconstuctionism.**

The reconstructionists sought systemic changes of a society that seemed to be off its tracks during the Depression years of the 1930s. Theodore Brameld saw the schools as the instrument needed for building a new social order, one that was more just and democratic. George S. Counts was skeptical of the values and information being imposed on learners by the prevailing culture, which benefited those with much at the detriment of those with little. Out of the reconstructionists sprang neo-Marxist thinkers, postmodernists, critical theorists, and liberationists. Of these, perhaps the one with the greatest long-term influence was Paulo Freire, the author of *Pedagogy of the Oppressed*.

For Freire there are two theories of education. He called the first one banking theory. where there are depositors of knowledge, the teachers; and depositories of knowledge, the students. The depositors are active. The depositories are passive. One knows, the others are known about. One has power, the others are powerless. The second theory is known as dialogic. Each teacher is also a student, and each student is also a teacher. Together, through dialog, teachers and students endeavor to "name" the world, to make it known and knowable.

EXISTENTIALISM

Existentialist thinking was born in the nineteenth century with Kierkegaard and Nietzsche. Kierkegaard, the lonely Dane, walked the town square knowing that a decision must be made either to stand in the sunshine or to cross over the square to the shade. A metaphor for life, we must take a stand either here or there, must make a commitment, without ever fully knowing all the potentialities of our choices. And, in the final analysis, we are the sum total of our life choices. We are our decisions. There are never any excuses in the end. We are forced to do nothing by others or by circumstances. We always have a choice, even if the only choice is to die.

Nietzsche wrote of the madman, like Diogenes, walking about the town in daylight with a lantern shining in townspeople's faces, looking for an honest man. Nietzsche, through the madman, foresaw the death of God. The god of the ancients and the Middle Ages could not survive the twentieth century, the bloodiest in human history, foretold Nietzsche. The god of optimism, of personal relationship and caring would be replaced by silence and the dark night of the soul.

Twentieth-century existentialists such as Buber, Frankl, Sartre, and Camus thought that life is structured individually through our choices. A key factor of consideration of existentialist thinkers is *authentic* being, being true to self and others. Authenticity is what gives order to an otherwise seeming chaotic and absurd world. What kinds of schools would grow from existentialist thought? Schools that focused on individual choice and responsibility would be the answer: schools that grew authentic human beings rather than preparing them for the workplace.

The Apology

—Plato translated by Benjamin Jowett

Men of Athens, I honor and love you; but I shall obey God rather than you, and while I have life and strength I shall never cease from the practice and teaching of philosophy, exhorting anyone whom I meet after my manner, and convincing him, saying: O my friend, why do you who are a citizen of the great and mighty and wise city of Athens, care so much about laying up the greatest amount of money and honor and reputation, and so little about wisdom and truth and the greatest improvement of the soul, which you never regard or heed at all? Are you not ashamed of this? And if the person with whom I am arguing says: Yes, but I do care; I do not depart or let him go at once; I interrogate and examine and cross-examine him, and if I think that he has no virtue, but only says that he has, I reproach him with undervaluing the greater, and overvaluing the less. And this I should say to everyone whom I meet, young and old, citizen and alien, but especially to the citizens, inasmuch as they are my brethren. For this is the command of God, as I would have you know; and I believe that to this day no greater good has ever happened in the state than my service to the God. For I do nothing but go about persuading you all, old and young alike, not to take thought for your persons and your properties, but first and chiefly to care about the greatest improvement of the soul. I tell you that virtue is not given by money, but that from virtue come money and every other good of man, public as well as private. This is my teaching, and if this is the doctrine which corrupts the youth, my influence is ruinous indeed. But if anyone says that this is not my teaching, he is speaking an untruth. Wherefore, O men of Athens, I say to you, do as Anytus bids or not as Anytus bids, and either acquit me or not; but whatever you do, know that I shall never alter my ways, not even if I have to die many times.

Men of Athens, do not interrupt, but hear me; there was an agreement between us that you should hear me out. And I think that what I am going to say will do you good: for I have something more to say, at which you may be inclined to cry out; but I beg that you will not do this. I would have you know that, if you kill such a one as I am, you will injure yourselves more than you will injure me. Meletus and Anytus will not injure me: they cannot; for it is not in the nature of things that a bad man should injure a better than himself. I do not deny that he may, perhaps, kill him, or drive him into exile, or deprive him of civil rights; and he may imagine, and others may imagine, that he is doing him a great injury: but in that I do not agree with him; for the evil of doing as Anytus is doing—of unjustly taking away another man's life—is greater far. And now, Athenians, I am not going to argue for my own sake, as you may think, but for yours, that you may not sin against the God, or lightly reject his boon by condemning me. For if you kill me you will not easily find another like me, who, if I may use such a ludicrous figure of speech, like a great and noble steed who is tardy in his motions owing to his very size, and requires to be stirred into life. I am that gadfly which God has given the state and all day long and in all places am always fastening upon you, arousing and persuading and reproaching you. And as you will not easily find another like me, I would advise you to spare me. I dare say that you may feel irritated at being suddenly awakened when you are caught napping; and you may think that if you were to strike me dead, as Anytus advises, which you easily might, then you would sleep on for the remainder of your lives, unless God in his care of you gives you another gadfly. And that I am given to you by God is proved by this:—that if I had been like other men, I should not have neglected all my own concerns, or patiently seen the neglect of them during all these years, and have been doing yours, coming to you individually, like a father or elder brother, exhorting you to regard virtue; this I say, would not be like human nature. And had I gained anything, or if my exhortations had been paid, there would have been some sense in that: but now, as you will perceive, not even the impudence of my accusers dares to say that I have ever exacted or sought pay of anyone; they have no witness of that. And I have a witness of the truth of what I say; my poverty is a sufficient witness.

Someone may wonder why I go about in private, giving advice and busying myself with the concerns of others, but do not venture to come forward in public and advise the state. I will tell you the reason of this. You have often heard me speak of an oracle or sign which comes to me, and is the divinity which Meletus ridicules in the indictment. This sign I have had ever since I was a child. The sign is a voice which comes to me and always forbids me to do something which I am going to do, but never commands me to do anything, and this is what stands in the way of my being a politician. And rightly, as I think. For I am certain, O men of Athens, that if I had engaged in politics, I should have perished long ago and done no good either to you or to myself. And don't be offended at my telling you the truth: for the truth is that no man who goes to war with you or any other multitude, honestly struggling against the commission of unrighteousness and wrong in the state, will save his life; he who will really fight for the right, if he would live even for a little while, must have a private station and not a public one.

I can give you as proofs of this, not words only, but deeds, which you value more than words. Let me tell you a passage of my own life, which will prove to you that I should never have yielded to injustice from any fear of death, and that if I had not yielded I should have died at once. I will tell you a story—tasteless, perhaps, and commonplace, but nevertheless true. The only office of state which I ever held, O men of Athens, was that of senator; the tribe Antiochis, which is my tribe, had the presidency at the trial of the generals who had not taken up the bodies of the slain after the battle of Arginusae; and you proposed to try them all together, which was illegal, as you all thought afterwards; but at the time I was the only one of the Prytanes who was opposed to the illegality, and I gave my vote against you; and when the orators threatened to impeach and arrest me, and have me taken away, and you called and shouted, I made up my mind that I would run the risk, having law and justice with me, rather than take part in your injustice because I feared imprisonment and death. This happened in the days of the democracy. But when the oligarchy of the Thirty was in power, they sent for me and four others into the rotunda, and bade us bring Leon the Salaminian from Salamis, as they wanted to execute him. This was a specimen of the sort of commands which they were always giving with the view of implicating as many as possible in their crimes; and then I showed, not in words only, but in deed, that, if I may be allowed to use such an expression, I cared not a straw for death, and that my only fear was the fear of doing an unrighteous or unholy thing.

For if I am really corrupting the youth, and have corrupted some of them already, those of them who have grown up and have become sensible that I gave them bad advice in the days of their youth should come forward as accusers and take their revenge; and if they do not like to come themselves, some of their relatives, fathers, brothers, or other kinsmen, should say what evil their families suffered at my hands. Now is their time. Many of them I see in the court. There is Crito, who is of the same age and of the same deme with myself; and there is Critobulus his son, whom I also see. Then again there is Lysanias of Sphettus, who is the father of Aeschines—he is present; and also there is Antiphon of Cephisus, who is the father of Epignes; and there are the brothers of several who have associated with me. There is Nicostratus the son of Theosdotides, and the brother of Theodotus (now Theodotus himself is dead, and therefore he, at any rate, will not seek to stop him); and there is Paralus the son of Demodocus, who had a brother Theages; and Adeimantus the son of Ariston, whose brother Plato is present; and Aeantodorus, who is the brother of Apollodorus, whom I also see. I might mention a great many others, any of whom Meletus should have produced as witnesses in the course of his speech; and let him still produce them, if he has forgotten—I will make way for him. And let him say, if he has any testimony of the sort which he can produce. Nay, Athenians, the very opposite is the truth. For all these are ready to witness on behalf of the corrupter, of the destroyer of their kindred, as Meletus and Anytus call me; not the corrupted youth only—there might have been a motive for that—but their uncorrupted elder relatives. Why should they too support me with their testimony? Why, indeed, except for the sake of truth and justice, and because they know that I am speaking the truth, and that Meletus is lying.

Well, Athenians, this and the like of this is nearly all the defence which I have to offer. Yet a word more. Perhaps there may be someone who is offended at me, when he calls to mind how he himself, on a similar or even a less serious occasion, had recourse to prayers and supplications with many tears, and how he produced his children in court, which was a moving spectacle, together with a posse of his relations and friends; whereas I, who am probably in danger of my life, will do none of these things. Perhaps this may come into his mind, and he may be set against me, and vote in anger because he is displeased at this.

Now if there be such a person among you, which I am far from affirming, I may fairly reply to him: My friend, I am a man, and like other men, a creature of flesh and blood, and not of wood or stone, as Homer says; and I have a family, yes, and sons. O Athenians, three in number, one of whom is growing up, and the two others are still young; and yet I will not bring any of them hither in order to petition you for an acquittal. And why not? Not from any self-will or disregard of you. Whether I am or am not afraid of death is another question, of which I will not now speak. But my reason simply is that I feel such conduct to be discreditable to myself, and you, and the whole state. One who has reached my years, and who has a name for wisdom, whether deserved or not, ought not to debase himself. At any rate, the world has decided that Socrates is in some way superior to other men. And if those among you who are said to be superior in wisdom and courage, and any other virtue, demean themselves in this way, how shameful is their conduct! I have seen men of reputation, when they have been condemned, behaving in the strangest manner: they seemed to fancy that they were going to suffer something dreadful if they died, and that they could be immortal if you only allowed them to live; and I think that they were a dishonor to the state, and that any stranger coming in would say of them that the most eminent men of Athens, to whom the Athenians themselves give honor and command, are no better than women. And I say that these things ought not to be done by those of us who are of reputation; and if they are done, you ought not to permit them; you ought rather to show that you are more inclined to condemn, not the man who is quiet, but the man who gets up a doleful scene, and makes the city ridiculous.

But, setting aside the question of dishonor, there seems to be something wrong in petitioning a judge, and thus procuring an acquittal instead of informing and convincing him. For his duty is, not to make a present of justice, but to give judgment; and he has sworn that he will judge according to the laws, and not according to his own good pleasure; and neither he nor we should get into the habit of perjuring ourselves—there can be no piety in that. Do not then require me to do what I consider dishonorable and impious and wrong, especially now, when I am being tried for impiety on the indictment of Meletus. For if, O men of Athens, by force of persuasion and entreaty, I could overpower your oaths, then I should be teaching you to believe that there are no gods, and convict myself, in my own defence, of not believing in them. But that is not the case; for I do believe that there are gods, and in a far higher sense than that in which any of my accusers believe in them. And to you and to God I commit my cause, to be determined by you as is best for you and me.

The jury finds Socrates guilty.

Socrates' Proposal for his Sentence

There are many reasons why I am not grieved, O men of Athens, at the vote of condemnation. I expected it, and am only surprised that the votes are so nearly equal; for I had thought that the majority against me would have been far larger; but now, had thirty votes gone over to the other side, I should have been acquitted. And I may say that I have escaped Meletus. And I may say more; for without the assistance of Anytus and Lycon, he would not have had a fifth part of the votes, as the law requires, in which case he would have incurred a fine of a thousand drachmae, as is evident.

And so he proposes death as the penalty. And what shall I propose on my part, O men of Athens? Clearly that which is my due.

Someone will say: Yes, Socrates, but cannot you hold your tongue, and then you may go into a foreign city, and no one will interfere with you? Now I have great difficulty in making you understand my answer to this. For if I tell you that this would be a disobedience to a divine command, and therefore that I cannot hold my tongue, you will not believe that I am serious; and if I say again that the greatest good of man is daily to converse about virtue, and all that concerning which you hear me examining myself and others, and that the life which is unexamined is not worth living—that you are still less likely to believe.

Wherefore, O judges, be of good cheer about death, and know this of a truth—that no evil can happen to a good man, either in life or after death. He and his are not neglected by the gods; nor has my own approaching end happened by mere chance. But I see clearly that to die and be released was better for me; and therefore the oracle gave no sign. For which reason also, I am not angry with my accusers, or my condemners; they have done me no harm, although neither of them meant to do me any good; and for this I may gently blame them. Still I have a favor to ask of them. When my sons are grown up, I would ask you, O my friends, to punish them; and I would have you trouble them, as I have troubled you, if they seem to care about riches, or anything, more than about virtue; or if they pretend to be something when they are really nothing,—then reprove them, as I have reproved you, for not caring about that for which they ought to care, and thinking that they are something when they are really nothing. And if you do this, I and my sons will have received justice at your hands.

The hour of departure has arrived, and we go our ways—I to die, and you to live. Which is better God only knows.

The Allegory of the Cave

Book VII of The Republic

—Plato translated by Benjamin Jowett

Here's a little story from Plato's most famous book, **The Republic**. Socrates is talking to a young follower of his named Glaucon, and is telling him this fable to illustrate what it's like to be a philosopher—a lover of wisdom: Most people, including ourselves, live in a world of relative ignorance. We are even comfortable with that ignorance, because it is all we know. When we first start facing truth, the process may be frightening, and many people run back to their old lives. But if you continue to seek truth, you will eventually be able to handle it better. In fact, you want more! It's true that many people around you now may think you are weird or even a danger to society, but you don't care. Once you've tasted the truth, you won't ever want to go back to being ignorant!

[Socrates is speaking with **Glaucon**]

[Socrates:] And now, I said, let me show in a figure how far our nature is enlightened or unenlightened: — Behold! human beings living in a underground den, which has a mouth open towards the light and reaching all along the den; here they have been from their childhood, and have their legs and necks chained so that they cannot move, and can only see before them, being prevented by the chains from turning round their heads. Above and behind them a fire is blazing at a distance, and between the fire and the prisoners there is a raised way; and you will see, if you look, a low wall built along the way, like the screen which marionette players have in front of them, over which they show the puppets.

[Glaucon:] I see.

And do you see, I said, men passing along the wall carrying all sorts of vessels, and statues and figures of animals made of wood and stone and various materials, which appear over the wall? Some of them are talking, others silent.

You have shown me a strange image, and they are strange prisoners.

Like ourselves, I replied; and they see only their own shadows, or the shadows of one another, which the fire throws on the opposite wall of the cave?

True, he said; how could they see anything but the shadows if they were never allowed to move their heads?

And of the objects which are being carried in like manner they would only see the shadows?

Yes, he said.

And if they were able to converse with one another, would they not suppose that they were naming what was actually before them?

Very true.

And suppose further that the prison had an echo which came from the other side, would they not be sure to fancy when one of the passers-by spoke that the voice which they heard came from the passing shadow?

No question, he replied.

To them, I said, the truth would be literally nothing but the shadows of the images.

That is certain.

And now look again, and see what will naturally follow if the prisoners are released and disabused of their error. At first, when any of them is liberated and compelled suddenly to stand up and turn his neck round and walk and look towards the light, he will suffer sharp pains; the glare will distress him, and he will be unable to see the realities of which in his former state he had seen the shadows; and then conceive some one saying to him, that what he saw before was an illusion, but that now, when he is approaching nearer to being and his eye is turned towards more real existence, he has a clearer vision,—what will be his reply? And you may further imagine that his instructor is pointing to the objects as they pass and requiring him to name them,—will he not be perplexed? Will he not fancy that the shadows which he formerly saw are truer than the objects which are now shown to him?

Far truer.

And if he is compelled to look straight at the light, will he not have a pain in his eyes which will make him turn away to take and take in the objects of vision which he can see, and which he will conceive to be in reality clearer than the things which are now being shown to him?

True, he said.

And suppose once more, that he is reluctantly dragged up a steep and rugged ascent, and held fast until he's forced into the presence of the sun himself, is he not likely to be pained and irritated? When he approaches the light his eyes will be dazzled, and he will not be able to see anything at all of what are now called realities.

Not all in a moment, he said.

He will require to grow accustomed to the sight of the upper world. And first he will see the shadows best, next the reflections of men and other objects in the water, and then the objects themselves; then he will gaze upon the light of the moon and the stars and the spangled heaven; and he will see the sky and the stars by night better than the sun or the light of the sun by day?

Certainly.

Last of he will be able to see the sun, and not mere reflections of him in the water, but he will see him in his own proper place, and not in another; and he will contemplate him as he is.

Certainly.

He will then proceed to argue that this is he who gives the season and the years, and is the guardian of all that is in the visible world, and in a certain way the cause of all things which he and his fellows have been accustomed to behold?

Clearly, he said, he would first see the sun and then reason about him.

And when he remembered his old habitation, and the wisdom of the den and his fellow-prisoners, do you not suppose that he would felicitate himself on the change, and pity them?

Certainly, he would.

And if they were in the habit of conferring honors among themselves on those who were quickest to observe the passing shadows and to remark which of them went before, and which followed after, and which were together; and who were therefore best able to draw conclusions as to the future, do you think that he would care for such honors and glories, or envy the possessors of them? Would he not say with Homer,

Better to be the poor servant of a poor master, and to endure anything, rather than think as they do and live after their manner?

Yes, he said, I think that he would rather suffer anything than entertain these false notions and live in this miserable manner.

Imagine once more, I said, such a one coming suddenly out of the sun to be replaced in his old situation; would he not be certain to have his eyes full of darkness?

To be sure, he said.

And if there were a contest, and he had to compete in measuring the shadows with the prisoners who had never moved out of the den, while his sight was still weak, and before his eyes had become steady (and the time which would be needed to acquire this new habit of sight might be very considerable) would he not be ridiculous? Men would say of him that up he went and down he came without his eyes; and that it was better not even to think of ascending; and if any one tried to loose another and lead him up to the light, let them only catch the offender, and they would put him to death.

No question, he said.

This entire allegory, I said, you may now append, dear Glaucon, to the previous argument; the prison-house is the world of sight, the light of the fire is the sun, and you will not misapprehend me if you interpret the journey upwards to be the ascent of the soul into the intellectual world according to my poor belief, which, at your desire, I have expressed whether rightly or wrongly God knows. But, whether true or false, my opinion is that in the world of knowledge the idea of good appears last of all, and is seen only with an effort; and, when seen, is also inferred to be the universal author of all things beautiful and right, parent of light and of the lord of light in this visible world, and the immediate source of reason and truth in the intellectual; and that this is the power upon which he who would act rationally, either in public or private life must have his eye fixed.

On Education Politics: Book Eight

—Aristotle translated by Benjamin Jowett

I

NO ONE will doubt that the legislator should direct his attention above all to the education of youth; for the neglect of education does harm to the constitution. The citizen should be molded to suit the form of government under which he lives. For each government has a peculiar character which originally formed and which continues to preserve it. The character of democracy creates democracy, and the character of oligarchy creates oligarchy; and always the better the character, the better the government.

Again, for the exercise of any faculty or art a previous training and habituation are required; clearly therefore for the practice of virtue. And since the whole city has one end, it is manifest that education should be one and the same for all, and that it should be public, and not private—not as at present, when every one looks after his own children separately, and gives them separate instruction of the sort which he thinks best; the training in things which are of common interest should be the same for all. Neither must we suppose that any one of the citizens belongs to himself, for they all belong to the state, and are each of them a part of the state, and the care of each part is inseparable from the care of the whole. In this particular as in some others the Lacedaemonians are to be praised, for they take the greatest pains about their children, and make education the business of the state.

II

That education should be regulated by law and should be an affair of state is not to be denied, but what should be the character of this public education, and how young persons should be educated, are questions which remain to be considered. As things are, there is disagreement about the subjects. For mankind are by no means agreed about the things to be taught, whether we look to virtue or the best life. Neither is it clear whether education is more concerned with intellectual or with moral virtue. The existing practice is perplexing; no one knows on what principle we should proceed—should the useful in life, or should virtue, or should the higher knowledge, be the aim of our training; all three opinions have been entertained. Again, about the means there is no agreement; for different persons, starting with different ideas about the nature of virtue, naturally disagree about the practice of it. There can be no doubt that children should be taught those useful things which are really necessary, but not all useful things; for occupations are divided into liberal and illiberal; and to young children should be imparted only such kinds of knowledge as will be useful to them without vulgarizing them. And any occupation, art, or science, which makes the body or soul or mind of the freeman less fit for the practice or exercise of virtue, is vulgar; wherefore we call those arts vulgar which tend to deform the body, and likewise all paid employments, for they absorb and degrade the mind. There are also some liberal arts quite proper for a freeman to acquire, but only in a certain degree, and if he attend to them too closely, in order to attain perfection in them, the same evil effects will follow. The object also which a man sets before him makes a great difference; if he does or learns anything for his own sake or for the sake of his friends, or with a view to excellence the action will not appear illiberal; but if done for the sake of others, the very same action will be thought menial and servile. The received subjects of instruction, as I have already remarked, are partly of a liberal and party of an illiberal character.

III

The customary branches of education are in number four; they are—(1) reading and writing, (2) gymnastic exercises, (3) music, to which is sometimes added (4) drawing. Of these, reading and writing and drawing are regarded as useful for the purposes of life in a variety of ways, and gymnastic exercises are thought to infuse courage. concerning music a doubt may be raised—in our own day most men cultivate it for the sake of pleasure, but originally it was included in education, because nature herself, as has been often said, requires that we should be able, not only to work well, but to use leisure well; for, as I must repeat once again, the first principle of all action is leisure. Both are required, but leisure is better than occupation and is its end; and therefore the question must be asked, what ought we to do when at leisure? Clearly we ought not to be amusing ourselves, for then amusement would be the end of life. But if this is inconceivable, and amusement is needed more amid serious occupations than at other times (for he who is hard at work has need of relaxation, and amusement gives relaxation, whereas occupation is always accompanied with exertion and effort), we should introduce amusements only at suitable times, and they should be our medicines, for the emotion which they create in the soul is a relaxation, and from the pleasure we obtain rest. But leisure of itself gives pleasure and happiness and enjoyment of life, which are experienced, not by the busy man, but by those who have leisure. For he who is occupied has in view some end which he has not attained; but happiness is an end, since all men deem it to be accompanied with pleasure and not with pain. This pleasure, however, is regarded differently by different persons, and varies according to the habit of individuals; the pleasure of the best man is the best, and springs from the noblest sources. It is clear then that there are branches of learning and education which we must study merely with a view to leisure spent in intellectual activity, and these are to be valued for their own sake; whereas those kinds of knowledge which are useful in business are to be deemed necessary, and exist for the sake of other things. And therefore our fathers admitted music into education, not on the ground either of its necessity or utility, for it is not necessary, nor indeed useful in the same manner as reading and writing, which are useful in money-making, in the management of a household, in the acquisition of knowledge and in political life, nor like drawing, useful for a more correct judgment of the works of artists, nor again like gymnastic, which gives health and strength; for neither of these is to be gained from music. There remains, then, the use of music for intellectual enjoyment in leisure; which is in fact evidently the reason of its introduction, this being one of the ways in which it is thought that a freeman should pass his leisure; as Homer says,

"But he who alone should be called to the pleasant feast,"

and afterwards he speaks of others whom he describes as inviting

"The bard who would delight them all."

And in another place Odysseus says there is no better way of passing life than when men's hearts are merry and The

"banqueters in the hall, sitting in order, hear the voice of the minstrel."

It is evident, then, that there is a sort of education in which parents should train their sons, not as being useful or necessary, but because it is liberal or noble. Whether this is of one kind only, or of more than one, and if so, what they are, and how they are to be imparted, must hereafter be determined. Thus much we are now in a position to say, that the ancients witness to us; for their opinion may be gathered from the fact that music is one of the received and traditional branches of education. Further, it is clear that children should be instructed in some useful things—for example, in reading and writing—not only for their usefulness, but also because many other sorts of knowledge are acquired through them. With a like view they may be taught drawing, not to prevent their making mistakes in their own purchases, or in order that they may not be imposed upon in the buying or selling of articles, but perhaps rather because it makes them judges of the beauty of the human form. To be always seeking after the useful does not become free and exalted souls. Now it is clear that in education practice must be used before theory, and the body be trained before the mind; and therefore boys should be handed over to the trainer, who creates in them the roper habit of body, and to the wrestling-master, who teaches them their exercises.

IV

Of those states which in our own day seem to take the greatest care of children, some aim at producing in them an athletic habit, but they only injure their forms and stunt their growth. Although the Lacedaemonians have not fallen into this mistake, yet they brutalize their children by laborious exercises which they think will make them courageous. But in truth, as we have often repeated, education should not be exclusively, or principally, directed to this end. And even if we suppose the Lacedaemonians to be right in their end, they do not attain it. For among barbarians and among animals courage is found associated, not with the greatest ferocity, but with a gentle and lion like temper. There are many races who are ready enough to kill and eat men, such as the Achaeans and Heniochi, who both live about the Black Sea; and there are other mainland tribes, as bad or worse, who all live by plunder, but have no courage. It is notorious that the Lacedaemonians themselves, while they alone were assiduous in their laborious drill, were superior to others, but now they are beaten both in war and gymnastic exercises. For their ancient superiority did not depend on their mode of training their youth, but only on the circumstance that they trained them when their only rivals did not. Hence we may infer that what is noble, not what is brutal, should have the first place; no wolf or other wild animal will face a really noble danger; such dangers are for the brave man. And parents who devote their children to gymnastics while they neglect their necessary education, in reality vulgarize them; for they make them useful to the art of statesmanship in one quality only, and even in this the argument proves them to be inferior to others. We should judge the Lacedaemonians not from what they have been, but from what they are; for now they have rivals who compete with their education; formerly they had none.

It is an admitted principle, that gymnastic exercises should be employed in education, and that for children they should be of a lighter kind, avoiding severe diet or painful toil, lest the growth of the body be impaired. The evil of excessive training in early years is strikingly proved by the example of the Olympic victors; for not more than two or three of them have gained a prize both as boys and as men; their early training and severe gymnastic exercises exhausted their constitutions. When boyhood is over, three years should be spent in other studies; the period of life which follows may then be devoted to hard exercise and strict diet. Men ought not to labor at the same time with their minds and with their bodies; for the two kinds of labor are opposed to one another; the labor of the body impedes the mind, and the labor of the mind the body.

V

Concerning music there are some questions which we have already raised; these we may now resume and carry further; and our remarks will serve as a prelude to this or any other discussion of the subject. It is not easy to determine the nature of music, or why any one should have a knowledge of it. Shall we say, for the sake of amusement and relaxation, like sleep or drinking, which are not good in themselves, but are pleasant, and at the same time 'care to cease,' as Euripides says? And for this end men also appoint music, and make use of all three alike—sleep, drinking, music—to which some add dancing. Or shall we argue that music conduces to virtue, on the ground that it can form our minds and habituate us to true pleasures as our bodies are made by gymnastic to be of a certain character? Or shall we say that it contributes to the enjoyment of leisure and mental cultivation, which is a third alternative? Now obviously youths are not to be instructed with a view to their amusement, for learning is no amusement, but is accompanied with pain. Neither is intellectual enjoyment suitable to boys of that age, for it is the end, and that which is imperfect cannot attain the perfect or end. But perhaps it may be said that boys learn music for the sake of the amusement which they will have when they are grown up. If so, why should they learn themselves, and not, like the Persian and Median kings, enjoy the pleasure and instruction which is derived from hearing others? (for surely persons who have made music the business and profession of their lives will be better performers than those who practice only long enough to learn). If they must learn music, on the same principle they should learn cookery, which is absurd. And even granting that music may form the character, the objection still holds: why should we learn ourselves? Why cannot we attain true pleasure and form a correct judgment from hearing others, like the Lacedaemonians?—for they, without learning music, nevertheless can correctly judge, as they say, of good and bad melodies. Or again, if music should be used to promote cheerfulness and refined intellectual enjoyment, the objection still remains—why should we learn ourselves instead of enjoying the performances of others? We may illustrate what we are saying by our conception of the Gods; for in the poets Zeus does not himself sing or play on the lyre. Nay, we call professional performers vulgar; no freeman would play or sing unless he were intoxicated or in jest. But these matters may be left for the present.

The first question is whether music is or is not to be a part of education. Of the three things mentioned in our discussion, which does it produce?—education or amusement or intellectual enjoyment, for it may be reckoned under all three, and seems to share in the nature of all of them. Amusement is for the sake of relaxation, and relaxation is of necessity sweet, for it is the remedy of pain caused by toil; and intellectual enjoyment is universally acknowledged to contain an element not only of the noble but of the pleasant, for happiness is made up of both. All men agree that music is one of the pleasantest things, whether with or without songs; as Musaeus says:

"Song to mortals of all things the sweetest."

Hence and with good reason it is introduced into social gatherings and entertainments, because it makes the hearts of men glad: so that on this ground alone we may assume that the young ought to be trained in it. For innocent pleasures are not only in harmony with the perfect end of life, but they also provide relaxation. And whereas men rarely attain the end, but often rest by the way and amuse themselves, not only with a view to a further end, but also for the pleasure's sake, it may be well at times to let them find a refreshment in music. It sometimes happens that men make amusement the end, for the end probably contains some element of pleasure, though not any ordinary or lower pleasure; but they mistake the lower for the higher, and in seeking for the one find the other, since every pleasure has a likeness to the end of action. For the end is not eligible for the sake of any future good, nor do the pleasures which we have described exist for the sake of any future good but of the past, that is to say, they are the alleviation of past toils and pains. And we may infer this to be the reason why men seek happiness from these pleasures.

But music is pursued, not only as an alleviation of past toil, but also as providing recreation. And who can say whether, having this use, it may not also have a nobler one? In addition to this common pleasure, felt and shared in by all (for the pleasure given by music is natural, and therefore adapted to all ages and characters), may it not have also some influence over the character and the soul? It must have such an influence if characters are affected by it. And that they are so affected is proved in many ways, and not least by the power which the songs of Olympus exercise; for beyond question they inspire enthusiasm, and enthusiasm is an emotion of the ethical part of the soul. Besides, when men hear imitations, even apart from the rhythms and tunes themselves, their feelings move in sympathy. Since then music is a pleasure, and virtue consists in rejoicing and loving and hating aright, there is clearly nothing which we are so much concerned to acquire and to cultivate as the power of forming right judgments, and of taking delight in good dispositions and noble actions. Rhythm and melody supply imitations of anger and gentleness, and also of courage and temperance, and of all the qualities contrary to these, and of the other qualities of character, which hardly fall short of the actual affections, as we know from our own experience, for in listening to such strains our souls undergo a change. The habit of feeling pleasure or pain at mere representations is not far removed from the same feeling about realities; for example, if any one delights in the sight of a statue for its beauty only, it necessarily follows that the sight of the original will be pleasant to him. The objects of no other sense, such as taste or touch, have any resemblance to moral qualities; in visible objects there is only a little, for there are figures which are of a moral character, but only to a slight extent, and all do not participate in the feeling about them. Again, figures and colors are not imitations, but signs, of moral habits, indications which the body gives of states of feeling. The connection of them with morals is slight, but in so far as there is any, young men should be taught to look, not at the works of Pauson, but at those of Polygnotus, or any other painter or sculptor who expresses moral ideas. On the other hand, even in mere melodies there is an imitation of character, for the musical modes differ essentially from one another, and those who hear them are differently affected by each. Some of them make men sad and grave, like the so-called Mixolydian, others enfeeble the mind, like the relaxed modes, another, again, produces a moderate and settled temper, which appears to be the peculiar effect of the Dorian; the Phrygian inspires enthusiasm. The whole subject has been well treated by philosophical writers on this branch of education, and they confirm their arguments by facts. The same principles apply to rhythms; some have a character of rest, others of motion, and of these latter again, some have a more vulgar, others a nobler movement. Enough has been said to show that music has a power of forming the character, and should therefore be introduced into the education of the young. The study is suited to the stage of youth, for young persons will not, if they can help, endure anything which is not sweetened by pleasure, and music has a natural sweetness. There seems to be in us a sort of affinity to musical modes and rhythms, which makes some philosophers say that the soul is a tuning, others, that it possesses tuning.

VI

And now we have to determine the question which has been already raised, whether children should be themselves taught to sing and play or not. Clearly there is a considerable difference made in the character by the actual practice of the art. It is difficult, if not impossible, for those who do not perform to be good judges of the performance of others. Besides, children should have something to do, and the rattle of Archytas, which people give to their children in order to amuse them and prevent them from breaking anything in the house, was a capital invention, for a young thing cannot be quiet. The rattle is a toy suited to the infant mind, and education is a rattle or toy for children of a larger growth. We conclude then that they should be taught music in such a way as to become not only critics but performers.

The question what is or is not suitable for different ages may be easily answered; nor is there any difficulty in meeting the objection of those who say that the study of music is vulgar. We reply (1) in the first place, that they who are to be judges must also be performers, and that they should begin to practice early, although when they are older they may be spared the execution; they must have learned to appreciate what is good and to delight in it, thanks to the knowledge which they acquired in their youth. As to (2) the vulgarizing effect which music is supposed to exercise, this is a question which we shall have no difficulty in determining, when we have considered to what extent freemen who are being trained to political virtue should pursue the art, what melodies and what rhythms they should be allowed to use, and what instruments should be employed in teaching them to play; for even the instrument makes a difference. The answer to the objection turns upon these distinctions; for it is quite possible that certain methods of teaching and learning music do really have a degrading effect. It is evident then that the learning of music ought not to impede the business of riper years, or to degrade the body or render it unfit for civil or military training, whether for bodily exercises at the time or for later studies.

The right measure will be attained if students of music stop short of the arts which are practiced in professional contests, and do not seek to acquire those fantastic marvels of execution which are now the fashion in such contests, and from these have passed into education. Let the young practice even such music as we have prescribed, only until they are able to feel delight in noble melodies and rhythms, and not merely in that common part of music in which every slave or child and even some animals find pleasure.

From these principles we may also infer what instruments should be used. The flute, or any other instrument which requires great skill, as for example the harp, ought not to be admitted into education, but only such as will make intelligent students of music or of the other parts of education. Besides, the flute is not an instrument which is expressive of moral character; it is too exciting. The proper time for using it is when the performance aims not at instruction, but at the relief of the passions. And there is a further objection; the impediment which the flute presents to the use of the voice detracts from its educational value. The ancients therefore were right in forbidding the flute to youths and freemen, although they had once allowed it. For when their wealth gave them a greater inclination to leisure, and they had loftier notions of excellence, being also elated with their success, both before and after the Persian War, with more zeal than discernment they pursued every kind of knowledge, and so they introduced the flute into education. At Lacedaemon there was a choragus who led the chorus with a flute, and at Athens the instrument became so popular that most freemen could play upon it. The popularity is shown by the tablet which Thrasippus dedicated when he furnished the chorus to Ecphantides. Later experience enabled men to judge what was or was not really conducive to virtue, and they rejected both the flute and several other old-fashioned instruments, such as the Lydian harp, the many-stringed lyre, the 'heptagon,' 'triangle,' 'sambuca,' the like—which are intended only to give pleasure to the hearer, and require extraordinary skill of hand. There is a meaning also in the myth of the ancients, which tells how Athene invented the flute and then threw it away. It was not a bad idea of theirs, that the Goddess disliked the instrument because it made the face ugly; but with still more reason may we say that she rejected it because the acquirement of flute-playing contributes nothing to the mind, since to Athene we ascribe both knowledge and art.

Thus then we reject the professional instruments and also the professional mode of education in music (and by professional we mean that which is adopted in contests), for in this the performer practices the art, not for the sake of his own improvement, but in order to give pleasure, and that of a vulgar sort, to his hearers. For this reason the execution of such music is not the part of a freeman but of a paid performer, and the result is that the performers are vulgarized, for the end at which they aim is bad. The vulgarity of the spectator tends to lower the character of the music and therefore of the performers; they look to him—he makes them what they are, and fashions even their bodies by the movements which he expects them to exhibit.

VII

We have also to consider rhythms and modes, and their use in education. Shall we use them all or make a distinction? And shall the same distinction be made for those who practice music with a view to education, or shall it be some other? Now we see that music is produced by melody and rhythm, and we ought to know what influence these have respectively on education, and whether we should prefer excellence in melody or excellence in rhythm. But as the subject has been very well treated by many musicians of the present day, and also by philosophers who have had considerable experience of musical education, to these we would refer the more exact student of the subject; we shall only speak of it now after the manner of the legislator, stating the general principles.

We accept the division of melodies proposed by certain philosophers into ethical melodies, melodies of action, and passionate or inspiring melodies, each having, as they say, a mode corresponding to it. But we maintain further that music should be studied, not for the sake of one, but of many benefits, that is to say, with a view to (1) education, (2) purgation (the word 'purgation' we use at present without explanation, but when hereafter we speak of poetry, we will treat the subject with more precision); music may also serve (3) for for enjoyment, for relaxation, and for recreation after exertion. It is clear, therefore, that all the modes must be employed by us, but not all of them in the same manner. In education the most ethical modes are to be preferred, but in listening to the performances of others we may admit the modes of action and passion also. For feelings such as pity and fear, or, again, enthusiasm, exist very strongly in some souls, and have more or less influence over all. Some persons fall into a religious frenzy, whom we see as a result of the sacred melodies—when they have used the melodies that excite the soul to mystic frenzy—restored as though they had found healing and purgation. Those who are influenced by pity or fear, and every emotional nature, must have a like experience, and others in so far as each is susceptible to such emotions, and all are in a manner purged and their souls lightened and delighted. The purgative melodies likewise give an innocent pleasure to mankind. Such are the modes and the melodies in which those who perform music at the theater should be invited to compete. But since the spectators are of two kinds—the one free and educated, and the other a vulgar crowd composed of mechanics, laborers, and the like—there ought to be contests and exhibitions instituted for the relaxation of the second class also. And the music will correspond to their minds; for as their minds are perverted from the natural state, so there are perverted modes and highly strung and unnaturally colored melodies. A man receives pleasure from what is natural to him, and therefore professional musicians may be allowed to practice this lower sort of music before an audience of a lower type. But, for the purposes of education, as I have already said, those modes and melodies should be employed which are ethical, such as the Dorian, as we said before; though we may include any others which are approved by philosophers who have had a musical education. The Socrates of the Republic is wrong in retaining only the Phrygian mode along with the Dorian, and the more so because he rejects the flute; for the Phrygian is to the modes what the flute is to musical instruments—both of them are exciting and emotional. Poetry proves this, for Bacchic frenzy and all similar emotions are most suitably expressed by the flute, and are better set to the Phrygian than to any other mode. The dithyramb, for example, is acknowledged to be Phrygian, a fact of which the connoisseurs of music offer many proofs, saying, among other things, that Philoxenus, having attempted to compose his Mysians as a dithyramb in the Dorian mode, found it impossible, and fell back by the very nature of things into the more appropriate Phrygian. All men agree that the Dorian music is the gravest and manliest. And whereas we say that the extremes should be avoided and the mean followed, and whereas the Dorian is a mean between the other modes, it is evident that our youth should be taught the Dorian music.

Two principles have to be kept in view, what is possible, what is becoming: at these every man ought to aim. But even these are relative to age; the old, who have lost their powers, cannot very well sing the high-strung modes, and nature herself seems to suggest that their songs should be of the more relaxed kind. Wherefore the musicians likewise blame Socrates, and with justice, for rejecting the relaxed modes in education under the idea that they are intoxicating, not in the ordinary sense of intoxication (for wine rather tends to excite men), but because they have no strength in them. And so, with a view also to the time of life when men begin to grow old, they ought to practice the gentler modes and melodies as well as the others, and, further, any mode, such as the Lydian above all others appears to be, which is suited to children of tender age, and possesses the elements both of order and of education. Thus it is clear that education should be based upon three principles—the mean, the possible, the becoming, these three.

Book One: Emile

—Rousseau translated by Barbara Foxley

Contents

Everything is good as it leaves the hands of the author of things, everything degenerates in the hands of man. He forces one soil to nourish the products of another, one tree to bear the fruits of another. He mixes and confuses the climates, the elements, the seasons. He mutilates his dog, his horse, his slave. He turns everything upside down, he disfigures everything, he loves deformities, monsters. He wants nothing as nature made it, not even man himself. For him man must be trained like a saddle-horse; he must be shaped according to the fashion, like trees in his garden.

Without this everything would be even worse; our species was not made to remain only half-finished. Under existing conditions a man left to himself from birth would be the most disfigured of all. Prejudice, authority, necessity, example—all the social conditions in which we find ourselves submerged—would stifle nature in him and put nothing in its place. Human nature would be like a seedling that chance had sown in the midst of the highway, bent this way and that and soon crushed by the passers-by.

It is you whom I address, tender, foresighted mother—you who know how to stay away from the busy highway and protect the growing seedling from the impact of human opinion! Cultivate and water the young plant before it dies; its fruit will one day be your delight. Early on, form an enclosure around your child's soul. Someone else can mark its circumference, but you alone must build the fence.

Plants are fashioned by cultivation, man by education. If a man were born tall and strong, his size and strength would be of no good to him until he had learned to use them; they would even harm him by preventing others from wanting to assist him. Left to himself he would die of misery before he knew his needs. We lament the helplessness of infancy; we fail to perceive that the human race would have perished had not man begun by being a child.

We are born weak, we need strength; we are born lacking everything, we need aid; we are born stupid, we need judgment. All that we lack at birth and that we need when we are grown is given by education.

This education comes to us from nature, from men, or from things. The inner growth of our organs and faculties is the education of nature, the use we learn to make of this growth is the education of men, and what we gain by our experience of our surroundings is the education of things.

Thus we are each taught by three masters. The pupil in whom their diverse lessons conflict is poorly raised and will never be in harmony with himself; he in whom they all agree on the same points and tend towards the same ends goes straight to his goal and lives consistently. The latter is well raised.

Now of these three factors in education, the education of nature is wholly beyond our control; that of things is only partly in our power; the education of men is the only one of which we are truly the master. And even here our power is largely illusory, for who can hope to direct every word and action of all those who surround a child?

As much therefore as education is an art, it is almost impossible that it succeed, since the coordination necessary to its success depends on no one person. All one can do by one's own efforts is to more or less approach the goal. One needs luck to attain it.

What is this goal? It is the goal of nature, that has just been proved. Since the coordination of the three educations is necessary to their perfection, the two that we can control must follow the lead of that which is beyond our control. Perhaps this word Nature has too vague a meaning. Let us try to define it.

Nature, we are told, is merely habit. What does this signify? Are there not habits formed under compulsion, habits which never stifle nature? Such, for example, is the habit of plants that have had their vertical direction altered. Once given liberty, the plant keeps the shape it was forced into. And yet for all that, the sap has not changed its original direction, and any new growth the plant makes will be vertical. It is the same with the inclinations of man. As long as we stay in the same condition we will keep those inclinations that result from habit and which are the least natural to us. But as soon as the situation changes, habit ceases and nature reasserts itself. Education is certainly only a habit, for there are people who forget or lose their education and others who keep it. Whence comes this difference? If we restrict the name of nature to those habits that conform to nature, we can spare ourselves any confusion.

We are born sensitive and from our birth onwards we are affected in various ways by the objects that surround us. As soon as we have, so to speak, consciousness of our sensations, we are disposed to seek out or shun the things that cause them, at first because they are pleasant or unpleasant, then because they suit us or not, and finally because of judgments of them formed by means of the ideas of happiness and goodness which reason gives us. These tendencies gain strength and permanence as we become more sensitive and more enlightened. But once they are constrained by our habits, they become more or less corrupted by our opinions. Before this change they are what I call nature within us.

It is thus to these primitive dispositions that everything should be related, and that would be possible if our three modes of education merely differed from one another. But what can be done when they are opposed, when instead of raising a man for himself one wishes to raise him for others? Then harmony becomes impossible. Forced to combat either nature or social institutions, you must choose between making a man and making a citizen, for you cannot do both at the same time.

All partial societies, when they are tightly knit and well united, are alienated from the larger society. Every patriot acts coldly towards foreigners; they are only men, and nothing to him. This defect is inevitable but of little importance. The essential thing is to be good to the people with whom one lives. Abroad, the Spartan was selfish, grasping, and unjust; yet unselfishness, justice, and harmony ruled within his home. Distrust those cosmopolitans who search far in their books for duties that they neglect to fulfil towards those around them. Such philosophers love the Tartars to so as to be spared from loving their neighbours.

Natural man is everything for himself. He is the numerical unit, the absolute whole, accountable only to himself or to his own kind. Civil man is only a fractional unit dependent on the denominator, whose value is in his relationship with the whole, that is, the social body. Good social institutions are those that know best how to denature man, to take away his absolute existence in order to give him a relative one, and to transport the "me" into a common unity so that each individual no longer regards himself as one but as a part of the unity and is sensitive only to the whole. A citizen of Rome was neither Caius nor Lucius, he was a Roman; he even loved his country better than his life. Regulus claimed he was a Carthaginian, as having become the property of his masters. In his status of foreigner he refused to sit in the Roman Senate; a Carthaginian had to order him to do so. He was indignant when they tried to save his life. He conquered, and returned in triumph to die by torture. There is no similarity between Regulus and the men of our own day.

The Spartan Pedaretes presented himself for admission to the council of the Three Hundred and was rejected; he went away rejoicing that there were three hundred Spartans better than himself. I suppose he was in earnest; there is no reason to doubt it. That was a citizen.

A Spartan mother had five sons in the army and awaited news of the battle. A Helot arrived; trembling she asked his news. "Your five sons have been killed." "Vile slave, was that what I asked you?" "We have won the victory." She ran to the temple to give thanks to the gods. That was a citizen.

He who in the civil order wishes to preserve the primacy of the sentiments of nature does not know what he wants. Always in contradiction with himself, always floating between his wishes and his duties, he will be neither a man nor a citizen. He will be good neither for himself nor for others. He will be a man of our day—a Frenchman, an Englishman, a bourgeois. He will be nothing.

To be something, to be oneself, and always at one with oneself, one must act as one speaks. One must be decisive about what course to take and must follow that course with vigour and persistence. I am waiting to be shown this prodigy to decide whether he is man or citizen, or how he manages to be both.

From these necessarily opposite aims come two contrary forms of education—one is public and common, the other individual and domestic.

Do you wish to get an idea of public education? Read Plato's *Republic*. Those who merely judge books by their titles take this for a treatise on politics, but it is the finest treatise on education ever written.

When people wish to go back to a land of fantasies they cite Plato's institutions. But had Lycurgus put forth his system only in writing, I would have found it to be far more impracticable than Plato's. Plato sought only to purify man's heart, whereas Lycurgus denatured it.

Public institutions do not and cannot exist, for where there is no longer a homeland there can no longer be citizens. These two words, homeland and citizen, ought to be erased from modern languages. I know very well the reason for this but I do not want to discuss it here; it has nothing to do with my subject.

I do not consider our ridiculous colleges as public institutions. Nor do I count the education of society, for this education, facing two ways at once, achieves nothing. It is only fit to turn out double men, always seeming to relate everything to others while actually relating nothing to anyone but themselves. These forms of display are common to everybody and deceive no one. They are so much wasted effort.

From these contradictions arise the one which we experience ceaselessly within ourselves. Drawn this way by nature and that way by men, forced to divide ourselves between divergent impulses, we make a compromise and reach neither goal. Thus buffeted and floating throughout the course of our lives, we end it without having been able to be in harmony with ourselves—and without having done anything good either for ourselves or for others.

There remains finally domestic education or the education of nature. But what will a man raised uniquely for himself become for others? If perhaps the proposed double aim could be resolved into one, then by removing man's contradictions we would remove a great obstacle to his happiness. To judge you must see this man full-grown; you must have observed his inclinations, watched his progress, followed his steps. In a word, natural man would have to be known. When you have read this work, I think you will have made some progress in this research.

What must be done to form this rare man? Without a doubt, very much: it is to prevent anything from being done. When one wishes to go against the wind one can tack; but to keep one's position in a stormy sea one must cast anchor. Beware, young pilot, lest your boat slip its cable or drag its anchor before you know it.

In the social order where each has his own place a man must be educated for it. If an individual formed for a particular social position happens to leave that position, he is fit for nothing else. His education is only useful when fate agrees with his parents' choice. If not, education harms the student, if only by the prejudices it has given him. In Egypt, where the son was compelled to adopt his father's calling, education had at least a settled aim. But with us, where only the social ranks remain and the men who form them are constantly changing, no one knows if raising one's son for his own class may actually be working against him.

In the natural order since men are all equal their common vocation is that of man. And whoever is well-raised for that calling cannot badly fulfill anything that relates to it. Whether my pupil is destined for the army, the church, or the law, is of little import. Before his parents chose a vocation for him, nature called him to human life. Life is the trade I want to teach him. Leaving my hands I grant you he will be neither a magistrate, a soldier, nor a priest; he will be first of all a man. All that a man ought to be he will learn as quickly as another. In vain can fortune change his station; he will always be in his right place. "*Ocupavi te, fortuna, atque cepi; omnesque aditus tuos interclusi, ut ad me aspirare non posses.*"

Our true study is that of the human condition. Those who can best endure the good and evil of life are in my view the best educated. Hence it follows that true education consists less in precept than in practice. We begin to learn when we begin to live; our education begins with ourselves. Our first teacher is our nurse. Moreover this word "educatio" had with the ancients another meaning that we no longer give it—it meant "nurture." "*Educit obstetrix,*" says Varro. "*Educat nutrix, instituit pedagogus, docet magister.*" Thus, education, discipline, and instruction are three things as different in their purpose as the nurse, the preceptor, and the master. But these distinctions are undesirable and the child should only follow one guide.

We must therefore look at the general rather than the particular, and consider our pupil as man in the abstract, man exposed to all the accidents of human life. If men were born attached to the soil of one country, if one season lasted all the year round, if every man's fortune were so firmly grasped that he could never lose it, then the established method of education would be good in certain ways: the child raised for his own place in society would never leave it, and he would never be exposed to the difficulties of another. But given the mobility of human affairs, the restless and uneasy spirit of this century which turns everything upside down with each generation, can we conceive a more senseless plan than to raise a child as if he will never leave his room, as if he will always have his servants about him? If the poor creature takes a single step on the ground, if he descends the social ladder by a single rung, he is lost. This is not teaching him to bear pain; it is training him to feel it.

People think only of preserving their child's life; this is not enough. He must be taught to preserve himself as a man, to bear the blows of fate, to brave wealth and poverty, to live if necessary among the snows of Iceland or on the scorching rocks of Malta. In vain you guard against death: he will nevertheless have to die, and even if you do not kill him with your precautions, they are ill-conceived. It is less a question of keeping him from dying than of making him live. To live is not to breathe but to act. It is to make use of our organs, our senses, our faculties, of all the parts of ourselves which give us the sentiment of our existence. The man who has lived the most is not he who has counted the most years but he who has most felt life. A man may be buried at a hundred who has been dead since his birth. He would have gained more by dying young: at least he would have lived up until that time.

All our wisdom consists of servile prejudices; our customs consist in subjection, discomfort, constraint. Civil man is born, lives, and dies in slavery. At his birth the infant is bound up in swaddling clothes; at his death he is nailed down in his coffin. As long as he keeps a human form he is enchained by by our institutions.

It is said that many midwives profess to improve the shape of the infant's head by rubbing, and they are allowed to do this. Our heads are not good enough as God made them; they must be moulded outside by the nurse and inside by the philosophers. The Caribs are better off than we are.

"The child has hardly left the mother's womb, it has hardly begun to move and stretch its limbs, when it is given new bonds. It is wrapped in swaddling bands, laid down with its head fixed, its legs stretched out, and its arms by its sides; it is wound round with linen and bandages of all sorts so that it cannot move. The child is fortunate if it has room to breathe and if it is laid on its side so that any water which should flow from its mouth can escape; for it is not free to turn its head on one side for this purpose."

The new-born child needs to stir and stretch his limbs to free them from the stiffness resulting from being curled up so long. His limbs are stretched indeed, but he is not allowed to move them. Even the head is confined by a cap. One would think they were afraid the child should look as if he were alive.

As a result the internal impulses which should lead to growth find an insurmountable obstacle in the way of the necessary movements. The child exhausts his strength in vain struggles, or he gains strength very slowly. He was freer and less constrained in the womb; he has gained nothing by birth.

The inaction, the constraint to which the child's limbs are subjected, can only hinder the circulation of the blood and bodily fluids; it can only limit the child's growth in size and strength and injure its constitution. In places where such absurd precautions are unknown, the men are tall, strong, and well-made. The countries where children are swaddled swarm with hunch-backs, the lame, the bowlegged, the arthritic, and people with every kind of deformity. In our fear that the body should become deformed by free movement, we hasten to deform it by putting it in a press. We willfully make our children crippled by preventing them from disabling themselves.

Might not such a cruel constraint influence their humor as well as their temperament? Their first feeling is one of sadness and of pain. They are confronted by obstacles with each necessary movement. More miserable than a criminal in chains, they make vain efforts, they become angry, they cry. Their first words you say are tears. I believe it. You thwart them from birth. The first gifts they receive from you are chains, the first treatment they experience is torture. Having nothing that is free but their voice, why wouldn't they use it to complain? They cry from the pains that you give them. Thus fettered you would cry louder than they.

Whence comes this unreasonable custom? From an unnatural practice. Since mothers despise their primary duty and do not wish to nurse their own children, they have had to entrust them to mercenary women. These women thus become mothers to a stranger's children, who by nature mean so little to them that they seek only to spare themselves trouble. A child unswaddled would need constant watching; well swaddled it is cast into a corner and its cries are ignored. As long as the nurse's negligence escapes notice, as long as the nursling does not break its arms or legs, what matter if it dies or becomes a weakling for life? Its limbs are kept safe at the expense of its body, and if anything goes wrong it is not the nurse's fault.

These gentle mothers, having gotten rid of their babies, devote themselves gaily to the pleasures of the town. Do they know how their children are being treated in the villages? If the nurse is at all busy, the child is hung up on a nail like a bundle of clothes and is left crucified while the nurse goes leisurely about her business. All those who have been found in this position were purple in the face. Their tightly bandaged chest prevented the circulation of the blood, and it went to the head. The patient was considered very quiet because he had not strength to cry. How long a child might survive under such conditions I do not know, but it could not be long. That, I suppose, is one of the chief advantages of swaddling clothes.

It is claimed that infants left free would assume faulty positions and make movements which might injure the proper development of their limbs. This is one of the vain rationalizations of our false wisdom which experience has never confirmed. Out of the multitude of children who grow up with the full use of their limbs among nations wiser than ourselves, you never find one who hurts himself or maims himself; their movements are too feeble to be dangerous, and when they assume an injurious position, pain warns them to change it.

We have not yet decided to swaddle our kittens and puppies; are they any the worse for this neglect? Children are heavier, I admit, but in proportion they are also weaker. They can scarcely move, how could they hurt themselves? If you lay them on their backs, they will lie there till they die, like turtles, unable to turn itself over.

Not content with having ceased to suckle their children, women no longer even wish to do it. The consequence is natural. Once motherhood becomes a burden means are found to avoid it. They will make their work useless in order to begin it over again, and they thus distort, to the prejudice of the species, the charm which was given them for its increase. This practice, along with other causes of depopulation, forebodes the coming fate of Europe. The sciences, arts, philosophy and customs that are generated will not be long in reducing Europe to a desert. It will be the home of wild beasts, and its inhabitants will hardly have changed for the worse.

I have sometimes watched the little manipulations of young wives who pretend that they wish to nurse their own children. They take care to be dissuaded from this whim. They contrive that husbands, doctors, and especially mothers should intervene. A man who dared to let his wife nurse her own baby would be lost; they would make him out a murderer who wanted to be rid of her. Prudent husbands, one must sacrifice paternal affection to domestic peace. Luckily there are women in the countryside who are more conscientious than your wives. You will be even more lucky if the time your wives thus gain is not intended for another than yourself!

There can be no doubt about a wife's duty, but considering the contempt in which it is held, it is doubtful whether it is not just as good for the child to be suckled by a stranger. This is a question for the doctors to settle, and in my opinion they have settled it according to the women's wishes. For my own part, I think it is better that if the child has any new ills to fear from the same blood out of which he was formed, he should suck the breast of a healthy nurse rather than of a spoiled mother.

However, should the question be considered only from the physical side? Does not the child need a mother's care as much as her milk? Other women, or even other animals, may give him the milk she denies him, but there is no substitute for a mother's love. The woman who nurses another's child in place of her own is a bad mother; how will she be a good nurse? She could become one, though slowly. For that it would be necessary for habit to change nature, and the child poorly cared for could perish a hundred times before his nurse had developed a mother's tenderness for him.

And this affection, when developed, has its drawbacks, which should make any feeling woman afraid to put her child out to nurse. Is she prepared to divide her mother's rights, or rather to abdicate them, in favour of a stranger? to see her child loving another more than herself? to feel that the affection he retains for his own mother is a favour, while his love for his foster-mother is a duty? For is not some affection due where there has been a mother's care?

To remove this difficulty, children are taught to look down on their nurses, to treat them as mere servants. When their task is completed the child is withdrawn or the nurse is dismissed. By receiving her badly, the parents discourage her from coming to see her nurseling. After a few years the child doesn't see her and knows nothing of her. The mother who expects to take her place and to repair neglect with cruelty deceives herself. Instead of making an affectionate son out of a denatured nurseling, she is teaching him ingratitude; she is teaching him to despise at a later day the mother who bore him just as he now despises his nurse.

How I would I insist on this point if it were not so discouraging to keep hammering at useful subjects! More depends on this than one thinks. If you wish to restore all men to their primary duties, begin with the mothers. The results will surprise you. Everything follows from this first deprivation: the whole moral order is disturbed, nature is quenched in every breast, the home becomes gloomy, the spectacle of a young family no longer stirs the husband's love and the stranger's reverence. The mother whose children are out of sight is less respected; there is no home life; the ties of nature are not strengthened by those of habit; fathers, mothers, children, brothers, and sisters cease to exist. They hardly know each other. How could they love one another? Each one thinks only of himself. When the home is only a sad solitude, one must go elsewhere to be gay.

But when mothers deign to nurse their own children, then morals will reforms themselves, natural feeling will revive in every heart, the state will be repopulated. This first point, this point alone, will bring everything together. The attractions of domestic life are the best antidote for bad morals. The noisy play of children, which one assumes to be bothersome, becomes agreeable; the mother and the father become more necessary, more dear to each other; the conjugal bonds are tightened. When the family is lively and animated domestic cares become the most cherished occupation of the wife and the sweetest amusement of the husband. Thus from this one corrected abuse would result a general reform; soon nature would have regained all of its rights. Once women become mothers again, men will become husbands and fathers.

A superfluous speech! When we are sick of worldly pleasures we do not return to the pleasures of the home. Women have ceased being mothers—they will no longer be and do not wish to be. Even if they wanted to they hardly could. Today the contrary custom is established. Each would have to overcome the opposition of those who approach her and who are leagued together against the example which some have never given and others do not desire to follow.

Yet there are still a few young women of natural goodness who on this point dare brave the empire of fashion and the clamors of their sex and, with virtuous boldness, do fulfill this sweet duty that nature imposes on them. May their number increase from the attraction of the benefits destined for those who do so! Based on consequences given by simple reasoning and upon observations I have never seen disputed, I dare promise these worthy mothers the firm and steadfast affection of their husbands, the truly filial love of their children, the estime and respect of the public, easy pregnancies without accident or misfortune, firm and vigorous health, and finally the pleasure of one day seeing their daughters follow their example and being cited as an example to the daughters of others.

No mother, no child. Between them their duties are reciprocal, and if they are poorly fulfilled by the one they will be neglected by the other. The child should love his mother before he knows that he should. If the voice of instinct is not strengthened by habit and care, it will die in the early years and the heart will die, so to speak, before being born. Here we are already stepping away from nature.

One also leaves nature by an opposite route when instead of neglecting a mother's care a woman carries it to excess. This is when she makes an idol of her child, when she augments and nurtures his weakness in order to prevent him from feeling it, and when hoping to protect him from the laws of nature she removes from him any painful impact—without thinking to what extent she is preserving him for a moment from a few inconveniences only to accumulate accidents and perils later on, and to what extent it is a barbarous precaution to add the weakness of childhood to a mature man's burdens. Thetis, according to the fable, plunged her son in the waters of Styx to make him invulnerable. This allegory is beautiful and clear. The cruel mothers I speak of do otherwise: by plunging their children into softness, they prepare them for suffering, they open their pores to every kind of ill which they will not fail to be a victim of when they grow up.

Observe nature, follow the route that it traces for you. Nature exercises children continually, it hardens their temperament by all kinds of difficulties, it teaches them early the meaning of pain and sorrow. Teething gives them fevers, sharp colics bring on convulsions, long coughing suffocates them, worms torment them, plethora corrupts their blood, various leavens ferment it and cause dangerous eruptions. Almost all of the first age is sickness and danger: one half of the children who are born die before their eighth year. The tests passed, the infant has gained strength, and as soon as he can make use of his life its principle becomes more secure.

This is the law of nature. Why would you contradict it? Do you not see that in your efforts to improve upon its work you are destroying it, that you impede the effect of its aims? To do from without what she does within is according to you to increase the danger twofold. On the contrary, it is the way to avert it. Experience shows that children delicately raised are more likely to die. Provided we do not overdo it, there is less risk in using their strength than in sparing it. Accustom them therefore to the hardships they will have to face; train them to endure extremes of temperature, climate, and condition, hunger, thirst, and weariness. Dip them in the waters of Styx. Before bodily habits are acquired you may teach what habits you will without danger. But once habits are established any change becomes perilous. A child will bear changes which a man cannot bear. The muscles of the one are soft and flexible and take whatever direction you give them without any effort. The muscles of the grown man are harder and they only change their accustomed mode of action when subjected to violence. One can thus make a child robust without risking his life or health; and even if there were some risk, one should not hesitate. Since risks are inseperable from human life, can we do better than face them at a time when they can do the least harm?

A child's worth increases with his years. To his personal value must be added the cost of the care bestowed upon him; to the loss of his life is joined in him the sentiment of death. It is therefore above all of the future that we must think in watching over his conservation; it is against the ills of childhood that he must be armed even before he gets there. For if the value of life increases until the child reaches an age when he can be useful, is it not crazy to spare some suffering in infancy only to multiply his pain when he reaches the age of reason? Are those the lessons of the master?

The fate of man is to suffer at all times. Even the effort to conserve himself is attached to pain. In infancy one is lucky to know only physical ills, ills much less cruel, much less painful, than the others and much less frequently than they to make us give up on life. One does not kill oneself over the pains of gout; it is only the pains of the soul that produce such despair. We pity the sufferings of childhood; we should pity ourselves. Our worst sorrows are of our own making.

In childbirth the infant cries; his early infancy is spent in crying. Sometimes we bustle about, we caress him in order to pacify him; at other times we threaten him, we hit him in order to make him be quiet. We do what pleases him, or we insist that he do what pleases us. Either we submit to his whims or subject him to our own. There is no middle way: he must give orders or receive them. Thus his earliest ideas are those of domination or servitude. Before knowing how to speak he commands; before knowing how to act he obeys; and sometimes we chastise him before he can know his faults or even commit them. It is thus that early on we pour into his young heart passions that we later attribute to nature, and that after having taken pains to make him evil we complain of having found him so.

A child passes six or seven years this way in the hands of women, the victim of their caprice or his own. And after having made him to learn this or that—that is to say after having burdened his memory with words that he cannot understand or with things that are good for nothing—after having stifled what is natural in him with passions that have been created, we give over this artificial being into the hands of a tutor. The tutor continues to develop these artificial germs that he found already formed and teaches the child everything except how to know himself, how to decide for himself, how to live and make himself happy. Finally when this child—both a slave and a tyrant, full of knowledge but lacking all sense, equally debilitated in body and soul—is thrown into the world, by showing his ineptitude, his pride and all his vices he makes us deplore human misery and perversity. We are wrong. This is a man based on our fantasies. One based on nature is made differently.

Do you wish, then, that he keep his original form? Watch over him from the moment he comes into the world. As soon as he is born take possession of him and do not leave him till he is a man; you will never succeed otherwise. Just as the real nurse is the mother, the real teacher is the father. Let them agree in the ordering of their functions as well as in their system; let the child pass from one to the other. He will be better educated by a sensible though limited father than by the cleverest teacher in the world. For zeal will make up for lack of knowledge better than knowledge for lack of zeal.

But business, jobs, duties . . . Duties indeed! Does a father's duty come last? It is not surprising that the man whose wife despises the duty of suckling her child should himself despise the child's education. There is no more charming picture than that of family life; but when one feature is lacking the whole is marred. If the mother is too delicate to nurse her child, the father will be too busy to teach him. Their children, scattered about in schools, convents, and colleges, will carry their love for their paternal home elsewhere, or rather they will form the habit of caring for nothing. Brothers and sisters will scarcely know each other; when they are together in company they will behave as strangers. When there is no confidence between relations, when the familiar society ceases to give favour to life, its place is soon usurped by bad morals. Is there any man so stupid that he cannot see how all this hangs together?

When a father begets children and provides a living for them he has done but a third of his task. He owes human beings to his species, social men to society, citizens to the state. A man who can pay this threefold debt and neglects to do so is guilty, more guilty, perhaps, if he pays it in part than when he neglects it entirely. He who cannot fulfil the duties of a father has no right to be a father. Neither poverty, work, nor human respect excuse a man from supporting his children and raising them himself. Readers, you can believe me. I predict that anyone who has visceral feelings and neglects such sacred duties will long weep bitter tears and will never be consoled.

But what does this rich man do, this father of a family, who is so busy and forced, according to him, to abandon his children? He pays another man to fulfil those duties which are his alone. Venal soul! Do you expect to purchase a second father for your child? Do not deceive yourself; it is not even a master you have hired for him, it is a flunkey. He soon will create a second one.

There is much discussion about the qualities of a good tutor. My first requirement, and it implies many more, is that he should not be a man who can be bought. There are callings so great that they cannot be undertaken for money without showing our unfitness for them; such callings are those of the soldier and the teacher. "But who must train my child?" I have just told you, you should do it yourself. "I cannot." You cannot! Then you must make a friend. I see no other resource.

A tutor! What a sublime soul . . . In truth to make a man one must either be a father or more than a man. It is this function you would calmly hand over to mercenaries.

The more one thinks about it the more one can see the difficulties. The tutor must have been trained for his pupil and his servants must have been trained for their master, so that all who come near him may have received the impression that they must communicate with him. Thus one must pass from education to education I know not how far. How can a child be well educated by one who has not been well educated himself?

Is this rare mortal impossible to find? I do not know. In these times of degradation who knows the height of virtue to which man's soul may attain? But let us assume that this prodigy has been found. It is in considering what he should do that we will see what he can be. What I think I see in advance is that the father who realises the value of a good tutor will contrive to do without one, for it will be harder to find one than to become such a tutor himself. Does he then want to find a friend? If he should raise his son to be one he need search no further and nature herself will have done half the work.

Someone whose rank alone is known to me suggested that I should educate his son. He did me a great honour, no doubt, but far from regretting my refusal, he ought to congratulate himself on my prudence. Had the offer been accepted and had I been mistaken in my method, there would have been an education ruined. Had I succeeded, things would have been worse-his son would have renounced his title and refused to be a prince.

I feel too deeply the importance of a tutor's duties and my own unfitness, ever to accept such a post, whoever offered it, and even the claims of friendship would be only an additional motive for my refusal. Few, I think, will be tempted to make me such an offer when they have read this book, and I beg any one who would do so to spare his pains. I have had enough experience of the task to convince myself of my own unfitness, and my circumstances would make it impossible even if my talents were such as to fit me for it. I have thought it my duty to make this public declaration to those who apparently refuse to do me the honour of believing in the sincerity of my determination.

Unable to undertake the more useful task, I will at least venture to attempt the easier one. I will follow the example of so many others and take up, not the task, but my pen; and instead of doing the right thing I will try to say it.

I know that in such an undertaking the author, always at home among systems that he is spared from putting into practice, painlessly provides nice-sounding precepts that are impossible to follow; and that lacking details and examples, even what is practicable remains unused when its application has not been demonstrated.

I have therefore decided to take an imaginary pupil, to assume on my own part the age, health, knowledge, and talents required for the work of his education, to guide him from birth to the point where, having become a man, he needs no other guide but himself. This method seems to me useful for an author who fears that he may be carried away by his visions, for as soon as he departs from common practice he has only to try his method on his pupil; he will soon know, or the reader will know for him, whether he is following the development of the child and the natural growth of the human heart.

This is what I have tried to do in all the difficulties that are presented here. Lest my book should be unduly bulky, I have been content to state principles whose truth everyone should sense. But as to the rules which call for proof, I have applied them to Emile or to others, and I have shown, in very great detail, how my theories may be put into practice. Such at least is my plan; the reader must decide whether I have succeeded.

At first I have said little about Emile, for my earliest maxims of education, though very different from those generally accepted, are so plain that it is hard for a man of sense to refuse to accept them. But as I advance, my scholar, having been led along differently from yours, is no longer an ordinary child; he needs a regime that is special for him. Then he appears upon the scene more frequently, and towards the end I never lose sight of him for a moment, until, whatever he may say, he hasn't the slightest need for me.

I pass over the qualities required in a good tutor; I take them for granted, and assume that I am endowed with them. As you read this book you will see how generous I have been to myself.

I will only remark that, contrary to the received opinion, a child's tutor should be young, even as young as a wise man can be. Were it possible, he should become a child himself, that he may become the companion of his pupil and win his confidences by sharing his games. Childhood and ripened age have too little in common for the formation of a really firm affection. Children sometimes flatter old men, but they never love them.

People seek a tutor who has already educated one pupil. This is too much; one man can only make one other man; if two were essential to success, what right would he have to undertake the first?

With more experience you may know better what to do, but you are less capable of doing it. Whoever has fulfilled this state one time well enough to know all its difficulties does not try to start again, and if he fulfilled it badly the first time it's a bad sign for the second.

It is one thing to follow a young man about for four years, another to be his guide for twenty-five. You find a tutor for your son when he is already formed; I want one for him before he is born. Your man may change his pupil every five years, mine will never have but one pupil. You distinguish between the teacher and the tutor. Another piece of folly! Do you make any distinction between the disciple and the pupil? There is only one science to teach children: it is that of the duties of man. This science is one, and, whatever Xenophon may say of the education of the Persians, it cannot be divided. Besides, I prefer to call the man who has this knowledge tutor rather than teacher, since for him it is less a question of instruction than of guidance. He must not give precepts, he must let them be found.

If the tutor is to be so carefully chosen, so may he be allowed to choose his pupil, especially when it is a question of proposing a model. This choice cannot depend on the child's genius or character, since I adopt him before he is born, and those things are only known when the task is finished. If I had my choice I would take a child of ordinary mind, such as I assume in my pupil. It is ordinary people who have to be educated, and their education alone can serve as a pattern for the education of their fellows. The others raise themselves no matter what one does.

One's native land is not a matter of indifference in the education of men; they are all that they can be only in temperate climates. The disadvantages of extremes are easily seen. A man is not planted in one place like a tree, to stay there the rest of his life, and to pass from one extreme to another you must travel twice as far as he who starts half-way.

If the inhabitant of a temperate climate passes in turn through both extremes his advantage is plain, for although he may be changed as much as he who goes from one extreme to the other, he only moves half-way from his natural condition. A Frenchman can live in New Guinea or in Lapland, but a negro cannot live in Tornea nor a Samoyed in Benin. It seems also as if the brain were less perfectly organised in the two extremes. Neither the negroes nor the Laps have the sense of the Europeans. So if I want my pupil to be an inhabitant of the earth I will choose him in the temperate zone, in France for example, rather than elsewhere.

In the north with its barren soil men devour much food; in the fertile south they eat little. From this arises another difference which makes the former industrious, the latter contemplative. Society shows us in a single place an image of these differences between the poor and the rich. The first live on unyielding soil, the others on fertile soil.

The poor man has no need of education. The education of his own station in life is forced upon him; he can have no other. The education received by the rich man from his own station is least fitted for himself and for society, whereas a natural education should fit a man for any position. Now it is more unreasonable to train a poor man for wealth than a rich man for poverty, for in proportion to their numbers more rich men are ruined and fewer poor men become rich. Let us choose our pupil among the rich; we will at least be sure to have made one more man, whereas the poor can become men on their own.

For the same reason I should not be sorry if Emile came of a good family. He will be another victim snatched from prejudice.

Emile is an orphan. No matter whether he has father or mother, having undertaken their duties I am invested with their rights. He must honour his parents, but he must obey only me. That is my first or rather my only only condition.

I must add that there is just one other point arising out of this; we must never be separated except by mutual consent. This clause is essential, and I would have tutor and scholar so inseparable that they should regard their fate as one. If once they perceive the time of their separation drawing near—the time which must make them strangers to one another, they will become strangers then and there. Each will make his own little world, and both of them being busy in thought with the time when they are no longer be together, they will remain together against their will. The pupil will regard his tutor as the sign and plague of childhood, the tutor will regard his scholar as a heavy burden which he longs to be rid of. Both will be looking forward to the time when they will part, and as there was never any real affection between them, one will have very little vigilance, the other very little docility.

But when they consider they must always live together, they must love one another, and in this way they will become dear to one another. The pupil will not be ashamed to follow as a child the friend who will be with him in manhood; the tutor will an interest in the efforts whose fruits he will harvest, and the merit he is cultivating in his pupil is a fund that he will profit from in his old age.

This agreement made beforehand assumes a normal birth, a well-formed, vigorous and healthy child. A father has no choice, and should have no preference within the limits of the family God has given him; all his children are equally his children and he owes them all the same care and affection. Crippled or not, languid or robust, each of them is a trust for which he is responsible to the hand from which it has been given, and marriage is a contract made with nature as well as between spouses.

But anyone who undertakes a duty not imposed upon him by nature must secure beforehand the means for its fulfillment; otherwise he makes himself accountable even for what he could not do. If you take the care of a sickly, unhealthy child, you become a sick nurse, not a tutor. To preserve a useless life you are wasting the time which should be spent in increasing its value; you risk the sight of a despairing mother reproaching you for the death of a child who ought to have died long ago.

I would not undertake the care of a feeble, sickly child, even if he should live for eighty years. I do not want a pupil who is useless alike to himself and others, one whose sole business is to keep himself alive, one whose body is always a hindrance to the training of his mind. If I vainly lavish my care upon him, what can I do but double the loss to society by robbing it of two men instead of one? Let another tend this weakling for me; I am quite willing, I approve his charity, but I myself have no gift for such a task. I could never teach the art of living to one who needs all his strength to keep himself alive.

The body must be strong enough to obey the mind; a good servant must be strong. I know that intemperance stimulates the passions; it also destroys the body in the long run. Fasting and penance often produce the same results in an opposite way. The weaker the body, the more imperious its demands; the stronger it is, the better it obeys. All sensual passions find their home in effeminate bodies. The less satisfied they are the more irritated they feel.

A frail body weakens the soul. Hence the influence of medicine, an art which does more harm to man than all the evils it professes to cure. I do not know what the doctors cure us of, but I know this: they infect us with very deadly diseases—cowardice, timidity, credulity, the fear of death. What if they can make corpses walk? It is men that we need, and we will never see them leaving the hands of a doctor.

Medicine is fashionable among us; it has to be. It is the amusement of idle and inactive people who do not know what to do with their time and so spend it in taking care of themselves. If by ill luck they had happened to be born immortal, they would have been the most miserable of men; a life they could not lose would be of no value to them. Such men must have doctors to threaten and flatter them, to give them the only pleasure they can enjoy—the pleasure of not being dead.

I have no intention of continuing on about the vanity of medicine. My aim is to consider its bearings on morals. Still I cannot refrain from saying that men employ the same sophism about medicine as they do about the search for truth. They assume that by treating the patient they cure him and that by seeking the truth they find it. They do not see that one must weigh the advantage of a cure that the doctor effects with the death of a hundred sick people he has killed, and the usefulness of one true discovery with the the errors which creep in with it. The science which instructs and the medicine which heals are no doubt excellent, but the science which misleads us and the medicine which kills us are evil. Teach us to tell them apart—that is the knot of the question. If we knew how to ignore truth we would not be the dupes of falsehood; if we did not want to be cured in spite of nature, we would never die at the hand of the doctor. We should do well to steer clear of both, and we should evidently be the gainers. I do not deny that medicine is useful to some men, but I say that it is fatal to mankind.

You will tell me, as usual, that the doctors are to blame, that medicine itself is infallible. Well and good, then give us the medicine without the doctor. For when we have both, the blunders of the artist are a hundredfold greater than our hopes from the art.

This lying art, invented rather for the ills of the mind than of the body, is useless to both alike; it does less to cure us of our diseases than to fill us with alarm. It does less to ward off death than to make us dread its approach. It exhausts life rather than prolongs it. Should it even prolong life it would only be to the prejudice of the race, since it makes us set its precautions before society and our fears before our duties. It is the knowledge of danger that makes us afraid. If we thought ourselves invulnerable we should know no fear. By arming Achilles against danger the poet robbed him of the merit of courage. Anyone else in his place would have been an Achilles at the same price.

Do you wish to find men with true courage? Seek them where there are no doctors, where the results of disease are unknown, and where death is little thought of. Naturally man knows how to constantly suffer and he dies in peace. It is the doctors with their rules, the philosophers with their precepts, the priests with their exhortations, who debase the heart and make us unlearn how to die.

Give me a pupil who has no need of these people or I will have nothing to do with him. No one else shall spoil my work. I wish to raise him myself or not at all. That wise man, Locke, who had devoted part of his life to the study of medicine, advises us strongly to give no drugs to the child, either as a precaution or on account of slight ailments. I will go farther and declare that, as I never call in a doctor for myself I will never send for one for Emile, unless his life is clearly in danger. For then a doctor can do no worse than to kill him.

I know the doctor will not fail to take advantage of this delay. If the child dies, he was called in too late; if he recovers, it is his doing. So be it; let the doctor boast, but do not call him in except in extremity.

For lack of knowing how to cure himself, let the child know how to be sick. The one art takes the place of the other and is often more successful; it is the art of nature. When an animal is sick it keeps quiet and suffers in silence; we see fewer sickly animals than sick men. How many men have been slain by impatience, fear, anxiety, and above all by medicine, men whom disease would have spared and time alone have cured? I shall be told that animals, who live according to nature, are less liable to disease than ourselves. Well, that way of living is just what I mean to teach my pupil; he should profit by it in the same way.

Hygiene is the only useful part of medicine, and hygiene is a virtue rather than a science. Temperance and industry are man's true remedies; work sharpens his appetite and temperance teaches him to control it.

To learn what regimen is most useful to life and to health, you have only to study the regimen followed by the peoples who are the healthiest, the most robust, and live the longest. If common observation shows us that medicine neither increases health nor prolongs life, it follows that this useless art is worse than useless, since it wastes time, men, and things on what is a pure loss. Not only must we deduct the time spent preserving life rather than using it, but if this time is spent in tormenting ourselves it is worse than wasted; it is adding to the bad; and to reckon fairly a corresponding share must be deducted from what remains to us. A man who lives ten years without doctors lives more for himself and others than one who spends thirty years as their victim. Having done a test of both ways I think I have a better right than most to draw my own conclusions.

For these reasons I decline to take any but a strong and healthy pupil, and these are my principles for keeping him in health. I will not stop to prove at length the value of manual labour and bodily exercise for strengthening the health and constitution; no one denies it. Nearly all the instances of long life are to be found among the men who have taken most exercise, who have endured fatigue and labour. Neither will I enter into details as to the care I shall take for this alone. It will be clear that it forms such an essential part of my practice that it is enough to get hold of the idea without further explanation.

When our life begins our needs begin too. The new-born infant must have a nurse. If his mother will do her duty, so much the better; her instructions will be given her in writing. This advantage has its drawbacks—it removes the tutor from his charge. But it is to be hoped that the child's own interests, and her respect for the person to whom she is about to confide so precious a treasure will induce the mother to follow the tutor's wishes, and whatever she does you may be sure she will do better than another. If we must have a stranger for a nurse, let us begin by choosing her well.

One of the misfortunes of the rich is to be deceived in everything. If they judge people poorly, should one be surprised? It is riches that corrupt men, and the rich are rightly the first to feel the defects of the only tool they know. Everything is done poorly for them, except what they do themselves, and they do next to nothing. Is it a question of selecting a nurse? She is chosen by the doctor. What happens? The best nurse is the one who offers the highest bribe. I will not consult the doctor about Emile's nurse; I will take care to choose her myself. I may not argue about it so elegantly as the surgeon, but for sure I will be more reliable, and my zeal will deceive me less than his greed.

There is no mystery about this choice; its rules are well known. But I think we ought probably to pay as much attention to the age of the milk as to its quality. The first milk is watery, it must be almost a laxative in order to purge the remains of the meconium curdled in the bowels of the new-born child. Little by little the milk thickens and supplies more solid food as the child is able to digest it. It is surely not without cause that nature changes the milk in the female of every species according to the age of the offspring.

Thus a new-born child requires a nurse who has recently become a mother. There is, I know, a difficulty here, but as soon as we leave the path of nature every attempt to do things well has its difficulties. The wrong course is the only right one under the circumstances, so we take it.

The nurse must be as healthy in her heart as in her body. The storms of the passions as well as the humors may spoil her milk. Moreover, to focus on the physical is to see only half of the object. The milk may be good and the nurse bad; a good character is as necessary as a good constitution. If you choose a vicious person, I do not say her foster-child will acquire her vices, but he will suffer for them. Should she not to bestow on him day by day, along with her milk, a care which calls for zeal, patience, gentleness, and cleanliness? If she is greedy and intemperate her milk will soon be spoiled; if she is careless and hasty what will become of a poor little thing left to her mercy, and unable either to protect himself or to complain? The wicked are never good for anything.

The choice is all the more important because her foster-child should have no other guardian, just as he should have no teacher but his tutor. This was the custom of the ancients, who talked less but acted more wisely than we. After having nursed female children their nurses never left them; this is why the nurse is the confidante in most of their plays. A child who passes through many hands in succession can never be well raised. At every change he makes a secret comparison, which continually tends to lessen his respect for those who control him and with it their authority over him. If once he thinks there are grown-up people with no more sense than children the authority of age is destroyed and his education is ruined. A child should know no superiors other than his father and mother, or failing them his foster-mother and his tutor, and even this is one too many, but this division is inevitable, and the best that can be done in the way of remedy is that the man and woman who control him shall be so well agreed with regard to him that they seem like one.

The nurse must live rather more comfortably. She must have rather more substantial food, but her whole way of living must not be altered, for a sudden change, even a change for the better, is dangerous to health, and since her usual way of life has made her healthy and strong, why change it?

Peasant women eat less meat and more vegetables than towns-women, and this vegetarian diet seems favourable rather than otherwise to themselves and their children. When they take nurslings from the upper classes they eat meat and broth with the idea that they will form better chyle and supply more milk. I am not at all of this sentiment and experience is on my side, for we do not find children fed in this way less liable to colic and worms.

That need not surprise us, for decaying animal matter swarms with worms, but this is not the case with vegetable matter. Milk, although manufactured in the body of an animal, is a vegetable substance. This is shown by analysis; it readily turns acid, and far from showing traces of any volatile alkali like animal matter, it gives a neutral salt like plants.

The milk of herbivorous creatures is sweeter and more wholesome than the milk of the carnivorous. Formed of a substance similar to its own, it keeps its goodness and becomes less liable to putrifaction. If quantity is considered, it is well known that farinaceous foods produce more blood than meat, so they ought to yield more milk. If a child were not weaned too soon, and if it were fed on vegetarian food, and its foster-mother were a vegetarian, I do not think it would be troubled with worms.

Milk derived from vegetable foods may perhaps be more liable to go sour, but I am far from considering sour milk an unwholesome food; whole nations have no other food and are none the worse, and all the array of absorbents seems to me mere humbug. There are constitutions which do not thrive on milk, others can take it without absorbents. People are afraid of the milk separating or curdling. That is absurd, for we know that milk always curdles in the stomach. This is how it becomes sufficiently solid to nourish children and young animals. If it did not curdle it would merely pass away without feeding them. In vain you dilute milk and use absorbents; whoever swallows milk digests cheese, this rule is without exception; rennet is made from calf's stomach.

Instead of changing the nurse's usual diet I think it would be enough to give food in larger quantities and better of its kind. It is not the nature of the food that makes a vegetable diet indigestible, but the flavoring that makes it unwholesome. Reform your cookery, use neither butter nor oil for frying. Butter, salt, and milk should never be cooked. Let your vegetables be cooked in water and only seasoned when they come to table. The vegetable diet, far from disturbing the nurse, will give her a plentiful supply of milk. If a vegetable diet is best for the child, how can meat food be best for his nurse? The things are contradictory.

Fresh air affects children's constitutions, particularly in early years. It enters every pore of a soft and tender skin; it has a powerful effect on their young bodies. Its effects can never be destroyed. So I should not agree with those who take a country woman from her village and shut her up in one room in a town and her nursling with her. I would rather send him to breathe the fresh air of the country than the foul air of the town. He will take his new mother's position, will live in her cottage, where his tutor will follow him. The reader will bear in mind that this tutor is not a paid servant but the father's friend. If this friend cannot be found, if this transfer is not easy, if none of my advice can be followed, you will say to me, "What shall I do instead?" I have told you already— "Do what you are doing;" no advice is needed there.

Men are not made to be crowded together in ant-hills, but scattered over the earth to till it. The more they are massed together, the more corrupt they become. Disease and vice are the sure results of over-crowded cities. Of all creatures man is least fitted to live in herds. Huddled together like sheep, men would very soon die. Man's breath is fatal to his fellows. This is literally as well as figuratively true.

Cities are the abysse of the human species. In a few generations the race dies out or becomes degenerate; it needs renewal, and it is always renewed from the country. Send your children to renew themselves, so to speak; send them to regain in the open fields the strength lost in the foul air of our crowded cities. Women hurry home that their children may be born in the town. They ought to do just the opposite, especially those who mean to nurse their own children. They would lose less than they think, and in more natural surroundings the pleasures associated by nature with maternal duties would soon destroy the taste for those that are not.

The new-born infant is first bathed in warm water to which a little wine is usually added. I think the wine might be dispensed with. As nature does not produce fermented liquors, it is not likely that they are of much value to her creatures.

In the same way it is unnecessary to take the precaution of heating the water. In fact among many races the new-born infants are bathed with no more ado in rivers or in the sea. Our children, made tender before birth by the softness of their parents, come into the world with a constitution already enfeebled, which cannot be at once exposed to all the trials required to restore it to health. By degrees they must be restored to their natural vigour. Begin then by following this custom, and depart from it little by little. Wash your children often, their dirty ways show the need of this. If they are only wiped their skin is injured; but as they grow stronger gradually reduce the heat of the water, till at last you bathe them winter and summer in cold, even in ice-cold water. To avoid risk this change must be slow, gradual, and imperceptible, so you may use the thermometer for exact measurements.

This habit of the bath, once established, should never be broken off; it must be kept up all through life. I value it not only on grounds of cleanliness and present health, but also as a wholesome means of making the muscles supple, and accustoming them to bear without risk or effort extremes of heat and cold. As he gets older I would have the child trained to bathe occasionally in hot water of every bearable degree, and often in every degree of cold water. Now water being a denser fluid touches us at more points than air, so that, having learnt to bear all the variations of temperature in water, we shall scarcely feel those of the air.

At the moment that the child first breathes when leaving its envelope do not allow anyone to give him other constraints that will hold him even tighter. No cap, no bandages, nor swaddling clothes. Instead, loose and flowing flannel wrappers, which heave his limbs free and are not too heavy to check his movements, not too warm to prevent his feeling the air. Put him in a big cradle, well padded, where he can move easily and safely. As he begins to grow stronger, let him crawl about the room; let him develop and stretch his tiny limbs. You will see him gain strength from day to day. Compare him with a well swaddled child of the same age and you will be surprised at the difference in their progress.

You must expect great opposition from the nurses, who find that a half strangled baby needs much less watching. Besides, his dirtyness is more perceptible in an open garment; he must be attended to more frequently. In the end, custom is an argument that will never be refuted in some lands and among all classes of people.

Do not argue with the nurses; give your orders, see them carried out, and spare no pains to make the attention you prescribe easy in practice. Why not take your share in it? With ordinary nurslings, where the body alone is thought of, nothing matters so long as the child lives and does not actually die. But with us, when education begins with life, the new-born child is already a pupil, not of his tutor, but of nature. The tutor merely studies under this master, and sees that his orders are not evaded. He watches over the infant, he observes it, he looks for the first feeble glimmering of intelligence, as the Moslem looks for the moment of the moon's rising in her first quarter.

We are born capable of learning, but knowing nothing, perceiving nothing. The mind, bound up within imperfect and half grown organs, is not even aware of its own existence. The movements and cries of the newborn child are purely reflex, without knowledge or will.

Suppose that a child had at its birth the stature and strength of a man, that he had entered life full grown like Pallas from the brain of Jupiter. Such a child-man would be a perfect idiot, an automaton, a statue without motion and almost without feeling. He would see and hear nothing, he would recognise no one, he could not turn his eyes towards what he wanted to see. Not only would he perceive no external object, he would not even be aware of sensation through the several sense-organs. His eye would not perceive colour, his ear sounds, his body would be unaware of contact with neighbouring bodies, he would not even know he had a body. What his hands handled would be in his brain alone; all his sensations would be united in one place, they would exist only in the common "sensorium." He would have only one idea, that of self, to which he would refer all his sensations; and this idea, or rather this sentiment, would be the only thing he had more of than an ordinary child.

This man, full grown at birth, would also be unable to stand on his feet. He would need a long time to learn how to keep his balance; perhaps he would not even be able to try to do it, and you would see the big strong body left in one place like a stone, or creeping and crawling like a young puppy.

He would feel the discomfort of bodily needs without knowing what was the matter and without knowing how to provide for these needs. There is no immediate connection between the muscles of the stomach and those of the arms and legs to make him take a step towards food or stretch a hand to seize it even were he surrounded with it. And as his body would be full grown and his limbs well developed he would be without the perpetual restlessness and movement of childhood, so that he might die of hunger without stirring to seek food. However little you may have thought about the order and development of our knowledge, you cannot deny that such a one would be in the state of almost primitive ignorance and stupidity natural to man before he has learnt anything from experience or from his fellows.

We know then, or we may know, the point of departure from which we each start towards the usual level of understanding; but who knows the other extreme? Each progresses more or less according to his genius, his taste, his needs, his talents, his zeal, and his opportunities for using them. No philosopher, so far as I know, has dared to say to man, "Thus far shalt thou go and no further." We know not what nature allows us to be, but none of us has measured the possible difference between man and man. Is there a mind so dead that this thought has never kindled it, that has never said in his pride, "How much have I already done, how much more may I achieve? Why should I lag behind my fellows?"

I repeat: man's education begins at birth; before he can speak or understand he is learning. Experience precedes instruction; when he recognises his nurse he has learnt much. The knowledge of the most ignorant man would surprise us if we had followed his course from birth to the present time. If all human knowledge were divided into two parts, one common to all, the other peculiar to the learned, the latter would seem very small compared with the former. But we scarcely reflect on these general acquisitions because they happen without us thinking about them and even before the age of reason. Moreover, knowledge only attracts attention by its differences; as in algebraic equations common factors count for nothing.

Even animals learn much. They have senses and must learn to use them; they have needs, they must learn to satisfy them; they must learn to eat, walk, or fly. Quadrupeds which can stand on their feet from the first cannot walk for all that; from their first attempts it is clear that they lack confidence. Canaries who escape from their cage are unable to fly, having never used their wings. Living and feeling creatures are always learning. If plants could walk they would need senses and knowledge, else their species would die out.

Children's first sensations are purely affective. They are only aware of pleasure and pain. Being unable to walk nor to grasp they need much time to form little by little the representative sensations that show them objects beyond themselves. But while waiting for these objects to become extended, become distanced, so to speak, from their eyes and take on for them dimension and shape, the recurrence of affective sensations begins to subject the child to the rule of habit. You see his eyes constantly follow the light, and if the light comes from the side the eyes turn towards it, so that one must be careful to turn his head towards the light lest he should squint. He must also be accustomed from the first to the dark, or he will cry if he misses the light. Food and sleep, too exactly measured, become necessary at regular intervals, and soon desire is no longer the effect of need, but of habit, or rather habit adds a fresh need to those of nature. This is what must be prevented.

The only habit the child should be allowed is that of contracting none. Let him be carried on either arm, let him be accustomed to offer either hand, to use one or other indifferently; let him not want to eat, sleep, or do anything at fixed hours, nor be unable to be left alone by day or night. Prepare from afar the reign of his liberty and the use of his own forces by letting his body keep its natural habit, by putting him in a condition of being always master of himself, of following his will in everything as soon as he has one.

From the moment that the child begins to take notice, what is shown him must be carefully chosen. Naturally all new objects interest man. He feels so feeble that he fears the unknown: the habit of seeing fresh things without ill effects destroys this fear. Children brought up in clean houses where there are no spiders are afraid of spiders, and this fear often lasts through life. I never saw peasants, man, woman, or child, afraid of spiders.

Since the mere choice of things shown him may make the child timid or brave, why should not his education begin before he can speak or understand? I would have him accustomed to see fresh things, ugly, repulsive, and strange animals, but little by little, and at a distance, until he is used to them, and until having seen others handle them he handles them himself. If in childhood he sees toads, snakes, and crayfish, he will not be afraid of any animal when he is grown up. Those who are continually seeing terrible things think nothing of them.

All children are afraid of masks. I begin by showing Emile a mask with a pleasant face. Then some one puts this mask before his face; I begin to laugh, they all laugh too, and the child with them. By degrees I accustom him to less pleasing masks, and at last to hideous ones. If I have arranged my stages skilfully, far from being afraid of the last mask, he will laugh at it as he did at the first. After that I am not afraid of people frightening him with masks.

When Hector bids farewell to Andromache, the young Astyanax, startled by the nodding plumes on the helmet, does not know his father; he flings himself weeping upon his nurse's bosom and wins from his mother a smile mingled with tears. What must be done to cure him of this terror? Just what Hector did: put the helmet on the ground and caress the child. In a calmer moment one would do more; one would go up to the helmet, play with the plumes, let the child feel them; at last the nurse would take the helmet and place it laughingly on her own head, if indeed a woman's hand dare touch the armour of Hector.

What if we need to get Emile used to the noise of a firearm? I first fire a pistol with a small charge. He is delighted with this sudden flash, this sort of lightning; I repeat the process with more powder; gradually I add a small charge without a wad, then a larger; in the end I accustom him to the sound of a gun, to fireworks, cannon, and the most terrible explosions.

I have observed that children are rarely afraid of thunder unless the claps are really terrible and actually hurt the ear. Otherwise this fear only comes to them when they know that thunder sometimes hurts or kills. When reason begins to cause fear, let use reassure them. By slow and careful stages man and child learn to fear nothing.

At the beginning of life, when memory and imagination have not begun to function, the child only attends to what affects its senses. His sense experiences are the raw material of thought. They should, therefore, be presented to him in fitting order, so that memory may at a future time present them in the same order to his understanding. But since he only attends to his sensations it is enough, at first, to show him clearly the connection between these sensations and the things which cause them. He wants to touch and handle everything. Do not oppose this restlessness; it suggests to him a very necessary learning. It is thus that he will learn to feel heat, cold, hardness, softness, weight, or lightness of bodies; to judge their size and shape and all their physical properties by looking, feeling, listening, and, above all, by comparing sight and touch, by judging with the eye what sensation they would cause to his hand.

It is only by movement that we learn that there are things which are not us; it is only by our own movements that we gain the idea of extension. It is because the child does not have this idea that he indifferently reaches out to grasp the object that touches him or the object that is a hundred feet away. You take this as a sign of tyranny, an attempt to make the thing come near him or to make you bring him to it; but it is not that. It is merely that the object first seen in his brain, then before his eyes, now seems close to his arms, and he has no idea of space beyond his reach. Be careful, therefore, to take him about, to move him from place to place, and to let him perceive the change in his surroundings so as to teach him to judge of distances. When he begins to perceive distances then you must change your method, and only carry him when you please, not when he pleases. For as soon as he is no longer deceived by his senses, the cause of his effort changes. This change is important and calls for explanation.

The discomfort of real needs expresses itself by signs when the help of others is necessary for us to provide for them. Hence the cries of children. They often cry; it must be so. Since all their feelings are affective, when those feelings are pleasant they enjoy them in silence; when they are painful they say so in their own way and demand relief. Now when they are awake they can scarcely be in a state of indifference; either they are asleep or else they are feeling something.

All our languages are the work of art. People have long searched whether there ever was a natural language common to all; no doubt there is, and it is the language of children before they begin to speak. This language is inarticulate, but it is accentuated, sonorous, intelligible. The use of our own language has led us to neglect it so far as to forget it altogether. Let us study children and we shall soon learn it afresh from them. Nurses are masters of this language; they understand all their nurslings say to them, they answer them, and keep up long conversations with them; and though they use words, these words are quite useless. It is not the hearing of the word, but its accompanying intonation that is understood.

To the language of the voice is added the no less forcible language of gesture. Such gestures are not in the child's weak hands, but in its face. It is astonishing how much expression is in such underdeveloped physiomonies; their features change from one moment to another with incredible speed. You see smiles, desires, terror, come and go like lightning; every time the face seems different. The muscles of the face are undoubtedly more mobile than our own. On the other hand the eyes are almost expressionless. Such must be the sort of signs they use at an age when their only needs are those of the body. Grimaces are the sign of sensation, the glance expresses sentiment.

As man's first state is one of misery and weakness, his first sounds are cries and tears. The child feels his needs and cannot satisfy them; he begs for help by his cries. If he is hungry or thirsty he cries; if is he is too cold or too hot he cries; if he needs movement and is kept quiet he cries; if he wants to sleep and is disturbed he cries. The less comfortable he is the more he demands change. He has only one language because he has, so to say, only one kind of discomfort. In the imperfect state of his sense organs he does not distinguish their several impressions; all ills produce one feeling of sorrow.

From these tears that we might think so little worthy of attention, arise man's first relation to all that surrounds him; here is forged the first link in the long chain that forms the social order.

When the child cries he is uncomfortable, he feels some need which he cannot satisfy. We examine him, we search out this need, find it, and provide for it. When we cannot find it or provide for it, the tears continue and become tiresome. We stroke the child to make him keep quiet, we rock him, we sing to him to make him fall asleep. If he persists, we get impatient, we threaten him; cruel nurses sometimes strike him. What strange lessons for him at his first entrance into life!

I shall never forget seeing one of these troublesome crying children thus beaten by his nurse. He was silent at once. I thought he was frightened, and said to myself, "This will be a servile being from whom nothing can be got but by harshness." I was wrong. The poor thing was choking with rage, he could not breathe, I saw him becoming blue in the face. A moment later there were bitter cries, every sign of the anger, rage, and the despair of this age was in his tones. I thought he would die from such agitation. Had I doubted the innate sense of justice and injustice in man's heart, this one instance would have convinced me. I am sure that a drop of boiling liquid falling by chance on that child's hand would have hurt him less than that blow, slight in itself, but clearly given with the intention of hurting him.

This disposition of children to fury, spite, and anger needs great care. Boerhaave thinks that most of the diseases of children are of the nature of convulsions, because the head being proportionally larger and the nervous system more extensive than in adults, they are more liable to nervous irritation. Take the greatest care to remove from them any servants who agitate them, irritate them, annoy them. They are a hundredfold more dangerous and more fatal than fresh air and changing seasons. As long as children find resistance only in things and never in wills, they will become neither rebellious nor angry and they will conserve their health better. This is one reason why the children of the people, who are freer and more independent, are generally less infirm, less delicate, and more vigorous than those who claim to raise them better by ceaselessly thwarting them. But one must always be aware that there is a big difference between obeying them and not thwarting them.

Children's first tears are prayers; if you are not careful they soon become commands. They begin by asking for help, they end by making themselves served. Thus from his own weakness, the source of his first sentiment of dependence, springs the later idea of empire and domination. But this idea being less aroused by his needs than by our service, we begin to see moral results whose immediate cause is not in nature, and we see how important it is, even at the earliest age, to discern the secret meaning of the gesture or cry.

When the child tries to seize something without speaking, he thinks he can reach the object, for he does not rightly judge its distance. When he cries and stretches out his hands he no longer misjudges the distance; he bids the object approach, or orders you to bring it to him. In the first case bring it to him slowly; in the second do not even seem to hear his cries. The more he cries the less you should heed him. He must learn in good time not to give commands to men, for he is not their master, nor to things, for they cannot hear him. Thus when the child wants something you mean to give him, it is better to carry him to it rather than to bring the thing to him. From this he will draw a conclusion suited to his age, and there is no other way of suggesting it to him.

The Abbé de Saint-Pierre calls men big children; one might also call children little men. These statements contain truth as sentences; as principles they require explanation. But when Hobbes calls the wicked man a strong child, he says something absolutely contradictory. All wickedness comes from weakness. The child is only wicked because he is weak; make him strong and he will be good. He who could do everything would never do wrong. Of all the attributes of the allpowerful divinity, goodness is the one without which we could least conceive him. All peoples who have recognized two principles have always regarded the evil as inferior to the good; otherwise their opinion would have been absurd. See below the creed of the Savoyard Vicar.

Reason alone teaches us to know good and evil. Therefore conscience, which makes us love the one and hate the other, although independent of reason, cannot develop without it. Before the age of reason we do good and bad without knowing it, and there is no morality in our actions, although there sometimes is in the sentiment of others' actions which relate to us. A child wants to overturn everything he sees. He breaks and smashes everything he can reach; he seizes a bird as he seizes a stone, and strangles it without knowing what he is doing.

Why is this? First of all philosophy will find a reason for this in the natural vices: pride, the spirit of domination, amour-propre, the wickedness of man. The sentiment of his own weakness, one could add, makes the child eager to act forcefully, to prove his own power to himself. But observe that broken old man reduced in the downward course of life to the weakness of a child; not only is he quiet and peaceful, he wants to have everything around him quiet and peaceful too; the least change disturbs and bothers him, he would like to see universal calm. How is it that similar feebleness and similar passions should produce such different effects in age and in infancy if the original cause were not different? And where can we find this difference in cause except in the bodily condition of the two? The active principle common to both is growing in one case and fading in the other; it is being formed in the one and destroyed in the other; one is moving towards life, the other towards death. The failing activity of the old man is centred in his heart, the child's is overflowing and spreads everywhere. He feels, if we may say so, strong enough to give life to everything around him. To make or to destroy, it is all one to him. Change is what he seeks, and all change involves action. If he seems to have more of a tendency to destroy it is only that it takes time to make things and very little time to break them, so that the work of destruction agrees more with his eagerness.

At the same time that the the Author of nature has given children this active principle, he takes care that it shall do little harm by giving them small power to use it. But as soon as they can think of people as instruments that depend on them to be set in action, they use them to carry out their wishes and to supplement their own weakness. This is how they become bothersome, tyranical, imperious, evil, and unmanageable—a development which does not spring from a natural spirit of domination but which is given them. For one does not need much experience to realise how agreeable it is to act with the hands of others and to need only to move one's tongue in order to make the universe move.

As the child grows it gains strength and becomes less restless and unquiet and turns more towards oneself. Soul and body become better balanced and nature no longer asks for more movement than is required for self-preservation. But the desire to command is not extinguished with the need that aroused it; domination arouses and flatters *amour-propre*, and habit strengthens it. Thus whim succeeds need; thus prejudice and opinion take their first roots.

The principle once known we see clearly the point where one leaves the path of nature. Let us see what must be done to stay on it.

First maxim: Far from having superfluous strength, children do not have enough enough for all that nature demands of them. One must, therefore, let them have the use of all the strength that they are given and which they cannot abuse.

Second Maxim. One must help them and supplement what is lacking either in intelligence or in strength regarding everything that has to do with physical need.

Third Maxim. The help that one gives them should be limited to what is real utility, without granting anything to whim or to desire without reason; for whim will not torment them as long as it has not been aroused, since it is no part of nature.

Fourth Maxim. One must study carefully their language and their signs, so that at an age when they are incapable of deception one may discriminate between those desires which come immediately from nature and those which spring from opinion.

The spirit of these rules is to give children more real freedom and less imperiousness, to let them do more for themselves and demand less of others. Thus accustoming them from the first to limiting their desires to their strengths, they will scarcely feel the deprivation of whatever is not in their power.

This is another very important reason for leaving children's limbs and bodies perfectly free, the only precaution being to keep them away from the danger of falls and to keep out of their hands everything that could hurt them.

Certainly the child whose body and arms are free will cry much less than a child tied up in swaddling clothes. He who knows only bodily needs only cries when in pain; and this is a great advantage, for then we know exactly when he needs help, and if possible we should not delay our help for an instant. But if you cannot relieve his pain, stay where you are and do not flatter him by way of soothing him. Your caresses will not cure his colic, but he will remember what he must do to win them; and if he once finds out how to gain your attention at will, he is your master; everything is lost.

Less constrained in their movements, children will cry less; less wearied with their tears, people will not take so much trouble to keep them quiet. With fewer threats and promises, children will be less timid and less obstinate, and will remain more nearly in their natural state. It is less in letting them cry than in rushing to appease them that makes them get hernias, and my proof for this is that the most neglected children are less subject to them than others. I am very far from wishing that they should be neglected; on the contrary, it is of the utmost importance that their wants should be anticipated, so that one need not be warned of their needs by their cries. But neither would I have unwise care bestowed on them. Why should they think it wrong to cry when they find that their cries are good for so many things? When they have learned the value of their silence they take good care not to waste it. In the end they will so exaggerate its importance that no one will be able to pay its price; then worn out with crying they become exhausted, and are at length silent.

Prolonged crying on the part of a child neither swaddled nor out of health, a child who lacks nothing, is merely the result of habit or obstinacy. Such tears are no longer the work of nature, but the work of the child's care-taker, who could not resist its importunity and so has increased it, without considering that while she quiets the child to-day she is teaching him to cry louder to-morrow.

The only way to cure or prevent this habit is to pay it no attention. No one likes to take useless pains, not even infants. They are obstinate in their attempts; but if you have more constancy than they have hardheadedness, they will give up and not try again. Thus one spares them tears and accustoms them to shed them only when pain forces them to do so.

Moreover, when whim or obstinacy is the cause of their tears, there is a sure way of stopping them by distracting their attention by some pleasant or conspicuous object which makes them forget that they want to cry. Most nurses excel in this art, and rightly used it is very useful. But it is of the utmost importance that the child should not perceive that you mean to distract his attention, and that he should be amused without suspecting you are thinking about him; now this is what most nurses cannot do.

Most children are weaned too soon. The time to wean them is when they cut their teeth. This generally causes pain and suffering. At this time the child instinctively carries everything he gets hold of to his mouth to chew it. To help forward this process he is given as a plaything some hard object such as ivory or a wolf's tooth. I think this is a mistake. Hard bodies applied to the gums do not soften them; far from it, they make the process of cutting the teeth more difficult and painful. Let us always take instinct as our guide; we never see puppies practising their budding teeth on pebbles, iron, or bones, but on wood, leather, rags, soft materials which yield to their jaws, and on which the tooth leaves its mark.

We can do nothing simply, not even for our children. Toys of silver, gold, coral, cut crystal, rattles of every price and kind; what vain and useless appliances! Nothing of all that. No bells, no rattles. A small branch of a tree with its leaves and fruit, a little poppy flower in which one can hear the seeds shake, a stick of liquorice which he may suck and chew, will amuse him as well as all those magnificent knick-knacks, and they will not have the disadvantage of accustoming him to luxury from his birth.

It has been recognized that porridge is not a very wholesome food. Boiled milk and uncooked flour cause gravel and do not suit the stomach. In porridge the flour is less thoroughly cooked than in bread and it has not fermented. I think bread and milk or rice-cream are better. If you absolutely must have porridge, the flour should be lightly cooked beforehand. In my own country they make a very pleasant and wholesome soup from flour thus heated. Meat-broth or soup is not a very suitable food and should be used as little as possible. The child must first get used to chewing his food; this is the right way to bring the teeth through, and when the child begins to swallow, the saliva mixed with the food helps digestion.

I would have them first chew dried fruit or crusts. I would give them as playthings little bits of dry bread or biscuits, like the Piedmont bread, known in the country as "grisses." By dint of softening this bread in the mouth some of it is eventually swallowed, the teeth come through of themselves, and the child is weaned al-most imperceptibly. Peasants have usually very good digestions, and they are weaned with very little trouble.

Children hear people speak from their birth. We speak to them not only before they can understand what is being said to them but before they can imitate the voices that they hear. The vocal organs are still stiff, and only gradually lend themselves to the reproduction of the sounds heard. It is even doubtful whether these sounds are heard distinctly as we hear them. I don't disapprove of the nurse amusing the child with songs and with very merry and varied intonation, but I object to her bewildering the child with a multitude of vain words of which he understands nothing but her tone of voice. I would have the first words he hears be few in number, distinct, and often repeated, while the words themselves be related to things which can first be shown to the child. That unfortunate facility in the use of words we do not understand begins earlier than we think. In the schoolroom the student listens to the verbiage of his master as he listened in the cradle to the babble of his nurse. I think it would be a very useful instruction to leave him in ignoranoc of both.

All sorts of ideas crowd in upon us when we try to consider the development of language and the child's first discourses. Whatever we do they all learn to talk in the same way, and all philosophical speculations are completely useless.

To begin with, children have, so to say, a grammar of their age whose syntax has more general rules than ours. And if one pays close attention one will be surprised to find how exactly they follow certain analogies, very much mistaken if you like, but very regular. These forms are grating only because of their crudeness or because they are not recognised by custom. I have just heard a child severely scolded by his father for saying, "Mon père, irai-je-t-y?" Now we see that this child was following the analogy more closely than our grammarians, for as they say to him, "Vas-y," why should he not say, "Irai-je-t-y? "Notice too the skilful way in which he avoids the hiatus in irai-je-y or y-irai-je? Is it the poor child's fault that we have so unskilfully deprived the phrase of this determinative adverb "y," because we did not know what to do with it? It is an intolerable piece of pedantry and most superfluous attention to detail to make a point of correcting all children's little sins against the customary expression, for they always cure themselves with time. Always speak correctly before them, let them never be so happy with any one as with you, and be sure that their speech will be imperceptibly modelled upon yours without any correction on your part.

But a much greater abuse, and one much less easy to prevent, is that they are urged to speak too much, as if people were afraid they would not learn to talk by themselves. This indiscreet pressure produces an effect directly opposite to what is meant. They speak later and more confusedly. The extreme attention paid to every-thing they say makes it unnecessary for them to speak distinctly, and as they will scarcely open their mouths, many of them contract bad pronunciation and a confused speech, which last all their life and make them almost unintelligible.

I have lived much among peasants, and I never knew one of them to lisp, man or woman, boy or girl. Why is this? Are their speech organs differently made from our own? No, but they are differently used. There is a little hill facing my window on which the children of the place assemble for their games. Although they are far enough away, I can distinguish perfectly what they say, and often get good notes for this book. Every day my ear deceives me as to their age. I hear the voices of children of ten; I look and see the height and features of children of three or four. This experience is not confined to me; the townspeople who come to see me, and whom I consult on this point, all fall into the same mistake.

This results from the fact that, up to five or six, children in town, brought up in a room and under the care of a nursery governess, do not need to speak above a whisper to make themselves heard. As soon as their lips move people take pains to make out what they mean. They are taught words which they repeat inaccurately, and by paying great attention to them the people who are always with them guess what they meant to say rather than what they said.

It is quite a different matter in the country. A peasant woman is not always with her child; he is obliged to learn to say very clearly and loudly what he wants if he is to make himself understood. Children scattered about the fields at a distance from their fathers, mothers and other children, gain practice in making themselves heard at a distance, and in adapting the loudness of the voice to the distance which separates them from those to whom they want to speak. This is the real way to learn pronunciation, not by stammering out a few vowels into the ear of an attentive governess. So when you question a peasant child, he may be too shy to answer, but what he says he says distinctly; while the nurse must serve as interpreter for the town child: without her one can understand nothing of what he is muttering between his teeth.

As they grow older, the boys are supposed to be cured of this fault at college, the girls in the convent schools; and indeed both usually speak more clearly than children brought up entirely at home. But what prevents them from acquiring as clear a pronunciation as the peasants in this way is the necessity of learning all sorts of things by heart and repeating aloud what they have learned. For when they are studying they get to babbling and pronouncing carelessly and wrong. In reciting their lessons it is even worse: they cannot find the right words, they drag out their syllables. It is impossible that when the memory vacillates the tongue will not stammer also. Thus they acquire or continue habits of bad pronunciation. You will see later on that Emile will not acquire such habits, or at least not from this cause.

I grant you that uneducated people and villagers often fall into the opposite extreme. They almost always speak too loud; their pronunciation is too exact and leads to rough and coarse articulation; their accent is too pronounced, they choose their expressions badly, etc.

But, to begin with, this extreme strikes me as much less dangerous than the other, for the first law of speech is to make oneself understood, and the chief fault is to fail to be understood. To pride ourselves on having no accent is to pride ourselves on ridding our phrases of strength and elegance. Emphasis is the soul of speech, it gives it its feeling and truth. Emphasis deceives less than words; perhaps that is why well-educated people are so afraid of it. From the custom of saying everything in the same tone has arisen that of poking fun at people without their knowing it. When emphasis is proscribed, its place is taken by all sorts of ridiculous, affected, and ephemeral pronunciations, such as those heard especially among the young people of the court. It is this affectation of speech and manner which makes Frenchmen disagreeable and repulsive to other nations on first acquaintance. Emphasis is found, not in their speech, but in their bearing. That is not the way to make themselves attractive.

All these little faults of speech, which you are so afraid the children will acquire, are nothing. They may be prevented or corrected with the greatest ease, but the faults that are taught them when you make them speak in a low, indistinct, and timid voice, when you are always criticising their tone and finding fault with their words, are never cured. A man who has only learned to speak from his side of a bed could never make himself heard at the head of his troops and would make little impression on the people during an uprising. First teach the child to speak to men; he will be able to speak to the women when required.

Nurtured in the country with all its pastoral rusticity, your children will gain a more sonorous voice; they will not acquire the hesitating stammer of town children, neither will they acquire the expressions nor the tone of the villagers. Or if they do they will easily lose them. Their tutor being with them from their earliest years and living with them from day to day ever more exclusively, will be able to prevent or efface, by speaking correctly himself, the impression of the peasants' talk. Emile will speak the purest French I know, but he will speak it more distinctly and with a better articulation than myself.

The child who is trying to speak should hear nothing but words he can understand, nor should he say words he cannot articulate. His efforts lead him to repeat the same syllable as if he were practising its clear pronunciation. When he begins to stammer, do not try to understand him. To expect to be always listened to is a form of tyranny which is not good for the child. See carefully to his real needs, and let him try to make you understand the rest. Still less should you hurry him into speech; he will learn to talk when he feels the usefulness of it.

It has indeed been remarked that those who begin to speak very late never speak so distinctly as others; but it is not because they talked late that they are hesitating. On the contrary, they began to talk late because they hesitate; if not, why did they begin to talk so late? Have they less need of speech, have they been less urged to it? On the contrary, the anxiety aroused with the first suspicion of this backwardness leads people to tease them much more to begin to talk than those who articulated earlier. This mistaken zeal may do much to make their speech confused, when with less haste they might have had time to bring it to greater perfection.

Children who are forced to speak too soon have no time to learn either to pronounce correctly or to understand what they are made to say. While left to themselves they first practise the easiest syllables, and then, adding to them little by little some meaning which their gestures explain, they teach you their own words before they learn yours. By this means they do not acquire your words till they have understood them. Being in no hurry to use them, they begin by carefully observing the sense in which you use them, and when they are sure of them they will adopt them.

The worst evil resulting from the precocious use of speech by young children is that we not only fail to understand the first words they use, we misunderstand them without knowing it. So that while they seem to answer us correctly, they fail to understand us and we them. This is the most frequent cause of our surprise at children's sayings; we attribute to them ideas which they did not attach to their words. This lack of attention on our part to the real meaning which words have for children seems to me the cause of their earliest misconceptions; and these misconceptions, even when corrected, colour their whole course of thought for the rest of their life. I will have several opportunities of illustrating these by examples later on.

Let the child's vocabulary, therefore, be limited. It is very undesirable that he should have more words than ideas, that he should be able to say more than he thinks. One of the reasons why peasants are generally shrewder than townsfolk is, I think, that their vocabulary is smaller. They have few ideas, but those few are thoroughly grasped.

The infant is progressing in several ways at once; he is learning to talk, eat, and walk about the same time. This is really the first epoque of his life. Formerly he was nothing more than what he was in the womb of his mother: he had no sentiments, no ideas, he scarcely had sensations; he could not even feel his own existence.

"Vivit, et est vitæ nescius ipse suæ" —*Ovid.*

Some Thoughts Concerning Education

—John Locke

Due care being had to keep the body in strength and vigour, so that it may be able to obey and execute the orders of the *mind;* the next and principal business is, to set the *mind* right, that on all occasions it may be dispos'd to consent to nothing but what may be suitable to the dignity and excellency of a rational creature.

If what I have said in the beginning of this discourse be true, as I do not doubt but it is, *viz.* That the difference to be found in the manners and abilities of men is owing more to their *education* than to any thing else, we have reason to conclude, that great care is to be had of the forming children's *minds,* and giving them that seasoning early, which shall influence their lives always after: For when they do well or ill, the praise and blame will be laid there; and when any thing is done awkwardly, the common saying will pass upon them, that it's suitable to their *breeding.*

As the strength of the body lies chiefly in being able to endure hardships, so also does that of the mind. And the great principle and foundation of all virtue and worth is plac'd in this: that a man is able to *deny himself* his own desires, cross his own inclinations, and purely follow what reason directs as best, tho' the appetite lean the other way.

The great mistake I have observ'd in people's breeding their children, has been, that this has not been taken care enough of in its *due season:* that the mind has not been made obedient to discipline, and pliant to reason, when at first it was most tender, most easy to be bow'd. Parents being wisely ordain'd by nature to love their children, are very apt, if reason watch not that natural affection very warily, are apt, I say, to let it run into fondness. They love their little ones and it is their duty; but they often, with them, cherish their faults too. They must not be cross'd, forsooth; they must be permitted to have their wills in all things; and they being in their infancies not capable of great vices, their parents think they may safe enough indulge their irregularities, and make themselves sport with that pretty perverseness which they think well enough becomes that innocent age. But to a fond parent, that would not have his child corrected for a perverse trick, but excus'd it, saying it was a small matter, *Solon* very well reply'd, *aye, but custom is a great one.*

The fondling must be taught to strike and call names, must have what he cries for, and do what he pleases. Thus parents, by humouring and cockering them when *little,* corrupt the principles of nature in their children, and wonder afterwards to taste the bitter waters, when they themselves have poison'd the fountain. For when their children are grown up, and these ill habits with them; when they are now too big to be dandled, and their parents can no longer make use of them as play-things, then they complain that the brats are untoward and perverse; then they are offended to see them wilful, and are troubled with those ill humours which they themselves infus'd and fomented in them; and then, perhaps too late, would be glad to get out those weeds which their own hands have planted, and which now have taken too deep root to be easily extirpated. For he that hath been us'd to have his will in every thing, as long as he was in coats, why should we think it strange, that he should desire it, and contend for it still, when he is in breeches? Indeed, as he grows more towards a man, age shews his faults the more; so that there be few parents then so blind as not to see them, few so insensible as not to feel the ill effects of their own indulgence. He had the will of his maid before he could speak or go; he had the mastery of his parents ever since he could prattle; and why, now he is grown up, is stronger and wiser than he was then, why now of a sudden must he be restrain'd and curb'd? Why must he at seven, fourteen, or twenty years old, lose the privilege, which the parents' indulgence 'till then so largely allow'd him? Try it in a dog or an horse or any other creature, and see whether the ill and resty tricks they have learn'd when young, are easily to be mended when they are knit; and yet none of those creatures are half so wilful and proud, or half so desirous to be masters of themselves and others, as man.

We are generally wise enough to begin with them when they are *very young,* and discipline *betimes* those other creatures we would make useful and good for somewhat. They are only our own offspring, that we neglect in this point; and having made them ill children, we foolishly expect they should be good men. For if the child must have grapes or sugar-plums when he has a mind to them, rather than make the poor baby cry or be out of humour; why, when, he is grown up, must he not be satisfy'd too, if his desires carry him to wine or women? They are objects as suitable to the longing of one of more years, as what he cry'd for, when little, was to the inclinations of a child. The having desires accommodated to the apprehensions and relish of those several ages, is not the fault; but the not having them subject to the rules and restraints of reason: the difference lies not in having or not having appetites, but in the power to govern, and deny ourselves in them. He that is not us'd to submit his will to the reason of others *when* he is *young,* will scarce hearken to submit to his own reason when he is of an age to make use of it. And what kind of a man such an one is like to prove, is easy to foresee.

These are oversights usually committed by those who seem to take the greatest care of their children's education. But if we look into the common management of children, we shall have reason to wonder, in the great dissoluteness of manners which the world complains of, that there are any footsteps at all left of virtue. I desire to know what vice can be nam'd, which parents, and those about children, do not season them with, and drop into 'em the seeds of, as soon as they are capable to receive them? I do not mean by the examples they give, and the patterns they set before them, which is encouragement enough; but that which I would take notice of here is, the downright teaching them vice, and actual putting them out of the way of virtue. Before they can go, they principle 'em with violence, revenge, and cruelty. *Give me a blow, that I may beat him,* is a lesson which most children every day hear; and it is thought nothing, because their hands have not strength to do any mischief. But I ask, does not this corrupt their mind? Is not this the way of force and violence, that they are set in? And if they have been taught when little, to strike and hurt others by proxy, and encourag'd to rejoice in the harm they have brought upon them, and see them suffer, are they not prepar'd to do it when they are strong enough to be felt themselves, and can strike to some purpose?

The coverings of our bodies which are for modesty, warmth and defence, are by the folly or vice of parents recommended to their children for other uses. They are made matters of vanity and emulation. A child is set a-longing after a new suit, for the finery of it; and when the little girl is trick'd up in her new gown and commode, how can her mother do less than teach her to admire herself, by calling her, *her little queen* and *her princess?* Thus the little ones are taught to be *proud* of their clothes before they can put them on. And why should they not continue to value themselves for their outside fashionableness of the taylor or tirewoman's making, when their parents have so early instructed them to do so?

Lying and equivocations, and excuses little different from lying, are put into the mouths of young people, and commended in apprentices and children, whilst they are for their master's or parents' advantage. And can it be thought, that he that finds the straining of truth dispens'd with, and encourag'd, whilst it is for his godly master's turn, will not make use of that privilege for himself, when it may be for his own profit?

Those of the meaner sort are hinder'd, by the straitness of their fortunes, from encouraging *intemperance* in their children by the temptation of their diet, or invitations to eat or drink more than enough; but their own ill examples, whenever plenty comes in their way, shew, that 'tis not the dislike of drunkenness or gluttony, that keeps them from excess, but want of materials. But if we look into the houses of those who are a little warmer in their fortunes, their eating and drinking are made so much the great business and happiness of life, that children are thought neglected, if they have not their share of it. Sauces and ragoos, and food disguis'd by all the arts of cookery, must tempt their palates, when their bellies are full; and then, for fear the stomach should be overcharg'd, a pretence is found for t'other glass of wine to help digestion, tho' it only serves to increase the surfeit.

Is my young master a little out of order, the first question is, *What will my dear eat? What shall I get for thee?* Eating and drinking are instantly press'd; and every body's invention is set on work, to find out something luscious and delicate enough to prevail over that want of appetite, which nature has wisely order'd in the beginning of distempers, as a defence against their increase; that being freed from the ordinary labour of digesting any new load in the stomach, she may be at leisure to correct and master the peccant humours.

And where children are so happy in the care of their parents, as by their prudence to be kept from the excess of their tables, to the sobriety of a plain and simple diet, yet there too they are scarce to be preserv'd from the contagion that poisons the mind; though, by a discreet management whilst they are under tuition, their healths perhaps may be pretty well secure, yet their desires must needs yield to the lessons which every where will be read to them upon this part of *epicurism.* The commendation that *eating well* has every where, cannot fail to be a successful incentive to natural appetites, and bring them quickly to the liking and expence of a fashionable table. This shall have from every one, even the reprovers of vice, the title of *living well.* And what shall sullen reason dare to say against the publick testimony? Or can it hope to be heard, if it should call that *luxury*, which is so much own'd and universally practis'd by those of the best quality?

This is now so grown a vice, and has so great supports, that I know not whether it do not put in for the name of virtue; and whether it will not be thought folly, or want of knowledge of the world, to open one's mouth against it? And truly I should suspect, that what I have here said of it, might be censur'd as a little satire out of my way, did I not mention it with this view, that it might awaken the care and watchfulness of parents in the education of their children, when they see how they are beset on every side, not only with temptations, but instructors to vice, and that, perhaps, in those they thought places of security.

I shall not dwell any longer on this subject, much less run over all the particulars that would shew what pains are us'd to corrupt children, and instil principles of vice into them: but I desire parents soberly to consider, what irregularity or vice there is which children are not visibly taught, and whether it be not their duty and wisdom to provide them other instructions.

It seems plain to me, that the principle of all virtue and excellency lies in a power of denying ourselves the satisfaction of our own desires, where reason does not authorize them. This power is to be got and improv'd by custom, made easy and familiar by an *early* practice. If therefore I might be heard, I would advise, that, contrary to the ordinary way, children should be us'd to submit their desires, and go without their longings, even *from their very cradles*. The first thing they should learn to know, should be, that they were not to have anything because it pleas'd them, but because it was thought fit for them. If things suitable to their wants were supply'd to them, so that they were never suffer'd to have what they once cry'd for, they would learn to be content without it, would never, with bawling and peevishness, contend for mastery, nor be half so uneasy to themselves and others as they are, because *from the first* beginning they are not thus handled. If they were never suffer'd to obtain their desire by the impatience they express'd for it, they would no more cry for another thing, than they do for the moon.

I say not this, as if children were not to be indulg'd in anything, or that I expected they should in hanging-sleeves have the reason and conduct of counsellors. I consider them as children, who must be tenderly us'd, who must play, and have play-things. That which I mean, is, that whenever they crav'd what was not fit for them to have or do, they should not be permitted it because they were *little*, and desir'd it: nay, whatever they were importunate for, they should be sure, for that very reason, to be deny'd. I have seen children at a table, who, whatever was there, never ask'd for anything, but contentedly took what was given them; and at another place, I have seen others cry for everything they saw; must be serv'd out of every dish, and that first too. What made this vast difference but this? that one was accustom'd to have what they call'd or cry'd for, the other to go without it. The *younger* they are, the less I think are their unruly and disorderly appetites to be comply'd with; and the less reason they have of their own, the more are they to be under the absolute power and restraint of those in whose hands they are. From which I confess it will follow, that none but discreet people should be about them. If the world commonly does otherwise, I cannot help that. I am saying what I think should be; which if it were already in fashion, I should not need to trouble the world with a discourse on this subject. But yet I doubt not, but when it is consider'd, there will be others of opinion with me, that the *sooner* this way is begun with children, the easier it will be for them and their governors too; and that this ought to be observ'd as an inviolable maxim, that whatever once is deny'd them, they are certainly not to obtain by crying or importunity, unless one has a mind to teach them to be impatient and troublesome, by rewarding them for it when they are so.

Those therefore that intend ever to govern their children, should begin it whilst they are *very little*, and look that they perfectly comply with the will of their parents. Would you have your son obedient to you when past a child; be sure then to establish the authority of a father *as soon* as he is capable of submission, and can understand in whose power he is. If you would have him stand in awe of you, imprint it in his *infancy*; and as he approaches more to a man, admit him nearer to your familiarity; so shall you have him your obedient subject (as is fit) whilst he is a child, and your affectionate friend when he is a man. For methinks they mightily misplace the treatment due to their children, who are indulgent and familiar when they are little, but severe to them, and keep them at a distance, when they are grown up: for liberty and indulgence can do no good to *children*; their want of judgment makes them stand in need of restraint and discipline; and on the contrary, imperiousness and severity is but an ill way of treating men, who have reason of their own to guide them; unless you have a mind to make your children, when grown up, weary of you, and secretly to say within themselves, *When will you die, father?*

What Knowledge Is of Most Worth?

Herbert Spencer

—Brian Holmes[1]

Herbert Spencer was a gifted amateur. Compared with his distinguished contemporaries, he was neither as precocious as J. S. Mill nor as well-educated as Charles Darwin and T. H. Huxley. Mill, a famous philosopher, was learning Greek at the age of 3 and had written a Roman history at the age of 6 (Bain, 1882). Both Darwin, who attended a famous public school—Shrewsbury (Barlow, 1958) and Huxley, who went to one of the best-known private schools in England (Bibby, 1959), received more formal education than Spencer. Yet at a time when, in the absence of popular publicly provided education, only a few boys acquired an education based on the classical languages, his schooling was not negligible. He attended a local school for three years but could not read until he was 7. At the age of 13 he went to stay with his uncle, Thomas Spencer, who had had a successful career at Cambridge University before becoming the priest of a parish near Bath. Young Herbert ran away when first left with his uncle but returned to acquire, on his own testimony (Spencer, 1850, p. 115), some knowledge of mathematics, physics and chemistry, a little French, some Greek grammar and an ability to translate some easy texts from Latin. Since, at the age of 16, Spencer declined the offer of a place at Cambridge University arranged by his uncle, he was obliged to look for a job. Fifty years later, he looked back on his educational achievements and was grateful for the stimulus to work provided by the school run by his uncle. His strictures about formal education were directed specifically to that type of schooling provided in the establishments attended by his subsequent adult friends who, in spite of it, had become world-famous professional philosophers and scientists. Formal schooling may not have been decisive in the careers of any of these nineteenth-century English intellectual giants; but Spencer was, however, an amateur among professionals.

For example, he learned much from experience. In roaming the countryside he collected specimens, acquired a tolerable knowledge of animal and insect life, and taught himself how to sketch from nature. Against the book knowledge acquired by his contemporaries, Spencer was proud to weigh the knowledge he had gained from things around him. At the same time it is clear that he benefited greatly from the intellectual atmosphere created by his father and uncle, and in which he grew up. His father, William George Spencer (1790–1866), was an apolitical radical who wanted to see society re-ordered. Though at one time a member of the Library Committee of the Derby Methodists, Spencer senior objected to the power that ministers exercised over the members of the congregation and began to attend Quaker services so that he could reflect quietly. He was by all accounts a good schoolmaster who, ahead of his time, advocated self-education. Free from doctrinal constraints, Spencer gave his father credit for the development in him of a scientific outlook which made him, like his father, hostile to supernatural explanations. As an agnostic, Spencer was more radical than his father, who could be regarded as a scientific deist. The two remained on good terms and corresponded regularly until his father died. The letters between them indicate mutual respect.

The influence of his uncle probably made Spencer even more radical since, for three years from the age of 13, Thomas Spencer (1796–1853), who was a lecturer and pamphleteer on matters of social reform, was in charge of Herbert's education. Thomas was interested in political action and favoured, among other things, church reform. Encouraged by his uncle, Spencer identified himself with most of the reform movements of the day. For example, his uncle was interested in the Complete Suffrage Union and, for a short time, Herbert was secretary of its Derby branch. His uncle also influenced his decision to write and at 16 he started a literary career with his short articles, critical of the Poor Laws, appearing in a local magazine.

By the time he was ready for work Spencer was already temperamentally opposed to all kinds of authority and was determined to pursue a literary career. His work as a railway engineer between 1837 and 1841 and again between 1845 and 1848 added another dimension to his education. The industrial revolution engaged the attention of a great many Englishmen. The construction of railway lines opening up the country was regarded

This document was originally published in *Prospects: The Quarterly Review of Comparative Education*, Vol. 24, No. 3/4, 1994, p. 533–554 (Paris UNESCO: International Bureau of Education). © UNESCO: International Bureau of Education.

by many Victorians as the single most important manifestation brought about by technological innovation in the nineteenth century. Spencer, engaged in surveying railway cuttings and inclines and preparing schemes for parliamentary approval, became aware of the ruthless drive to spread the network of railways. Some of his views on the social implications of this aspect of industrial development, of which he had first-hand experience, appeared in his article Railway Morals and Railway Policy in the Edinburgh Review of October 1854. Many years later, in 1892, he wrote a letter to an Earl of the Realm opposing the extension of a railway line through an inner London suburb unless the local residents were safeguarded from the enormous evil inflicted upon them by railway companies at every town in the kingdom (Duncan, 1908, p. 314).

In addition to his interest in social affairs, work on the railways also added to his scientific knowledge. The fossils he unearthed in the railway cuttings stimulated Spencer's study of geology. Thus, his brief experience of industrial life enabled him to speak to his fellow Victorians with some authority. At the same time, he missed no opportunity to increase his knowledge of the natural sciences.

From an early age Spencer appears to have been determined to give up engineering for a literary career, and between 1841 and 1845 he tried without much success to make his living as a journalist. His first work of any consequence a series of letters entitled the Proper Sphere of Government was published in The Nonconformist, to which he also contributed reports about the Complete Suffrage Union. Nevertheless, his initial failure to enter the literary field was not, in retrospect, without its compensations. He went back to engineering for a short time before becoming sub-editor of The Economist in 1848. This periodical had just been founded by an opponent of the Corn Laws and its editorial policy consistently and determinedly advocated laissez-faire as the correct way of running society. According to J. D. Y. Peel, Spencer simply amassed and presented factual material for The Economist and was more influenced by, rather than an influence on it or rather, was simply in accord with it (Peel, 1971, p. 77). The extreme position of the periodical was evident in its attacks on legislation which Arrested on ignorance of the laws of nature, and could have no beneficial consequences (ibid., p. 78).

The view that society should be organized in accordance with the laws of nature and that the best government was that which interfered least in the lives of individuals were convictions advanced consistently by Spencer in his subsequent writings. It was his aim to discover, within his evolutionary framework, natural scientific laws in accordance with which individuals could, without interference from the State, run their own affairs.

These views found expression in his first book, *Social Statics,* which was published in 1850, when he was 30. The book's contents were clearly in line with those espoused in The Economist up until the time he left it in 1853. For example, in *Social Statics* Spencer enunciated the equal-freedom doctrine which asserted that the freedom of each person was limited only to the extent that the liberties of other people were not infringed. This view he reaffirmed at the age of 79 when he reviewed his life's work. His chapter on education in *Social Statics,* in which he applied his principles, was from the start controversial; some critics became particularly incensed by his view that there should be no state involvement in education. As national systems developed throughout the nineteenth century, his view was ignored or considered bizarre, except perhaps in the United States where the power of the federal government in education was resisted. Today, the dangers of state control of education are more clearly recognized, at least as it operated in the former Soviet Union. In the United Kingdom, too, the rights of parents to decide how their children should be educated in state schools are running up against the power of local authorities to run schools. While Spencer's extreme views about parental influence and state control are contrary to established opinion today, his warnings are reflected in the desire of present-day educational policy-makers to decentralize educational control and increase parental freedom of choice.

In 1853 a legacy from his Uncle Thomas made it possible for Spencer to leave The Economist and subsequently to devote himself, as had long been his wish, to writing. By this time his self-education had been completed. Compared with his contemporaries, Spencer lacked many of the formal educational ingredients required of a potential philosopher or scientist. By philosophers, he was not regarded as a true philosopher; by scientists, he was not considered a professional scientist. On the other hand, through his own observations, the intellectual atmosphere provided by his father and uncle, industrial life as an engineer and his work for a radical periodical, he had educated himself admirably for the monumental task he set himself when, in 1853, he became a professional author.

In the absence of an institutional position in which he would have been required to teach or undertake research, his achievements were enormous. On the one hand, he was a radical critic of the *status quo* and against authority of any kind. On the other hand he had, by 1860, deduced an intellectual conception of the whole universe and spent the next thirty-six years of his life filling in the details of his system. As an extremely talented amateur, elements of his the Synthetic Philosophy, finally completed in 1896, together with his correspondence with distinguished scientists like Darwin, Huxley and John Tyndall, and philosophers like J. S. Mill, testify to the fact that, without being one of them, he was accepted as being in their league. It was a remarkable achievement.

THE SOCIO-ECONOMIC AND POLITICAL CONTEXT

As a self-educated academic, Spencer had many counterparts in the commercial and economic life of his day. In the United Kingdom, the nineteenth century was a period when the application of science in industry, which had started in the eighteenth century, gained momentum. Many self-made men, with minimal formal education, contributed to the growth of industry and its infrastructure; the rural society was transformed into an urban society. The abundance of coal facilitated the development of the iron industry; between 1788 and 1839 the production of pig iron grew from 68,000 to 1,347,000 tons. Steam-driven machines revolutionized the production of wool and cotton. Lancashire became the centre of the cotton industry; the West Riding of Yorkshire the centre of the woollen industry. In 1835 England produced over 60% of the cotton goods consumed in the world. The network of canals was extended to link the industrial districts in the north of England with the centres of distribution and the ports. To these developments was added the growth of a railway system first opened in 1825, founded by George Stephenson, an engineer for a railway company in northern England. Spencer, as stated, was employed for some time as a railway engineer

In the field of industrial development, there were great opportunities for enterprising men to make their own careers. Many of them from small beginnings helped to build up successful industries. These opportunities and their attendant success help to explain the optimism of the time and a disregard of the social evils that were fictionalized in such novels as *A Christmas Carol* and Oliver Twist by Charles Dickens. As a social reformer, Dickens revealed the dirt and brutality of schools, particularly those in the north of England. The squalor of Dickensian city life for the underprivileged is the other side of a situation in which a prosperous middle class grew in size and demanded for its children schools comparable to the ancient public schools, of which Eton, Harrow and Winchester were among the best known. Spencer criticized the schools of his day, but his commitment to economic liberalism and non-interference by the state prevented him from advocating the establishment of appropriate social services for those disadvantaged by the uncontrolled development of industry and commerce. Paradoxically, the population explosion, giving rise to Malthusian predictions of disaster, was seen by Spencer as a cause of progress and made social organization inevitable.

Politically, Spencer lived in an age of dissent and, as we have seen, was from an early age associated with many local radical movements. For the dissenters, the abolition of hereditary social advantages was the key to greater opportunities and self-betterment. Various groups were able to unite against the aristocracy, the landowners and the hereditary principle. On the issue of control of education, the Methodists aligned themselves with dissent. Spencer's family were Methodists. Faced with radical alternatives to the status quo, Spencer opted for co-operative individualism rather than socialism. He was, for example, against free libraries and state education on the grounds that they were socialist. And much as I abhor war, I abhor socialism in all its forms quite as much (Duncan, 1908, p. 422). As a radical in an age of radicalism, Spencer was a conservative. Yet he captured the mood of the times and spoke for the members of the growing middle class.

SPENCER'S SYNTHETIC PHILOSOPHY

Spencer's philosophy was in tune with his individualism and optimism. Individuals free to adapt to a changing society made progress inevitable. When complete, *The Synthetic Philosophy* represented his life's work. During the 1850s, he had published enough to make his views well-known. In 1855 his *The Principles of Psychology* appeared. His earlier psychology had its origins in phrenology in vogue at the time through George Combe's *The Constitution of Man* which, because it asserted that an understanding of a person could be gained by studying the shape of their head, no doubt appealed to Spencer's interest in making the study of psychology scientific. Combe's view of education as similar to that of Spencer in that he thought it should be secular and scientific. Spencer's evolutionary psychology broke new ground but, according to Harold Barrington, should now be regarded as pre-psychology. In any case, it was extended and incorporated into his the Synthetic Philosophy which had been conceived in its entirety by about 1858

In the preface to First Principles, which appeared in 1862, Spencer laid out his scheme. At regular intervals he filled in its component parts by publishing *The Principles of Biology* in two parts in 1864 and 1867, the first part of *The Principles of Sociology* in 1876 and *The Principles of Ethics* in two volumes between 1892 and 1893. As mentioned, *The Principles of Psychology* had already been published in 1855. The whole scheme, planned to take twenty-four years, took him thirty-six years to complete. In addition, he also published a great many articles on social issues and scientific topics. His book *Education: Intellectual, Moral and Physical*, bought together previously published articles, appeared in 1861.

Descriptive Sociology, prepared with the help of several collaborators, included comparative studies of races throughout the world.

Spencer pioneered the scientific study of psychology and sociology but, from his first essay on *The Proper Sphere of Government* (1843), his ultimate purpose 'lying behind all proximate purposes [was] that of finding for the principles of right and wrong, in conduct at large, a scientific basis' (Spencer, 1879, p. iii). Science informed all his work.

He provoked controversy, having something to say on most of the issues of the day. In his own lifetime, his work was recognized by scientists and philosophers at home and abroad. He was offered honorary degrees and membership in scientific academies in the United Kingdom and in more than a dozen foreign countries. He refused all these invitations. In the United Kingdom, the publication of the last volume of *The Synthetic Philosophy* evoked an outburst of sympathetic appreciation from a wide range of scholars in recognition of his intellectual power and his high moral purpose. More than eighty of the most distinguished academics, politicians and literary figures in the country asked him to sit for a portrait with a view to its being deposited in one of our national collections for the benefit of ourselves and those who come after us (Duncan, 1908, p. 383). William Gladstone, a distinguished prime minister, went so far as to break his rule of not joining groups of signatories and agreed to be set down as an approver of the request to Mr. Spencer (ibid.). Spencer eventually reluctantly agreed to have his portrait painted; in any event, he did not like it.

Further evidence of the liking and respect shown him by s contemporaries was revealed when he found it difficult to continue publication of *The Synthetic Philosophy*. An appeal for money was launched on his behalf and signed by distinguished academics, such as J. S. Mill, George Grote, Charles Darwin, T. H. Huxley, Alexander Bain, John Herschel, G. H. Lewes, John Tyndall, Charles King, T. H. Buckle and William De Morgan. With some of these men Huxley, for example he had prolonged disputes. His letters reveal, however, that he drew a sharp distinction between personal and impersonal criticism. He discussed issues on their merits and seldom descended to personal attacks. The tone in which he conducted debates helps to explain why, in spite of his critical rejection of established positions and his personal foibles, he was on good terms with the English intelligentsia. For example, he was a member of the exclusive X Club, of which there were only nine members, all of whom, with the exception of Spencer, were members of the most prestigious scientific organization in the United Kingdom: the Royal Society. Attempts were made to induce Spencer to become a member of that society, but he refused (as he did with many other honours) on the grounds that had the society invited him earlier, instead of hindering his work, he might have accepted. Members of the X Club wielded an enormous influence over scientific affairs. Spencer was, indeed, a member of the intellectual "establishment."

His position was recognized when, in 1868, he was elected to the Athenaeum, a London club where intellectuals met and for some time he was on its committee. He spent a great deal of time at the club and, by all accounts, became a good clubman, even if a pedantic member of the committee. Although claiming himself to be brusque and, certainly, in refusing the many honours he was offered by institutions in many countries he did not mince words he was described as sympathetic, companionable, hospitable, considerate and generous (ibid., p. 499–500). He liked children and enjoyed staying with friends. A keen sportsman, he was particularly fond of fishing and billiards. His was a complex character, yet his qualities outweighed his defects.

His foibles were well known. He was cantankerous, vain, sensitive to criticism, dogmatic and very self-confident. Some of his characteristics were, however, endearing. Huxley wrote: if ever Spencer wrote a tragedy, its plot would be the slaying of a beautiful deduction by an ugly fact (ibid., p. 502). Again, when Beatrice Webb commented on Spencer's contribution to the theory of evolution, Huxley remarked: He is the most original of thinkers, though he has never invented a new thought (Webb, 1926, p. 27). His willingness to tell more experienced people how to do such things as bring up their children gave rise to some amusing situations. While paying great attention to the smallest detail of domestic management, he was most impracticable administrator. His serious nature was well known. On one occasion in Spencer's presence John Tyndall said of him: "He'd be a much nicer fellow if he had a good swear now and then" (Duncan, 1908, p. 510). The thought of Spencer swearing caused hilarity among those present.

SPENCER'S THEORY OF EVOLUTION

Spencer's originality lies in his formulation and application of the laws of evolution to the scientific study of psychology, sociology, biology, education and ethics. John Dewey, in a chapter entitled The Work of Herbert Spencer in his *Characters and Events* (1929), pointed out that the theory of evolution had a long history in European philosophy. In its nineteenth-century reformulation, it created enormous controversy because it ran contrary to Christian belief in the story of creation. Charles Darwin is regarded as the nineteenth century scientist who re-discovered evolution. His *On the Origin of Species* appeared in 1859. Very modestly, Spencer pointed out that his version of evolution had been published some years before Darwin's book appeared. Certainly, the theory was fully developed in First Principles published in 1862. What is clear, however, in the words of Darwin himself, is that in *On the Origin of Species* he restricted the application of the theory to biological changes. Spencer did not. Analyzing change in First Principles, he deduced the laws of evolution from changes in the solar system, the Earth's structure and climate, in plants and animals, in individual men and in society. Change, in accordance with these universal laws, included processes of integration and differentiation.

Integrative changes in the social organism were clearly and abundantly exemplified by Spencer. "Uncivilized societies display them when wandering families, such as we see among the Bushmen, join into tribes of considerable numbers" (Spencer, 1862, p. 316). 'The progress from rude to, small, and simple tools to perfect, complex and large machines in a progress in integration' (ibid., p.324). In modern machines, a number of smaller simple machines are united. 'Evolution then, under its primary aspect, is a change from a less coherent form to a more coherent form', (ibid., p. 327). This is a universal process.

Of more consequence to an understanding of modern societies is the process of differentiation as change from a homogeneous state to a heterogeneous state. As before, Spencer took his examples from all fields of scientific knowledge: in geology a molten mass is changed into mountains; in geography there is a differentiation of climates. Differentiation takes place in plants and animals. Man has grown more heterogeneous; for example, civilized man has a more heterogeneous nervous system and his thoughts are more heterogeneous than uncivilized man. In the human being this change from an indefinite, herent homogeneity, to a definite coherent heterogeneity (ibid., p. 389) was illustrated by changes from homogeneous infant noises to more and more differentiated and definite sounds.

Social change from homogeneity to heterogeneity was exemplified in the progress of civilization in every tribe and nation. Society, in its first and lowest form, was a homogeneous aggregate of individuals. Every man, for example, was a warrior, tool-maker, fisherman and builder. All women performed the same drudgeries. Every family was self-sufficient and may well have lived apart from the rest. Chieftainship was the first sign of a differentiation of function. Power then became hereditary and religion co-existed with government. The next stage of social evolution was characterized by laws, manners and ceremonial usages. The specialization of labour occurred. Transport systems stimulated the development of districts with their own occupational characteristics. Society eventually became differentiated into classes. Spencer concluded:

> *Comparing the rule of a savage chief with that of a civilized government, aided by its subordinate local governments and their officers, down to the police in the streets, we see how, as men have advanced from tribes of tens to nations of millions, the regulative process has grown large in amount; how, guided by written laws, it has passed from vagueness and irregularity to comparative precision; and how it has subdivided into processes increasingly multiform (ibid., 395).*

These forms of differentiation were accompanied by differentiation in language, painting and sculpture, dancing and poetry. Spencer concluded: "From the remotest past which Science can fathom, up to the novelties of yesterday, an essential trait of Evolution has been the transformation of the homogeneous into the heterogeneous" (ibid., p. 359). Along with change from homogeneity to heterogeneity, Spencer recognized moves from the indefinite to the definite, from simplicity to complexity, and from confusion to order.

Darwin is usually credited with what is called social Darwinism. It could more accurately be termed "social Spencerism." The examples of his analysis of social change given here are designed to demonstrate the wealth of examples Spencer used to establish his deductive hypothesis that societies, like everything else, change according to the scientific laws of evolution.

He also applied the biological notion of "survival of the fittest" to societies. Modifications arise as a consequence of social differentiation and persist if they are well-adapted to the environment. They will eventually perish if they are not well-adapted. Spencer also held steadfastly, against scientific consensus, to a hotly contested biological theory advanced by Lamarck, who maintained that acquired characteristics were passed on to one's offspring. A majority of scientists rejected this view as the century progressed. In social affairs it has major implications. It means that characteristics acquired by parents through education can be inherited by their children. Thus, the characteristics of national character—a concept used by nineteenth century comparative educators—could be inherited. Racial characteristics, if not genetic, may also be passed on from one generation to the next. It is an assumption that can be used by both racists and anti-racists.

Convinced that all changes are evolutionary, Spencer argued from analogy in the absence of direct evidence. He used the analogy of the simple homogeneous human ovum which grows into an adult with specialized features—legs, arms, muscles, brain and so on— which help the human adult to adapt to his/her environment and survive; this justified his argument that, as societies evolve, functions become more specialized. In fact, his own sociological evidence was enough to persuade not only him, but the nineteenth-century sociologists in America and Europe, that homogeneous rural communities were changing to complex urban societies. Men like William Graham Sumner, Emile Durkheim, Ferdinand Tonnies, Karl Marx and Lester Ward, each in his own way, pointed to the fact that the political and economic functions once performed by all people had become the responsibility of specialists. Specialist agencies, like national and local governments and factories, had emerged in which could be performed specialist functions. The theories of social change favoured by Sumner and William Ogburn (in *Social Change*) owed something to Spencer's theory. Indeed, his theory of social evolution was itself a significant forerunner of the theories of social change enunciated by a succession of nineteenth and twentieth century sociologists, who saw differentiation of function as the key to an understanding of change.

SPENCER ON EDUCATION

Spencer became interested in education when still young. He thought at one time of becoming a teacher. At another point in time there was a plan to set up a school with his father. He taught for a mere three months. Without any real experience in teaching, he denounced state education in letters published in *The Nonconformist* in 1842, when he was only 22 years old. Spencer argued that truth had always originated from the clash of different minds and that 'establishment' education would, by its very nature, inhibit change.

During the 1850s, in various articles he consistently argued the laissez-faire case against the dangers of state interference in the lives of individuals through state education. If this was a political argument, Spencer also questioned the need for formal education in the light of his emerging theory of evolution. Arguing from analogy, he asked in *Social Statics* (1850, p. 208–09) why education was necessary at all since in biology the seed and the embryo grow to maturity without external aid. Why should not a child grow spontaneously into a normal human being? In their evolution, children show all the characteristics of aboriginal man as mankind has evolved from an uncivilized state to a civilized one. Spencer considered that, in the stage of transition from one state to another, individuals had lost the dispositions appropriate to the life of savages and had not yet acquired those needed for civilized life. Under these conditions education should restrain uncivilized characteristics in children. Born, therefore, of man's imperfections, education as a form of coercion would become unnecessary. In the short term, in accordance with the laws of nature, education would evolve through its adaptation to changes in society.

Some comparative educationists have insisted, in a less deterministic way, that the evolution of education reflected changes in society. Since 1945, the climate of opinion has changed. According to the views of academics from the United States and UNESCO, many practitioners have asserted that the provision of education could change society. Spencer would have disagreed. As already stated, he considered that, as society evolved in accordance with these laws, organized education would not be needed at all. Even in a period of transition, all that education can do is to retard the process of social change. To add to his political objections about the role of the state in education, Spencer found convincing arguments from his theory of evolution.

His views would not be accepted by the planners of today. There is little evidence, however, to support the optimistic claims of the founders of UNESCO that universal literacy would raise standards of living, promote democracy and ensure peace. Spencer's analysis of the role of education in social change was apparent even during the 1850s when he prepared four articles on education which were published in: *The North British Review,* ('The Art of Education', May 1854); the *British Quarterly Review* ('Moral Discipline for Children'), April 1858 and *Physical Training,* April 1859) and the *Westminister Review* ('What Knowledge Is of Most Worth?', July 1859). These articles were brought together in an extremely popular book entitled Education: *Intellectual, Moral and Physical,* on which Spencer's fame as an educator rests. Published in 1861, it went into many editions and sold any thousands of copies.

As was his wont, Spencer confidently attacked established educational orthodoxy. True to form, while his experience of teaching was minimal and his serious professional study of education negligible, he was prepared to pronounce aggressively on child development, the curriculum and methods of teaching. His contacts with the children of his friends were not universally successful, but he did not hesitate in giving advice on how they should be brought up. It cannot be said, therefore, that his educational proposals were induced from experience. They were, however, very much in line with progressive educational thought today. Gabriel Compayre, who had prepared books on several distinguished educators, including Rousseau and Pestalozzi, maintained in his book *Herbert Spencer and Scientific Education* that Spencer's ideas on education had been anticipated by Rousseau. Spencer denied having read *Emile* and claimed that he owed none of his ideas on education to it. He did, however, make frequent and favourable reference to Pestalozzi's theory of education, while deploring the extent to which the Swiss educator's practice fell short of it.

In education, as in other fields, the amateur attracted attention. In view of Spencer's very critical comments on the educational establishment, it is surprising that in 1868, within eight years of the appearance *of Education,* he had been included in R. H. Quick's *Essays on Educational Reformers* as one of the significant European educational innovators. Spencer, along with Richard Mulcaster, Roger Ascham and John Locke, was one of the Englishman to warrant a chapter to himself in Quick's history. John Milton, J. Dury and Dr Arnold were mentioned, as it were, in passing. Quick's account of Spencer's little book was hostile, but he concluded:

> *I have ventured in turn to differ on some points from Mr Spencer; but I have failed to give an adequate notion of the work I have been discussing if he reader has not perceived that it is not only one of the most readable, but also one of the most important books on education in the English language (Quick, 1904, p. 469).*

At the beginning of the twentieth century, a pioneer in the teaching of science, H. E. Armstrong, in his book (again now in vogue in the United Kingdom) *The Teaching of Scientific Method* (1903), advised all teachers to read Spencer's *Education* so that 'they may have clear ideas on the subject of education' (ibid., p. 381). Many years later, F.A. Cavenagh, in his introduction to a 1932 edition of Spencer's book, stated that while Spencer's views no longer impress, *Education* 'is still read; popular editions continue to appear; and every year students in training find it stimulating and provocative' (Spencer, 1861/1932, p. xx). J. A. Lauwerys, closely involved in the establishment of UNESCO and himself a scientific humanist in Spencer's tradition, wrote in a lecture at the University of London in 1951: "For two generations, students in our training colleges and departments of education were brought up on a diet of which Spencer's *Education* was an important ingredient. And this is strange because the very people who prescribed it for study were its harshest critics" (Lauwerys, 1952, p. 162). It must be assumed that Spencer's views had some influence on the young teachers who read his book.

His assertion that science should replace the classical languages in the curriculum, and indeed should constitute the whole curriculum, antagonized the teachers of his day. It has also alienated twentieth-century educators who were prepared to accept that science subjects should occupy more of the school curriculum than previously but were not prepared to accept that they should replace language studies or, more generally, the humanities. Perhaps only in the former Soviet Union was science accorded the position in education that Spencer considered it deserved. Certainly, his views on science in the school curriculum cannot be said to have influenced British educational practice in secondary schools to any great extent.

On the contrary, many of his other assertions, based, again by analogy, on the evolution of an embryo into a mature adult, find expression in British primary schools. The answer to this apparent paradox lies in the extent to which Spencer had a vogue (of which more later) in the United States and his ideas were subsequently reintroduced into the United Kingdom through the writings of Dewey and other progressive educators from that country. In British primary schools today many practitioners acknowledge their debt to Rousseau, Dewey and Piaget, but not to Spencer.

Even though his *First Principles,* in which the laws of evolution were fully explained, was published somewhat later than the articles that constitute *Education,* two of the principles of evolution inform his analysis of education. Spencer himself claimed: "The theory of evolution furnished guidance [in writing the article on education] as the ascent through lower forms of life has been affected by the discipline of enjoying the pleasure and suffering the pains which follow this or that form of conduct" (1904, p. 18).

Two other fundamental evolutionary principles permeate his analysis of education. The first is that education evolves in a way similar to that in which individuals and society evolve. Indeed: "There cannot fail to be a relationship between the successive systems of education, and the successive social states with which they have co-existed" (Spencer, 1861/1932, p. 61). Secondly, Spencer frequently wrote about the increased heterogeneity and complexity of education systems in the process of their evolution. Perhaps, if his articles on education had been written a few years later, his view that homogeneous education had given way to greater heterogeneity might have received greater attention. This has evidently been the case in science. Natural philosophy became, in the hands of specialists, astronomy, physics, chemistry and biology. In each of these subjects special fields of inquiry, like heat, light, sound and electricity emerged in physics; the two branches of chemistry—inorganic and organic—became further differentiated; and in biology, special fields like physiology and morphology emerged. Again, in accordance with his evolutionary principle, in many countries the primary school curriculum is far less differentiated than that offered in secondary schools. Secondary school teachers are more specialized than primary school teachers.

Spencer, somewhat inconsistently, considered that education lagged behind social change—a view taken by twentieth century followers of William Ogburn who accepted his theory of "social lag." Much of what Spencer wrote about the education of his day was negative. His positive recommendations were very similar to those expressed by Rousseau in *Emile.* Today, teachers in the United Kingdom and the United States accept them uncritically as part of a new orthodoxy. It is, therefore, worthwhile to examine in some detail what he wrote in the four articles that make up *Education* about the aims or purpose of education, attitudes to children, methods of teaching, discipline and the curriculum. Spencer complained that what was taught in schools was of no practical value. He used many examples to show that ornamental or decorative subjects were more prized than useful ones. In nine cases out of ten, he claimed, the Latin and Greek learned at school served no practical purpose. Indeed, boys were drilled in these subjects to show that they had received the education of a gentleman—a badge indicating a certain social position which commanded respect. Dancing, deportment, piano playing, singing and drawing served the same purpose in the education of girls. It was not the intrinsic value of knowledge that determined what was taught, but the respect and social power that its possession conferred on individuals. Knowledge as an instrument of social control is the theme of much sociological analysis today. The chapter on "Intellectual Education" in *Education* was really about methods of teaching and attitudes toward children. Its recommendations were most obviously derived from Spencer's theory of evolution. For example, he pointed out that in the evolution of societies an increase in political liberty and the abolition of laws restricting individual action had been accompanied by progress towards non-coercive education—though it must be remembered that the latter lagged behind the former. Old educational practices based on a belief in the wickedness of children were in line with repressive social systems. Uniformity of belief—religious, political and educational—influenced by Aristotle had, however, under Protestantism given way to a multiplicity of sects and political parties.

In his analysis of its evolution, Spencer contrasted the characteristics of education in the past with the characteristics of education in the present. Learning by rote had given way to learning through the child's spontaneous processes. Teaching the rules had been replaced by the teaching of principles. It was accepted that for children the learning of grammar should come last, not first. Having grasped the principles, young people would be able to solve a variety of new cases as they arise, as well as being able to deal with old ones.

Learning through independent inquiry and discovery are advocated in British primary schools today. It was one of the changes in education observed with approval by Spencer. So too was the importance given to the cultivation in children of their powers of observation. The spontaneous activity of children—in the form of play—was at last being recognized as a legitimate way of acquiring knowledge.

Object lessons were favoured by Spencer, although he considered that they were badly conducted in practice. The old method presenting truths in the abstract had been replaced by presenting them in the concrete. He illustrated this change by referring to geographical and geometrical models. Finally, for Spencer, the most significant change in the evolution of education was the desire to make learning enjoyable rather than painful. This was shown in the interest taken in play, nursery rhymes, fairy tales and in lessons which should be brought to an end before the children showed signs of weariness. Most of these beliefs inform the rhetoric of British primary school teachers today.

Spencer concluded that the common characteristic of these changes was that they showed an increasing conformity with the methods of nature, that is, in accordance with the natural mental development of children. He stated: 'there is a certain sequence in which the faculties spontaneously develop, and a certain kind of knowledge which each requires during its development; and it is for us to ascertain this sequence, and supply this knowledge' (ibid., p. 71). Today, Piagetian theories of child development are widely accepted as the grounds on which to establish sequences of learning.

Spencer himself maintained that it was not possible to perfect a system of education until a rational psychology had been established. In accordance with his epistemology, he was prepared to specify some of the principles on which good teaching should be based. Since the mind moves from homogeneity towards heterogeneity, education should proceed from the simple to the complex; teaching should begin at once with a few subjects, to which other subjects should be progressively added. Secondly, since in its process of development the mind advances from the indefinite to the definite, so:

> in education we must be content to set out with crude notions. These we must aim to make gradually clearer by facilitating the acquisition of experiences such as will correct, first their greatest errors, and afterwards their successively less marked errors. And the scientific formulae must be given only as fast as the conceptions are perfected (ibid., p. 81).

He repeated his contention that lessons should move from the concrete to the abstract so that, through the medium of examples, the mind is led from the particular to the general.

More controversially, Spencer maintained that the education of the child should follow the education of mankind, considered historically. In short the individual's mind should pass through the same stages as the general mind—"education should be a repetition of civilization in little" (ibid., p. 83). There is no doubt that, until recently, the content of science syllabuses in most countries followed the historical development of the subject; in physics the sequence in which topics were taught was: mechanics, heat, light, sound, magnetism and electricity.

Spencer's fifth recommendation stemmed from his assertion that organized scientific knowledge can be achieved only after a fund of observations had been accumulated.

In the light of present-day approaches to primary education in the United Kingdom, what Spencer wrote is very significant. He said that the process of self-development should be encouraged through education. 'Children should be led to make their own investigations, and to draw their own inferences. They should be told as little as possible, and induced to discover as much as possible' (ibid., p. 94). There can be few such succinct statements of modern methods of learning by discovery, which should be pleasurable and based upon the spontaneous activity to which children are prone. Courses in which pupils show no interest should be abandoned. Self-instruction was a fundamental principle held by Spencer in the recommendations he made about methods of teaching. This would enable the child to evolve in accordance with the natural development of its faculties.

Spencer proposed that instead of acquiring knowledge for the social prestige and power it conferred, education should be of practical use to its recipients. To the question "of what use is it?", Spencer answered that it should help individuals to live satisfactorily. 'To prepare us for complete living is the function which education has to discharge; and the only rational mode of judging of an educational course is to judge in what degree it discharges such function' (ibid., p. 10). Spencer claimed that before a rational curriculum could be established with this aim in mind, it was necessary to determine the relative values of knowledge.

His curriculum theory broke new ground. Unlike the essentialism of Plato and Aristotle and the encyclopaedism of Comenius and Condorcet, it was not subject-centred but rather activity-centred.

In asking the question 'what knowledge is of most worth?', Spencer answered that it is the knowledge needed to pursue the leading kinds of activity which constitute human life. He wrote:

> [These activities] may be naturally arranged into: 1) those activities which directly minister to self-preservation; 2) those activities which, by securing the necessaries of life, indirectly administer to self-preservation; 3) those activities which have for their end the rearing and discipline of offspring; 4) those activities which are involved in the maintenance of proper social and political relations; 5) those miscellaneous activities which fill up the leisure part of life, devoted to the gratification of the tastes and feelings (ibid.).

The order in which Spencer listed the activities corresponded to their order of importance; however, he recognized that they were not definitely separable but were inextricably mixed. In all these areas of activity, nonetheless, a knowledge of science is essential. Satisfactory, direct self-preservation demands a knowledge of physiology. Indirect self-preservation requires a knowledge of those sciences—mechanics, biology, geology, chemistry and physics—on which industrial life depends. Spencer asserted: "Some acquaintance with the first principles of physiology and the elementary truths of psychology is indispensable for the right bringing up of children" (ibid., p. 36).

Spencer was appalled by the failure of education to prepare parents for parenthood. As for citizens, history, as taught, threw no light on the science of society. What was needed if people were to discharge their civic functions was an education in descriptive and comparative sociology, both of which must be interpreted in the light of biology and physiology. Spencer also saw a science component in the activities undertaken by individuals during their leisure time. Art, music and poetry evoke emotions, but they can best be appreciated through a knowledge of science. Science not only underlies sculpture, painting and music, but true poetry is itself scientific. To be good, poetry must pay attention to those laws of nervous action which speech obeys. While Spencer took the argument to extremes, there is a way in which knowledge of science makes it possible to better appreciate the fine arts. Extreme though Spencer's views may seem, a case can be made that today every societal problem has a scientific component and that finding solutions involves an understanding of some elements of science.

R. H. Quick criticized Spencer's advocacy of the exclusive use of science in all five of the activities he identified. Although he conceded that science had an important role to play in industry, he considered it was impossible to teach all the sciences to everyone and that young people about to enter the world of work would be better prepared if their minds had been equipped to acquire knowledge rather than being given a great deal of special information. This view, that education should prepare individuals to acquire knowledge when it was needed, has only recently been challenged by educators in the United Kingdom, some of whom now want schools to equip pupils to enter industry through vocational training. To Spencer's argument, Quick's second response was that, in many cases, a knowledge of science was of no practical value; this indicated that neither Spencer nor Quick recognized the difference between a knowledge of science which enables a person to perform a task and a knowledge which enables them to appreciate or judge the effectiveness of a job undertaken by somebody else. Pericles drew such a distinction in politics. For him, only a few can formulate policy, but in a democracy everyone should be in a position to evaluate it. Today, in the industrial world, few are in a position to invent machines and manufacture consumer goods, but everybody should be able to assess the consequences of introducing modern machines into the industrial processes. The difference is between the science needed by experts to produce goods and the science needed by everyone to evaluate the products produced by the few.

Perhaps the most serious weakness in Spencer's account of an activity-based curriculum is the fact that he failed, in accordance with his own theory of child development, to state clearly at what stage in the evolution of children scientific knowledge should be provided. When should physiology or education be introduced? And at what levels of sophistication? Spencer did not say. His curriculum seems too demanding for primary school children. It might meet the needs of secondary school pupils, but it seems better designed for adults preparing to become teachers. For many years, health education was part of the course for aspiring teachers; it included information on how children might learn the elements of self-preservation. In the 1960s in the United Kingdom, many university departments of education exposed students to training in the so-called "disciplines" psychology, philosophy, sociology and history. Spencer would have approved.

Teachers should be aware of the implications of these studies for education. Wherever necessary they should be able to pass on, in an appropriate form, the findings of sociology and psychology to their pupils. Activity-based learning in British primary schools following Piagetian stages of child development, including an emphasis on art, has lacked the scientific content that Spencer thought essential. Experience in the United States has shown how difficult it was to introduce a Spencerian curriculum in high schools. Progressive educators in that country have tried to do so throughout the twentieth century. Spencer's ideas in the United States Spencer wanted his work to be known in the United States. He found a staunch ally in Edward Livingston Youmans who, when he read Spencer's circular in 1860 on the plan for his *Synthetic Philosophy,* immediately promised support. It was the start of a long, cordial friendship during which Youmans promoted Spencer's writings, often in the face of opposition from the author, and arranged for him to visit the United States. Spencer was acclaimed with traditional American generosity. He recounted his reception in his *Autobiography.* Managers of railways and hotel proprietors went out of their way to make him welcome. He received the most generous private hospitality and was guest at a magnificent banquet held in his honour by leading members of American society. While genuinely touched by the warmth of his welcome, Spencer 'never felt quite at ease with the demonstrative activities of some of his American admirers' (Duncan, 1908, p. 228) and reminded them that things that would be considered quite normal on one side of the Atlantic were treated differently on the other side. The theory of evolution was a case in point. Youmans wrote to him saying: 'Evidently, there is more religious independence of thought in England than here [America]. For your critics, at any rate, take interest in the subject, while there is too much timidity here to venture upon either side of the discussion' (ibid., p. 254). On the other hand, Henry Ward Beecher, in a letter to Spencer in 1866, wrote: 'The peculiar condition of American society has made your writings far more fruitful and quickening here than in Europe' (ibid., p. 128).

Beecher's opinion was probably nearer the truth than that expressed by Youmans, who had no wish to offend Spencer. Evolution was a topic that aroused deep passions and furious debate in the United States. Woodbridge Riley, in *American Thought from Puritanism to Pragmatism and Beyond,* claimed that "from the day of Puritanism to the day of pragmatism there have been so many skirmishes, battles, and general engagements as almost to merit the name of warfare between evolution and revelation in America" (1925, p. 173). In particular, with reference to the British contribution to the debate, he wrote:

> The outburst of controversy upon the appearance of On the Origin of Species in 1859 was, therefore, no unexpected thing. . . . The battle was extended and furious . . . there was a [nationwide] continuous campaign of scientific controversy which lasted even longer than the civil strife which rent the country (ibid.).

Certainly Spencer's writings were required reading for many American university courses during the second half of the nineteenth century. Not all theologians were convinced and, indeed, the college authorities at Yale objected when William Sumner, a follower of Spencer, prescribed the latter's *Study of Sociology* for one of his classes because of its anti-religious bias (Duncan, 1908, p. 208). Spencer's writings undoubtedly added to a debate that revolved around Darwin's biological theory.

Certainly, the pragmatists entered the debate, as was shown by Wiener in his *Evolution and the Founders of Pragmatism* and R. Hofstadter in *Social Darwinism in American Thought.* According to Wiener, "the chief question discussed by the founders of pragmatism, beginning with Chauncey Wright, was how far one could legitimately apply Darwin's hypothesis of natural selection to subjects other than biology" (Wiener, 1965, p. 6). Pragmatists, like William James, John Dewey, George Herbert Mead, Boyd H. Bode and William Heard Kilpatrick, were the intellectual children of Darwin who, like Spencer, had demonstrated the importance of change in evolution. The pragmatists concluded that they could do away with permanence, eternal values and all forms of absolutism. Again, to quote Wiener: "Darwinism and pragmatism were able to combat their conservative theological adversaries only because of the powerful impetus of scientific advances in the second half of the nineteenth century" (ibid., p. 1).

Among the founders of pragmatism, opinions of Spencer's work varied. J. L. Childs claimed that one of the "primary cultural factors which has conditioned the thought of Dr Dewey is the theory of organic evolution" (1949). Dewey himself admired Spencer's single-mindedness. Dewey recognized that Spencer had conceived a whole system—an idea of all that is in the universe; but, with no interest in history and an isolation from the intellectual currents of the day, he filled in the details over a period of thirty-six years. But such work, according to Dewey, was possible only if the author was immune to the changing play of ideas and cross-currents of interests. For Dewey, the inevitable weakness in Spencer's position was that it eliminated the individual and the subjective.

Charles S. Peirce, one of the most distinguished logicians and scientists among the founders of pragmatism, was scathing in his criticism of Spencer's attempt in *First Principles* to show that evolution was a consequence of the mechanical principle of the conservation of energy. He wrote: "But his chapter on the subject is mathematically absurd, and convicts him of being a man who will talk pretentiously of what he knows nothing about" (Wiener, 1965). William James was, according to Ann Low-Beer, carried away by *First Principles*, but subsequently became disenchanted. She stated that James continued to use Spencer's books in his courses but, in a final examination paper, invited students to mention all the inconsistencies in one of Spencer's books. In effect, James abandoned the simplistic behavioural psychology of Spencer in favour of a dynamic view of the mind that can change as well as be influenced by the environment. Thus, while Spencer was required reading in American universities for most of the second half of the nineteenth century, by its end his work in philosophy and science had been replaced by that of specialists in the natural and social sciences.

If the pragmatists were influenced by evolution, their influence on education was greater than on any other aspect of American society. In the climate of opinion created by the pragmatists, Spencer was given credit for inspiring reform in education. Paul Monroe, in his *History of Education*, linked the work of Spencer with that of T. H. Huxley in promoting the scientific tendency in education. Of Spencer, he wrote that among those pressing the claims of science in the nineteenth century, "the first of these, and yet the most influential at least for Anglo-Saxon thought, was that by Herbert Spencer" (Monroe, 1919, p. 684). Monroe was not alone in his judgement; L.A. Cremin in *The Transformation of the School* (1961) went so far as to claim that the revolution in American educational thought at the end of the nineteenth century had its origins in the work of Herbert Spencer. As in United Kingdom, not only the progressives took notice of him. He is referred to favourably by conservative thinkers, such as C. A. Bagley, even though he considered Spencer's assertion that teaching should start with the concrete as pernicious and believed, as in England, that enjoyment was merely an accessory in life (1911).

Many of the subjects advocated by Spencer, such as physiology, were introduced into American schools. Most historians of education in the United States, however, associate Spencer's name with a curriculum theory held by progressive educationists. It was articulated in a committee set up by the National Education Association. The Commission on the Reorganization of Secondary Education issued its report, usually called "The (Seven) Cardinal Principles of Education," in which it was asserted that in primary and secondary schools the aim of the curriculum should be to enable pupils to cope with: (a) their health; (b) fundamental processes; (c) worthy home membership; (d) vocational efficiency; (e) civic participation; (f) the worthy use of leisure time; and (g) ethical behaviour. These seven areas could be reduced, without distortion, to Spencer's five areas of activity. Members of the Progressive Education Association, set up in 1918, of which Dewey was the leading figure, adopted the latter's problem-solving approach to operationalize the "seven Cardinal Principles." Instead of identifying activities in these areas, progressive educators identified the problems young people were likely to face as adults in the areas of health, earning a living, taking care of a family, civic participation, leisure time activities and moral behaviour. In some schools, experimental curricula were worked out collectively in discussions between teachers and pupils. In the absence of established models, the originality of a somewhat modified version of Spencer's curriculum theory created major difficulties when attempts were made to apply it in practice.

The Progressive Education Association tried to do so in its *Eight-year Study* from 1933 to 1941. The study was designed to show whether the customary college entrance requirements were essential to college success, or if pupils on a broader course favoured by progressive educationists could succeed as well as pupils from the college preparatory course in the ordinary high school. The results were inconclusive, but at least they showed that pupils from progressive schools did not inevitably perform less well in college than those from regular schools. The fact remains that the selection of curriculum content has presented secondary school curriculum developers with a formidable task in view of the traditional demands universities and other institutions of higher education place on potential entrants to higher education.

Dewey considered that problems should be solved collectively and scientifically, but the role of science in the progressive school curricula was not as great as Spencer would have wished. Nevertheless, when the Progressive Education Association was disbanded in the 1950s, after its members had been accused by Senator McCarthy of un-American activities, it was true to say that it had completed its reforming task, having disseminated progressive views very widely among American teachers. Criticism of high school curricula, which follow Spencer's 'activity-based' approach—considered repetitious and lacking in rigour reached a crescendo in the United States from time to time. Criticism during the McCarthy era in the 1950s is one example. *A Nation at Risk,* prepared by a Presidential committee in the early 1980s, was another recent example of such criticism. Spencer was ahead of his time in curriculum theory. He can be regarded as one of the important pioneers of modern education. In practice his ideas find uneven expression. In primary schools in the United Kingdom most of his prescriptions about methods of teaching and the treatment of children have been accepted. Curricula in British primary schools were until the 1988 Education Reform Act based on the activities of children and overtly in accordance with their mental and physical development. In American junior and senior high schools there has been continuous tension between the advocates of a curriculum based on problems relevant to children and young adults, and the more conservative educators who want to see a return to the established school subjects or disciplines. In so far as Spencer influenced progressive educators in the United Kingdom and the United States of America he can, as Quick perceived, be regarded as one of the most influential educational reformers. Not a bad achievement for an amateur.

NOTE

1. *Brian Holmes (United Kingdom).* First worked as a secondary school science teacher and wrote several school text books. After four years as a lecturer in science teaching at the University of Durham, he joined the University of London Institute of Education in 1953. He eventually became Professor of Comparative Education. From the 1960s, onward, he became a central figure in the field of international comparative education. Upon retirement he was made Dean of the College of Preceptors. Apart from the editorship of several journals, his most significant publications were *Problems in Education* (1965), *International Guide to Education Systems* (1979), *Comparative Education: Some Considerations of Method* (1981) and *Educational Development Trends* (1983). He died in 1993.

WORKS BY HERBERT SPENCER

In chronological order

1850. *Social Statics.* London.

1855. *The Principles of Psychology.* London, Williams and Norgate.

1861. *Education: Intellectual, Moral and Physical.* London, Williams and Norgate. Reprinted in 1932 with an Introduction by F.A. Cavenagh. Cambridge, Cambridge University Press.

1862. *First Principles.* London, Williams & Norgate.

1864–67. *The Principles of Biology.* London.

1872. *The Study of Sociology.* London.

1873–81. *Descriptive Sociology.* London, Williams & Norgate.

1876–96. *The Principles of Sociology.* London, Williams & Norgate.

1892–93. *The Principles of Ethics.* 2 v. New York, Hurst.

1904. *Autobiography. 1* v. London, Williams and Norgate.

WORKS ABOUT HERBERT SPENCER

Armstrong, H. E. 1903. *The Teaching of Scientific Method.* London,

Macmillan. Bagley, C. A. 1911. *Educational Values.* New York, Macmillan.

Bain, A. 1882. *J. S. Mill.* London, Longmans, Green.

Barlow, N. (ed.). 1958. *The Autobiography of Charles Darwin.* London,

Collins. Bibby, C. 1959. *T. H. Huxley.* London, Watts.

Childs, J.L. 1949. 'Cultural factors in Dewey's Philosophy of Education'. *Teachers College Record* (New York), Vol. 51, No. 3, December.

Combe, G. 1828. *The Constitution of Man.* London.

Compayre, G. 1908. *Herbert Spencer and Scientific Education.* Trans, by M.E.F. Findlay. London, Harrap.

Cremin, L. A. 1961. *The Transformation of the School.* New York, A. Knopf.

Darwin, C. 1859. *On the Origin of Species.* Harmondsworth, Penguin, 1968 ed.

Dewey, J. 1929. 'The Philosophical Work of Herbert Spencer'. In: *Characters and Events.* New York, Holt.

Duncan, D. 1908. *The Life and Letters of Herbert Spencer.* London, Methuen.

Hofstadter, R. 1955. *Social Darwinism in American Thought.* Boston, Beacon.

Huxley, T. H. 1901. *Evolution and Ethics and Other Essays* London.

Lauwerys, J. A. 1952. 'Herbert Spencer and the Scientific Movement' In: A. V. Judges (ed.). *Pioneers of English Education.* London, Faber.

Lewes, G. H. 1883. *Comte's Philosophy of the Sciences.* London, Bell.

Low-Beer, A. 1969. *Spencer.* London, Collier-Macmillan.

Monroe, p. 1919. *History of Education.* New York, Macmillan.

Ogburn, W. F. 1966. *Social Change.* New York, Delta.

Payne, W. H. 1907. *Compayre's History of Pedagogy.* London, Swan Sonnenshein.

Peel, J. D. Y. 1971. *Herbert Spencer: the Evolution of a Sociologist.* London, Heinemann.

Quick, R. H. 1904. *Essays on Educational Reformers.* London, Longmans

Green. Riley, W. 1925. *American Thought from Puritanism to Pragmatism and Beyond'.* New York, Henry Holt.

Sumner, W. G. 1906. *Folkways.* New York, Dover.

Webb, B. *1926. My Apprenticeship.* London, Longmans Green.

Wiener, p. P. 1965. *Evolution and the Founders of Pragmatism.* New York, Harper.

——— . (ed.) 1958. *Values in a Universe of Choice: Selected Writings of Charles S. Peirce.* New York, Doubleday Anchor.

Education and Discipline

—Bertrand Russell

Any serious educational theory must consist of two parts: a conception of the ends of life, and a science of psychological dynamics, i.e. of the laws of mental change. Two men who differ as to the ends of life cannot hope to agree about education. The educational machine, throughout Western civilization, is dominated by two ethical theories: that of Christianity, and that of nationalism. These two, when taken seriously, are incompatible, as is becoming evident in Germany. For my part, I hold that, where they differ, Christianity is preferable, but where they agree, both are mistaken. The conception which I should substitute as the purpose of education is civilization, a term which, as I mean it, has a definition which is partly individual, partly social. It consists, in the individual, of both intellectual and moral qualities: intellectually, a certain minimum of general knowledge, technical skill in one's own profession, and a habit of forming opinions on evidence; morally, of impartiality, kindliness, and a modicum of self-control. I should add a quality which is neither moral nor intellectual, but perhaps physiological: zest and joy of life. In communities, civilization demands respect for law, justice as between man and man, purposes not involving permanent injury to any section of the human race, and intelligent adaptation of means to ends. If these are to be the purpose of education, it is a question for the science of psychology to consider what can be done towards realizing them, and, in particular, what degree of freedom is likely to prove most effective.

On the question of freedom in education there are at present three main schools of thought, deriving partly from differences as to ends and partly from differences in psychological theory. There are those who say that children should be completely free, however bad they may be; there are those who say they should be completely subject to authority, however good they may be; and there are those who say they should be free, but in spite of freedom they should be always good. This last party is larger than it has any logical right to be; children, like adults, will not all be virtuous if they are all free. The belief that liberty will ensure moral perfection is a relic of Rousseauism, and would not survive a study of animals and babies. Those who hold this belief think that education should have no positive purpose, but should merely offer an environment suitable for spontaneous development. I cannot agree with this school, which seems to me too individualistic, and unduly indifferent to the importance of knowledge. We live in communities which require co-operation, and it would be utopian to expect all the necessary co-operation to result from spontaneous impulse. The existence of a large population on a limited area is only possible owing to science and technique; education must, therefore, hand on the necessary minimum of these. The educators who allow most freedom are men whose success depends upon a degree of benevolence, self-control, and trained intelligence which can hardly be generated where every impulse is left unchecked; their merits, therefore, are not likely to be perpetuated if their methods are undiluted. Education, viewed from a social standpoint, must be something more positive than a mere opportunity for growth. It must, of course, provide this, but it must also provide a mental and moral equipment which children cannot acquire entirely for themselves.

The arguments in favour of a great degree of freedom in education are derived not from man's natural goodness, but from the effects of authority, both on those who suffer it and on those who exercise it. Those who are subject to authority become either submissive or rebellious, and each attitude has its drawbacks.

The submissive lose initiative, both in thought and action; moreover, the anger generated by the feeling of being thwarted tends to find an outlet in bullying those who are weaker. That is why tyrannical institutions are self-perpetuating: what a man has suffered from his father he inflicts upon his son, and the humiliations which he remembers having endured at his public school he passes on to Ònatives" when he becomes an empire-builder. Thus an unduly authoritative education turns the pupils into timid tyrants, incapable of either claiming or tolerating originality in word or deed. The effect upon the educators is even worse: they tend to become sadistic disciplinarians, glad to inspire terror, and content to inspire nothing else. As these men represent knowledge, the pupils acquire a horror of knowledge, which, among the English upper-class, is supposed to be part of human nature, but is really part of the well-grounded hatred of the authoritarian pedagogue.

Rebels, on the other hand, though they may be necessary, can hardly be just to what exists. Moreover, there are many ways of rebelling, and only a small minority of these are wise. Galileo was a rebel and was wise; believers in the flat-earth theory are equally rebels, but are foolish. There is a great danger in the tendency to suppose that opposition to authority is essentially meritorious and that unconventional opinions are bound to be correct: no useful purpose is served by smashing lamp-posts or maintaining Shakespeare to be no poet. Yet this excessive rebelliousness is often the effect that too much authority has on spirited pupils. And when rebels become educators, they sometimes encourage defiance in their pupils, for whom at the same time they are trying to produce a perfect environment, although these two aims are scarcely compatible.

What is wanted is neither submissiveness nor rebellion, but good nature, and general friendliness both to people and to new ideas. These qualities are due in part to physical causes, to which old-fashioned educators paid too little attention; but they are due still more to freedom from the feeling of baffled impotence which arises when vital impulses are thwarted. If the young are to grow into friendly adults, it is necessary, in most cases, that they should feel their environment friendly. This requires that there should be a certain sympathy with the child's important desires, and not merely an attempt to use him for some abstract end such as the glory of God or the greatness of one's country. And, in teaching, every attempt should be made to cause the pupil to feel that it is worth his while to know what is being taught-at least when this is true. When the pupil co-operates willingly, he learns twice as fast and with half the fatigue. All these are valid reasons for a very great degree of freedom.

It is easy, however, to carry the argument too far. It is not desirable that children, in avoiding the vices of the slave, should acquire those of the aristocrat. Consideration for others, not only in great matters, but also in little everyday things, is an essential element in civilization, without which social life would be intolerable. I am not thinking of mere forms of politeness, such as saying "please" and "thank you": formal manners are most fully developed among barbarians, and diminish with every advance in culture. I am thinking rather of willingness to take a fair share of necessary work, to be obliging in small ways that save trouble on the balance. Sanity itself is a form of politeness and it is not desirable to give a child a sense of omnipotence, or a belief that adults exist only to minister to the pleasures of the young. And those who disapprove of the existence of the idle rich are hardly consistent if they bring up their children without any sense that work is necessary, and without the habits that make continuous application possible.

There is another consideration to which some advocates of freedom attach too little importance. In a community of children which is left without adult interference there is a tyranny of the stronger, which is likely to be far more brutal than most adult tyranny. If two children of two or three years old are left to play together, they will, after a few fights, discover which is bound to be the victor, and the other will then become a slave. Where the number of children is larger, one or two acquire complete mastery, and the others have far less liberty than they would have if the adults interfered to protect the weaker and less pugnacious. Consideration for others does not, with most children, arise spontaneously, but has to be taught, and can hardly be taught except by the exercise of authority. This is perhaps the most important argument against the abdication of the adults.

I do not think that educators have yet solved the problem of combining the desirable forms of freedom with the necessary minimum of moral training. The right solution, it must be admitted, is often made impossible by parents before the child is brought to an enlightened school. just as psychoanalysts, from their clinical experience, conclude that we are all mad, so the authorities in modern schools, from their contact with pupils whose parents have made them unmanageable, are disposed to conclude that all children are "difficult" and all parents utterly foolish. Children who have been driven wild by parental tyranny (which often takes the form of solicitous affection) may require a longer or shorter period of complete liberty before they can view any adult without suspicion. But children who have been sensibly handled at home can bear to be checked in minor ways, so long as they feel that they are being helped in the ways that they themselves regard as important. Adults who like children, and are not reduced to a condition of nervous exhaustion by their company, can achieve a great deal in the way of discipline without ceasing to be regarded with friendly feelings by their pupils.

I think modern educational theorists are inclined to attach too much importance to the negative virtue of not interfering with children, and too little to the positive merit of enjoying their company. If you have the sort of liking for children that many people have for horses or dogs, they will be apt to respond to your suggestions, and to accept prohibitions, perhaps with some good-humoured grumbling, but without resentment. It is no use to have the sort of liking that consists in regarding them as a field for valuable social endeavour, or what amounts to the same thingÑas an outlet for power-impulses. No child will be grateful for an interest in him that springs from the thought that he will have a vote to be secured for your party or a body to be sacrificed to king and country. The desirable sort of interest is that which consists in spontaneous pleasure in the presence of children, without any ulterior purpose. Teachers who have this quality will seldom need to interfere with children's freedom, but will be able to do so, when necessary, without causing psychological damage.

Unfortunately, it is utterly impossible for over-worked teachers to preserve an instinctive liking for children; they are bound to come to feel towards them as the proverbial confectioner's apprentice does towards macaroons. I do not think that education ought to be anyone's whole profession: it should be undertaken for at most two hours a day by people whose remaining hours are spent away from children. The society of the young is fatiguing, especially when strict discipline is avoided. Fatigue, in the end, produces irritation, which is likely to express itself somehow, whatever theories the harassed teacher may have taught himself or herself to believe. The necessary friendliness cannot be preserved by self-control alone. But where it exists, it should be unnecessary to have rules in advance as to how "naughty" children are to be treated, since impulse is likely to lead to the right decision, and almost any decision will be right if the child feels that you like him. No rules, however wise, are a substitute for affection and tact.

John Dewey's Famous Declaration Concerning Education

First published in The School Journal, Volume LIV, Number 3 (January 16, 1897), pages 77-80.

ARTICLE I—WHAT EDUCATION IS

I believe that all education proceeds by the participation of the individual in the social consciousness of the race. This process begins unconsciously almost at birth, and is continually shaping the individual's powers, saturating his consciousness, forming his habits, training his ideas, and arousing his feelings and emotions. Through this unconscious education the individual gradually comes to share in the intellectual and moral resources which humanity has succeeded in getting together. He becomes an inheritor of the funded capital of civilization. The most formal and technical education in the world cannot safely depart from this general process. It can only organize it or differentiate it in some particular direction.

I believe that the only true education comes through the stimulation of the child's powers by the demands of the social situations in which he finds himself. Through these demands he is stimulated to act as a member of a unity, to emerge from his original narrowness of action and feeling, and to conceive of himself from the standpoint of the welfare of the group to which he belongs. Through the responses which others make to his own activities he comes to know what these mean in social terms. The value which they have is reflected back into them. For instance, through the response which is made to the child's instinctive babblings the child comes to know what those babblings mean; they are transformed into articulate language and thus the child is introduced into the consolidated wealth of ideas and emotions which are now summed up in language.

I believe that this educational process has two sides—one psychological and one sociological; and that neither can be subordinated to the other or neglected without evil results following. Of these two sides, the psychological is the basis. The child's own instincts and powers furnish the material and give the starting point for all education. Save as the efforts of the educator connect with some activity which the child is carrying on of his own initiative independent of the educator, education becomes reduced to a pressure from without. It may, indeed, give certain external results, but cannot truly be called educative. Without insight into the psychological structure and activities of the individual, the educative process will, therefore, be haphazard and arbitrary. If it chances to coincide with the child's activity it will get a leverage; if it does not, it will result in friction, or disintegration, or arrest of the child nature.

I believe that knowledge of social conditions, of the present state of civilization, is necessary in order properly to interpret the child's powers. The child has his own instincts and tendencies, but we do not know what these mean until we can translate them into their social equivalents. We must be able to carry them back into a social past and see them as the inheritance of previous race activities. We must also be able to project them into the future to see what their outcome and end will be. In the illustration just used, it is the ability to see in the child's babblings the promise and potency of a future social intercourse and conversation which enables one to deal in the proper way with that instinct.

I believe that the psychological and social sides are organically related and that education cannot be regarded as a compromise between the two, or a superimposition of one upon the other. We are told that the psychological definition of education is barren and formal—that it gives us only the idea of a development of all the mental powers without giving us any idea of the use to which these powers are put. On the other hand, it is urged that the social definition of education, as getting adjusted to civilization, makes of it a forced and external process, and results in subordinating the freedom of the individual to a preconceived social and political status.

I believe that each of these objections is true when urged against one side isolated from the other. In order to know what a power really is we must know what its end, use, or function is; and this we cannot know save as we conceive of the individual as active in social relationships. But, on the other hand, the only possible adjustment which we can give to the child under existing conditions, is that which arises through putting him in complete possession of all his powers. With the advent of democracy and modern industrial conditions, it is impossible to foretell definitely just what civilization will be twenty years from now. Hence it is impossible to prepare the child for any precise set of conditions. To prepare him for the future life means to give him command of himself; it means so to train him that he will have the full and ready use of all his capacities; that his eye and ear and hand may be tools ready to command, that his judgment may be capable of grasping the conditions under which it has to work, and the executive forces be trained to act economically and efficiently. It is impossible to reach this sort of adjustment save as constant regard is had to the individual's own powers, tastes, and interests-say, that is, as education is continually converted into psychological terms.

In sum, I believe that the individual who is to be educated is a social individual and that society is an organic union of individuals. If we eliminate the social factor from the child we are left only with an abstraction; if we eliminate the individual factor from society, we are left only with an inert and lifeless mass. Education, therefore, must begin with a psychological insight into the child's capacities, interests, and habits. It must be controlled at every point by reference to these same considerations. These powers, interests, and habits must be continually interpreted—we must know what they mean. They must be translated into terms of their social equivalents—into terms of what they are capable of in the way of social service.

ARTICLE II—WHAT THE SCHOOL IS

I believe that the school is primarily a social institution. Education being a social process, the school is simply that form of community life in which all those agencies are concentrated that will be most effective in bringing the child to share in the inherited resources of the race, and to use his own powers for social ends.

I believe that education, therefore, is a process of living and not a preparation for future living.

I believe that the school must represent present life—life as real and vital to the child as that which he carries on in the home, in the neighborhood, or on the playground.

I believe that education which does not occur through forms of life, or that are worth living for their own sake, is always a poor substitute for the genuine reality and tends to cramp and to deaden.

I believe that the school, as an institution, should simplify existing social life; should reduce it, as it were, to an embryonic form. Existing life is so complex that the child cannot be brought into contact with it without either confusion or distraction; he is either overwhelmed by the multiplicity of activities which are going on, so that he loses his own power of orderly reaction, or he is so stimulated by these various activities that his powers are prematurely called into play and he becomes either unduly specialized or else disintegrated.

I believe that as such simplified social life, the school life should grow gradually out of the home life; that it should take up and continue the activities with which the child is already familiar in the home.

I believe that it should exhibit these activities to the child, and reproduce them in such ways that the child will gradually learn the meaning of them, and be capable of playing his own part in relation to them.

I believe that this is a psychological necessity, because it is the only way of securing continuity in the child's growth, the only way of giving a back-ground of past experience to the new ideas given in school.

I believe that it is also a social necessity because the home is the form of social life in which the child has been nurtured and in connection with which he has had his moral training. It is the business of the school to deepen and extend his sense of the values bound up in his home life.

I believe that much of present education fails because it neglects this fundamental principle of the school as a form of community life. It conceives the school as a place where certain information is to be given, where certain lessons are to be learned, or where certain habits are to be formed. The value of these is conceived as lying largely in the remote future; the child must do these things for the sake of something else he is to do; they are mere preparation. As a result they do not become a part of the life experience of the child and so are not truly educative.

I believe that the moral education centers upon this conception of the school as a mode of social life, that the best and deepest moral training is precisely that which one gets through having to enter into proper relations with others in a unity of work and thought. The present educational systems, so far as they destroy or neglect this unity, render it difficult or impossible to get any genuine, regular moral training.

I believe that the child should be stimulated and controlled in his work through the life of the community.

I believe that under existing conditions far too much of the stimulus and control proceeds from the teacher, because of neglect of the idea of the school as a form of social life.

I believe that the teacher's place and work in the school is to be interpreted from this same basis. The teacher is not in the school to impose certain ideas or to form certain habits in the child, but is there as a member of the community to select the influences which shall affect the child and to assist him in properly responding to these influences.

I believe that the discipline of the school should proceed from the life of the school as a whole and not directly from the teacher.

I believe that the teacher's business is simply to determine on the basis of larger experience and riper wisdom, how the discipline of life shall come to the child.

I believe that all questions of the grading of the child and his promotion should be determined by reference to the same standard. Examinations are of use only so far as they test the child's fitness for social life and reveal the place in which he can be of the most service and where he can receive the most help.

ARTICLE III—THE SUBJECT-MATTER OF EDUCATION

I believe that the social life of the child is the basis of concentration, or correlation, in all his training or growth. The social life gives the unconscious unity and the background of all his efforts and of all his attainments.

I believe that the subject-matter of the school curriculum should mark a gradual differentiation out of the primitive unconscious unity of social life.

I believe that we violate the child's nature and render difficult the best ethical results, by introducing the child too abruptly to a number of special studies, of reading, writing, geography, etc., out of relation to this social life.

I believe, therefore, that the true center of correlation on the school subjects is not science, nor literature, nor history, nor geography, but the child's own social activities.

I believe that education cannot be unified in the study of science, or so called nature study, because apart from human activity, nature itself is not a unity; nature in itself is a number of diverse objects in space and time, and to attempt to make it the center of work by itself, is to introduce a principle of radiation rather than one of concentration.

I believe that literature is the reflex expression and interpretation of social experience; that hence it must follow upon and not precede such experience. It, therefore, cannot be made the basis, although it may be made the summary of unification.

I believe once more that history is of educative value in so far as it presents phases of social life and growth. It must be controlled by reference to social life. When taken simply as history it is thrown into the distant past and becomes dead and inert. Taken as the record of man's social life and progress it becomes full of meaning. I believe, however, that it cannot be so taken excepting as the child is also introduced directly into social life.

I believe accordingly that the primary basis of education is in the child's powers at work along the same general constructive lines as those which have brought civilization into being.

I believe that the only way to make the child conscious of his social heritage is to enable him to perform those fundamental types of activity which make civilization what it is.

I believe, therefore, in the so-called expressive or constructive activities as the center of correlation.

I believe that this gives the standard for the place of cooking, sewing, manual training, etc., in the school.

I believe that they are not special studies which are to be introduced over and above a lot of others in the way of relaxation or relief, or as additional accomplishments. I believe rather that they represent, as types, fundamental forms of social activity; and that it is possible and desirable that the child's introduction into the more formal subjects of the curriculum be through the medium of these activities.

I believe that the study of science is educational in so far as it brings out the materials and processes which make social life what it is.

I believe that one of the greatest difficulties in the present teaching of science is that the material is presented in purely objective form, or is treated as a new peculiar kind of experience which the child can add to that which he has already had. In reality, science is of value because it gives the ability to interpret and control the experience already had. It should be introduced, not as so much new subject-matter, but as showing the factors already involved in previous experience and as furnishing tools by which that experience can be more easily and effectively regulated.

I believe that at present we lose much of the value of literature and language studies because of our elimination of the social element. Language is almost always treated in the books of pedagogy simply as the expression of thought. It is true that language is a logical instrument, but it is fundamentally and primarily a social instrument. Language is the device for communication; it is the tool through which one individual comes to share the ideas and feelings of others. When treated simply as a way of getting individual information, or as a means of showing off what one has learned, it loses its social motive and end.

I believe that there is, therefore, no succession of studies in the ideal school curriculum. If education is life, all life has, from the outset, a scientific aspect, an aspect of art and culture, and an aspect of communication. It cannot, therefore, be true that the proper studies for one grade are mere reading and writing, and that at a later grade, reading, or literature, or science, may be introduced. The progress is not in the succession of studies but in the development of new attitudes towards, and new interests in, experience.

I believe finally, that education must be conceived as a continuing reconstruction of experience; that the process and the goal of education are one and the same thing.

I believe that to set up any end outside of education, as furnishing its goal and standard, is to deprive the educational process of much of its meaning and tends to make us rely upon false and external stimuli in dealing with the child.

ARTICLE IV—THE NATURE OF METHOD

I believe that the question of method is ultimately reducible to the question of the order of development of the child's powers and interests. The law for presenting and treating material is the law implicit within the child's own nature. Because this is so I believe the following statements are of supreme importance as determining the spirit in which education is carried on:

1. I believe that the active side precedes the passive in the development of the child nature; that expression comes before conscious impression; that the muscular development precedes the sensory; that movements come before conscious sensations; I believe that consciousness is essentially motor or impulsive; that conscious states tend to project themselves in action.

    I believe that the neglect of this principle is the cause of a large part of the waste of time and strength in school work. The child is thrown into a passive, receptive, or absorbing attitude. The conditions are such that he is not permitted to follow the law of his nature; the result is friction and waste.

    I believe that ideas (intellectual and rational processes) also result from action and devolve for the sake of the better control of action. What we term reason is primarily the law of orderly or effective action. To attempt to develop the reasoning powers, the powers of judgment, without reference to the selection and arrangement of means in action, is the fundamental fallacy in our present methods of dealing with this matter. As a result we present the child with arbitrary symbols. Symbols are a necessity in mental development, but they have their place as tools for economizing effort; presented by themselves they are a mass of meaningless and arbitrary ideas imposed from without.

2. I believe that the image is the great instrument of instruction. What a child gets out of any subject presented to him is simply the images which he himself forms with regard to it.

   I believe that if nine tenths of the energy at present directed towards making the child learn certain things, were spent in seeing to it that the child was forming proper images, the work of instruction would be indefinitely facilitated.

   I believe that much of the time and attention now given to the preparation and presentation of lessons might be more wisely and profitably expended in training the child's power of imagery and in seeing to it that he was continually forming definite, vivid, and growing images of the various subjects with which he comes in contact in his experience.

3. I believe that interests are the signs and symptoms of growing power. I believe that they represent dawning capacities. Accordingly the constant and careful observation of interests is of the utmost importance for the educator.

   I believe that these interests are to be observed as showing the state of development which the child has reached.

   I believe that they prophesy the stage upon which he is about to enter.

   I believe that only through the continual and sympathetic observation of childhood's interests can the adult enter into the child's life and see what it is ready for, and upon what material it could work most readily and fruitfully.

   I believe that these interests are neither to be humored nor repressed. To repress interest is to substitute the adult for the child, and so to weaken intellectual curiosity and alertness, to suppress initiative, and to deaden interest. To humor the interests is to substitute the transient for the permanent. The interest is always the sign of some power below; the important thing is to discover this power. To humor the interest is to fail to penetrate below the surface and its sure result is to substitute caprice and whim for genuine interest.

4. I believe that the emotions are the reflex of actions.

   I believe that to endeavor to stimulate or arouse the emotions apart from their corresponding activities, is to introduce an unhealthy and morbid state of mind.

   I believe that if we can only secure right habits of action and thought, with reference to the good, the true, and the beautiful, the emotions will for the most part take care of themselves.

   I believe that next to deadness and dullness, formalism and routine, our education is threatened with no greater evil than sentimentalism.

   I believe that this sentimentalism is the necessary result of the attempt to divorce feeling from action.

ARTICLE V—THE SCHOOL AND SOCIAL PROGRESS

I believe that education is the fundamental method of social progress and reform.

I believe that all reforms which rest simply upon the enactment of law, or the threatening of certain penalties, or upon changes in mechanical or outward arrangements, are transitory and futile.

I believe that education is a regulation of the process of coming to share in the social consciousness; and that the adjustment of individual activity on the basis of this social consciousness is the only sure method of social reconstruction.

I believe that this conception has due regard for both the individualistic and socialistic ideals. It is duly individual because it recognizes the formation of a certain character as the only genuine basis of right living. It is socialistic because it recognizes that this right character is not to be formed by merely individual precept, example, or exhortation, but rather by the influence of a certain form of institutional or community life upon the individual, and that the social organism through the school, as its organ, may determine ethical results.

I believe that in the ideal school we have the reconciliation of the individualistic and the institutional ideals.

I believe that the community's duty to education is, therefore, its paramount moral duty. By law and punishment, by social agitation and discussion, society can regulate and form itself in a more or less haphazard and chance way. But through education society can formulate its own purposes, can organize its own means and resources, and thus shape itself with definiteness and economy in the direction in which it wishes to move.

I believe that when society once recognizes the possibilities in this direction, and the obligations which these possibilities impose, it is impossible to conceive of the resources of time, attention, and money which will be put at the disposal of the educator.

I believe that it is the business of every one interested in education to insist upon the school as the primary and most effective interest of social progress and reform in order that society may be awakened to realize what the school stands for, and aroused to the necessity of endowing the educator with sufficient equipment properly to perform his task.

I believe that education thus conceived marks the most perfect and intimate union of science and art conceivable in human experience.

I believe that the art of thus giving shape to human powers and adapting them to social service, is the supreme art; one calling into its service the best of artists; that no insight, sympathy, tact, executive power, is too great for such service.

I believe that with the growth of psychological service, giving added insight into individual structure and laws of growth; and with growth of social science, adding to our knowledge of the right organization of individuals, all scientific resources can be utilized for the purposes of education.

I believe that when science and art thus join hands the most commanding motive for human action will be reached; the most genuine springs of human conduct aroused and the best service that human nature is capable of guaranteed.

I believe, finally, that the teacher is engaged, not simply in the training of individuals, but in the formation of the proper social life.

I believe that every teacher should realize the dignity of his calling; that he is a social servant set apart for the maintenance of proper social order and the securing of the right social growth.

I believe that in this way the teacher always is the prophet of the true God and the usherer in of the true kingdom of God.

Part 2

History of Education

Introduction to History of American Education

There are millions of individual histories of American education that could be told. For many, the schoolhouse door has always been the portal to greater and better things. For some, the schoolhouse door was closed for hundreds of years. For others, although the door was open a crack, their time in schools brought only frustration and tears.

This section traces some important moments in the history of American education from the early years in the seventeenth century in New England; through the eighteenth century in the Middle Atlantic colonies and the South and then the birth of the Nation and the westward movement; to the fight for equal access for schooling to all races; and the continuing argument over what should be taught to U.S. youth and what should they know and be able to do.

NEW ENGLAND

The Puritans of the New England colonies had a clear understanding from their very beginnings on this continent what role education must play in the lives of all citizens. Because of their religious understandings, the Puritans saw life on earth as a test for the next life and felt the devil was determined that they fail this test. Their only hope for salvation and avoidance of eternal damnation came through daily reading of the Bible.

Thus within a few years of their landing on these shores, the Puritans passed laws that required a basic education for all children. Education meant learning to read. Reading was seen as the key to deciphering God's will as expressed in the pages of the Bible. It was the adults' responsibility to ensure that all children had an opportunity for eternal life. First, it was the responsibility of parents that children be educated, but beyond that it was the responsibility of those whom children were apprenticed to and working for. Lastly, it was the responsibility of the whole community to ensure that every child had at least a rudimentary education and that bright children be educated as far as their talents would take them.

The passage of the Old Deluder Satan Act in 1647 set the stage for the next 350 years of U.S. education. The Old Deluder Satan Act ensured that each community of size would hire a teacher for its children. This act took the responsibility for educating children away from individual families only and put it on the community as its charge. The Old Deluder Satan Act also allowed for taxation of all citizens, not just those who had children of school age, to pay for schools.

MIDDLE ATLANTIC COLONIES

The cities of the Middle Atlantic Colonies began to thrive as commerce grew and saw heterogeneity of languages and ethnicities not allowed in New England by the Puritans. Thus, in places such as Philadelphia and New York City, schools sprang up to teach the skills needed not for the next life but for this one. Accounting, foreign languages, and navigation were taught in these schools along with basic reading and ciphering. These schools were private and entrepreneurial and open to those who could pay for them, although often with limited access to females and African Americans. It was here that the focus changed from education for salvation to education for nation building and making this life one of riches and rewards through hard work.

THE SOUTH

The Southern Colonies were largely agricultural, where cotton and tobacco were grown on large tracts of land. These crops required many workers, but this work did not require their minds as much as their strong backs. Slavery was the mechanism used to ensure a large and ready supply of workers, and education was forbidden to them as one more way of keeping them from breaking those bonds. Education in the South was seen as the privilege of those who owned land. Private tutors were hired for the sons of the wealthy, and some were sent back to Europe to further their education. For the daughters of the landowners, an education in becoming a lady was seen as most proper. It wasn't until after the War between the States that public education and schooling for most children was available. The battle for equal education for African American children and white children has continued to the present time.

THE GROWTH OF THE NATION

From the end of the eighteenth century through much of the nineteenth century, the movement West and expansion of the nation was a major focus. From the Northwest Ordinance, which set aside land for schools in the new territories, to the movement for common schools in all communities and the drive for female teachers, there was a growing common vision that through education the United States could become the greatest nation on earth. To be sure, there were continuing arguments over who would pay for schools, who should be sent to them and who should be excluded, and what the curriculum of the schools should be.

As the nation grew, so too did the need for more schooling. When the vast majority of workers were involved in agriculture in some way, only a rudimentary knowledge of reading and writing was seen as sufficient. With the shift from agriculture to industry came a need for greater numbers of workers to have the knowledge and skills that would come with more years of schooling. From 1850 to 1950, formal schooling for most people went from a modest number of days a year for a few years to a few years of elementary schooling to, in the twentieth century, most of the population attending high school and an ever-increasing number moving on to higher education. Along the way, links were made between elementary and secondary education and battles were fought over who would pay the bills of what had become a vast network of schools.

Once the infrastructure of America's schools was in place, there continued to be long arguments over which children should be educated in what ways. The pendulum swung from the recommendations at the close of the nineteenth century that all children should be given a college preparatory education, the same education for all, to—in the early decades of the twentieth century—the idea that only the brightest (and wealthiest) children should receive a college preparatory education and the rest should be prepared to take their places in the world of work and family life through "life-adjustment" education. These arguments can still be heard on a continuing basis around the country.

In the mid-twentieth century, two mighty forces steered the course of American education. One was the cry for equal education for all U.S. children. The other was spurred by the Cold War and America's place in an ever-competitive world stage. The last two decades of the century closed still focused on equity and equality in education, often seen through the lens of accountability and results. The first decade of the twenty-first century continued this focus, with an increasing concern for spiraling costs to burdened taxpayers.

Northwest Ordinance

The governor, judges, legislative council, secretary, and such other officers as Congress shall appoint in the district, shall take an oath or affirmation of fidelity and of office; the governor before the president of congress, and all other officers before the Governor. As soon as a legislature shall be formed in the district, the council and house assembled in one room, shall have authority, by joint ballot, to elect a delegate to Congress, who shall have a seat in Congress, with a right of debating but not voting during this temporary government.

And, for extending the fundamental principles of civil and religious liberty, which form the basis whereon these republics, their laws and constitutions are erected; to fix and establish those principles as the basis of all laws, constitutions, and governments, which forever hereafter shall be formed in the said territory: to provide also for the establishment of States, and permanent government therein, and for their admission to a share in the federal councils on an equal footing with the original States, at as early periods as may be consistent with the general interest:

It is hereby ordained and declared by the authority aforesaid, That the following articles shall be considered as articles of compact between the original States and the people and States in the said territory and forever remain unalterable, unless by common consent, to wit:

ART. 1.

No person, demeaning himself in a peaceable and orderly manner, shall ever be molested on account of his mode of worship or religious sentiments, in the said territory.

ART. 2.

The inhabitants of the said territory shall always be entitled to the benefits of the writ of habeas corpus, and of the trial by jury; of a proportionate representation of the people in the legislature; and of judicial proceedings according to the course of the common law. All persons shall be bailable, unless for capital offenses, where the proof shall be evident or the presumption great. All fines shall be moderate; and no cruel or unusual punishments shall be inflicted. No man shall be deprived of his liberty or property, but by the judgment of his peers or the law of the land; and, should the public exigencies make it necessary, for the common preservation, to take any person's property, or to demand his particular services, full compensation shall be made for the same. And, in the just preservation of rights and property, it is understood and declared, that no law ought ever to be made, or have force in the said territory, that shall, in any manner whatever, interfere with or affect private contracts or engagements, bona fide, and without fraud, previously formed.

ART. 3.

Religion, morality, and knowledge, being necessary to good government and the happiness of mankind, schools and the means of education shall forever be encouraged. The utmost good faith shall always be observed towards the Indians; their lands and property shall never be taken from them without their consent; and, in their property, rights, and liberty, they shall never be invaded or disturbed, unless in just and lawful wars authorized by Congress; but laws founded in justice and humanity, shall from time to time be made for preventing wrongs being done to them, and for preserving peace and friendship with them.

ART. 4.

The said territory, and the States which may be formed therein, shall forever remain a part of this Confederacy of the United States of America, subject to the Articles of Confederation, and to such alterations therein as shall be constitutionally made; and to all the acts and ordinances of the United States in Congress assembled, conformable thereto. The inhabitants and settlers in the said territory shall be subject to pay a part of the federal debts contracted or to be contracted, and a proportional part of the expenses of government, to be apportioned on them by Congress according to the same common rule and measure by which apportionments thereof shall be made on the other States; and the taxes for paying their proportion shall be laid and levied by the authority and direction of the legislatures of the district or districts, or new States, as in the original States, within the time agreed upon by the United States in Congress assembled. The legislatures of those districts or new States, shall never interfere with the primary disposal of the soil by the United States in Congress assembled, nor with any regulations Congress may find necessary for securing the title in such soil to the bona fide purchasers. No tax shall be imposed on lands the property of the United States; and, in no case, shall nonresident proprietors be taxed higher than residents. The navigable waters leading into the Mississippi and St. Lawrence, and the carrying places between the same, shall be common highways and forever free, as well to the inhabitants of the said territory as to the citizens of the United States, and those of any other States that may be admitted into the confederacy, without any tax, impost, or duty therefor.

ART. 5.

There shall be formed in the said territory, not less than three nor more than five States; and the boundaries of the States, as soon as Virginia shall alter her act of cession, and consent to the same, shall become fixed and established as follows, to wit: The western State in the said territory, shall be bounded by the Mississippi, the Ohio, and Wabash Rivers; a direct line drawn from the Wabash and Post Vincents, due North, to the territorial line between the United States and Canada; and, by the said territorial line, to the Lake of the Woods and Mississippi. The middle State shall be bounded by the said direct line, the Wabash from Post Vincents to the Ohio, by the Ohio, by a direct line, drawn due north from the mouth of the Great Miami, to the said territorial line, and by the said territorial line. The eastern State shall be bounded by the last mentioned direct line, the Ohio, Pennsylvania, and the said territorial line: Provided, however, and it is further understood and declared, that the boundaries of these three States shall be subject so far to be altered, that, if Congress shall hereafter find it expedient, they shall have authority to form one or two States in that part of the said territory which lies north of an east and west line drawn through the southerly bend or extreme of Lake Michigan. And, whenever any of the said States shall have sixty thousand free inhabitants therein, such State shall be admitted, by its delegates, into the Congress of the United States, on an equal footing with the original States in all respects whatever, and shall be at liberty to form a permanent constitution and State government: Provided, the constitution and government so to be formed, shall be republican, and in conformity to the principles contained in these articles; and, so far as it can be consistent with the general interest of the confederacy, such admission shall be allowed at an earlier period, and when there may be a less number of free inhabitants in the State than sixty thousand.

ART. 6.

There shall be neither slavery nor involuntary servitude in the said territory, otherwise than in the punishment of crimes whereof the party shall have been duly convicted: Provided, always, That any person escaping into the same, from whom labor or service is lawfully claimed in any one of the original States, such fugitive may be lawfully reclaimed and conveyed to the person claiming his or her labor or service as aforesaid.

Be it ordained by the authority aforesaid, That the resolutions of the 23rd of April, 1784, relative to the subject of this ordinance, be, and the same are hereby repealed and declared null and void.

Compulsory Education in the Southern Colonies

—Marcus W. Jernegan

I. VIRGINIA

If one turns to the existing accounts of the history of American education in the colonial period of our history, he will observe that many writers assume that most of those persons who received any instruction attended organized schools. That such an inference is entirely erroneous is easily realized by the performance of a simple arithmetical problem—namely, that of dividing the population at any given date by the number of schools *known* to have been in existence at that date. The percentage of persons receiving a part of their education in such institutions would be highest in the New England colonies, but even in this section it would surprise most students if they were aware of how many learned how to read or write through some other agency than organized schools.[1]

If we pass beyond New England to the middle and southern colonies, it is safe to say that a still smaller percentage of the total number who secured the rudiments of an education received it in an organized school. It is doubtless true that there were many private schools whose existence we shall never be able to prove, but, even allowing for this possibility, it is not believed that the point made above would be greatly modified. It is therefore important to stress the agencies other than schools if we are to gain a proper perspective of the evolution of American education. The well-known tendency to read into the past the ideals, and even the institutions, of the present is responsible for a very common fallacy—that of mistaking the special for the general fact. Contemporary conditions, not later theories, govern and explain the development of institutions; and the general fact, the typical institution, cannot vary widely from the general conditions, which must in the long run determine what is general and what exceptional.

During the colonial period much the larger proportion of the people at any one time were living under frontier conditions. Wherever such conditions were the controlling factor, organized institutions, such as the church and school, were not general, except perhaps in portions of New England, notwithstanding the assertions of our enthusiastic and imaginative racial, sectarian, and other types of historians, who often assert the contrary but fail to produce the evidence.[2] When a given area ceased to be governed by frontier conditions, then organized institutions gradually became the general rather than the special fact. Frontier conditions imply, among other things, a sparse population; absorption of energies, time, and thought in satisfying material needs—shelter, subsistence, and protection; occupations largely connected with agriculture or extractive industries; lack of easy means of communication, and hence isolation, particularly in the late fall, winter, and early spring months; and, finally, conservation of labor, even of children, during those months of the year in which the farming operations are pressing. If we realize also the weak cultural ideals, inevitable and inherent in frontier groups, and the impossibility of locating organized schools so that any large proportion of those of school age could be reached, under such conditions, even supposing the desire to exist, we can easily see that a great many persons who learned how to read and write must have taken advantage of other agencies than schools. Two were of the greatest importance—namely, home instruction given by the parents, and the apprenticeship system, instruction given by the master or his agent.

Both of these agencies were in common and voluntary use in every colony. Voluntary education through apprenticeship occurred when, through custom or agreement, an indenture was drawn so as to secure for the apprentice book or religious instruction, with or without instruction in a trade, and his maintenance, the latter being one of the main purposes of the system in its historical development. No special law concerning the enforcement of the indenture was needed in such cases, for indentures were almost universally looked upon as contracts, became a matter of public record, and hence were enforceable in the courts. In some of the colonies parental education was made compulsory through laws passed to this effect as in New England. In this study we are concerned with the system of *compulsory* education in the southern colonies, Virginia in particular, as it was

---

[1] We find little or no recognition of the fact that there were other agencies for education than organized schools in such general histories of American education as those by Dexter or Boone; nor even in most state histories of education, like those of Steiner for Connecticut or Smith for North Carolina.

[2] Compare A. B. Faust, *History of the German Element in the United States*, II, 203–4; G. L. Jackson, *The Privilege of Education*, p. 67.

From *School Review, 27, June 1919* by Marcus W. Jernegan.

instituted by law through the agencies of parents, guardians, and overseers, and particularly through masters and mistresses in connection with the system of apprenticeship.

Having discussed the general factors[3] which influenced the development of education in the southern colonies, we will now note how far they enacted laws involving the principle of compulsory education, and first with respect to Virginia. In view of the factors mentioned, it is not surprising that laws of this character referred to *special*, rather than to *all*, classes of children, as was generally the case at first in New England.[4] The classes provided for were orphans, poor children, and those of illegitimate birth, in the last case with respect to three classes: first, those born of free white women and white servants, second, those born of convict servant women, and third, mulatto children born of a free, or white servant, mother. The conception that the state was in part responsible for the education of the classes mentioned was expressed in compulsory laws, specifying the machinery for enforcement, similar to those in New England.

ORPHANS

The first class provided for was orphans. The legislation respecting these unfortunates is relatively large in the southern and middle colonies as compared with New England, where there is hardly a reference to such children. No less than seventeen acts were passed by Virginia alone relating to this class, most of them involving the principle of compulsory education. The principal reason for the increase of orphans was the presence of the white servant, and to some extent the negro slave.[5] A little less than one year after Massachusetts passed her first act on compulsory education, that of June 14, 1642, Virginia enacted one in March, 1642/3,[6] relating to orphans, the first of many laws relating to this class. Because guardians and overseers had neglected and "very much abused" orphans' estates, they were ordered to report annually an account of the estate and their service to the commissioners of the county court. They were also ordered "to educate and instruct them according to their best endeavours in Christian religion and in rudiments of learning." If they were found delinquent in their duties in these respects, the commissioners were ordered to see that the said orphans were provided for "according to their estates and qualities."

The act of 1656[7] provided that orphans must be educated on the interest of their estates according to its proportion, but if "so meane and inconsiderable that it will not reach to a free education," then such orphans must be bound out as apprentices until twenty-one years of age, to learn some manual trade, unless friends or relatives agreed to keep them for the interest of their estate. The court was ordered to take sufficient security for orphans' estates, inquire yearly of the security, whether orphans were "educated according as their estates will beare," remove them to other guardians if notorious defect were found, and change the master of orphans bound as apprentices if he used them "rigourously" or neglected to teach them his trade.

It will be noticed that the degree of education varied with the estate and quality of the orphan, and that in case of orphans apprenticed no book education is specified, though the law seems to imply that the court should provide for such education in the indenture. It was not until 1705, however, that specific instructions were given to this effect. The act of 1656 is clearly compulsory in character, as it is mandatory and provides for education and for a penalty for neglect by the guardian or master, that is, removal of the child. An order of the assembly of 1659[8] required sheriffs to summon all persons to bring in their accounts of orphans' estates, and clerks of county courts to register these accounts. An "Orphan's Court,"[9] to consider cases concerning orphans, was held

---

[3] *School Review*, May, 1919, article by the author on "The Educational Development of the Southern Colonies, Introduction."

[4] See *School Review*, December, 1918, and January, 1919, for articles by the author on the legislation of the New England colonies on compulsory education. Some of the laws passed by the southern colonies, bearing on the compulsory education of special classes, are omitted in Clews, *Educational Legislation and Administration of the Colonial Governments*, New York, 1899.

[5] See Section below "Poor Children." The acts relating to orphans are concerned especially with the security of their estates. Minute regulations are set forth governing guardians, in order that the orphan might have the largest income possible from his estate and its increase, and that he might be maintained and educated in the best manner possible.

[6] W. W. Hening, *Statutes at Large* (Virginia), I, 260–61. Editions—N. Y., 1823, Vols. I-II; Phil., 1823, Vol. III; Richmond, 1814–21, Vols. IV-VIII.

[7] W. W. Hening, *Statutes at Large* (Virginia), I, 416.

[8] *Ibid.*, p. 551.

[9] *William and Mary College Quarterly*, V, 221.

in one county as early as 1648.[10] A general act of 1645/6 had already provided that commissioners of county courts, neglecting to punish offenders "according to the merit of the cause," upon complaint could be fined at the discretion of the governor and council.[11]

An act of 1705[12] again repeated most of the provisions of the two earlier acts, but added for the first time a specific requirement respecting the education of apprenticed orphans; namely, that "the master of every such orphan shall be obliged to teach him to read and write." That of 1730[13] also reiterated the powers conferred in previous acts, declared that "great abuses" had been committed by guardians of orphans and justices of county courts, who had been negligent, and called again for annual reports by guardians, gave them custody of their "tuition," and gave power to the county court to make additional rules "for the better education and usage of orphans" when complaint was made that guardians were "neglecting the care of their education," with power to appoint another guardian, if the former did not "take due care of the educating and maintaining of any orphan, according to his degree and circumstances." The act of 1740,[14] for enforcing the execution of laws for better managing of orphans' estates, because of neglect by the justice of many county courts, recapitulated the previous orders and provided for an annual return to the August court of accounts of guardians, ordered the justices to direct process to issue against all guardians failing to appear, and provided for a penalty to be imposed on justices of county courts who neglected their duty, a forfeit of five thousand pounds of tobacco, one half to the use of the county and the other half to the informer.

The act of 1705 was the first to provide definitely for book education, and apparently made it *compulsory* only for boys. A failure to carry out the educational terms of the indenture, as in the case of those referring to trade education, might lead to the removal of an orphan apprenticed, as is proved by cases on record. The neglect by justices mentioned in the act of 1730 doubtless continued and led to that of 1740, providing for a severe penalty to be levied upon negligent justices. By this date then, the imposing of penalties was highly developed, as guardians, masters, and justices could all be penalized for neglect of orphans.

The last act passed before the Revolution was that of 1748,[15] in effect June 10, 1751. It was a codification of previous laws, and in fact repealed all former acts. Nearly all the former orders mentioned were repeated, and there was added this clause referring to orphans apprenticed: "Every male [to be apprenticed] to some tradesman, merchant, mariner, or other person approved by the court," to twenty-one years of age, and "every female to some suitable trade or employment" to eighteen years of age, and the master or mistress of such servant "shall find and provide for him or her, diet, cloathes, lodgings and accommodations fit and necessary, and shall teach, or cause him or her to be taught to read and write." This was the most comprehensive law enacted in the colonies on the education of orphans, and shows unexpected concern by Virginia for the education of girls as well as boys, of this class.

POOR CHILDREN

It has already been shown[16] that the nature of the population of Virginia, and of the South in general, was made up of several groups, such as the higher planter class, the smaller planter with a few slaves, the independent farmer, the white servant, who after his term of service of four or five years usually became a small farmer,

[10]An orphan's court was in existence in London in 1625/6. See *Fourth Report of Hist. Mss. Commission* (London, 1874), p. 7.

[11]Hening, I, 310. The act of 1661/2 which appears in the revisal of the laws of 1661/2 (*ibid.*, 41–43) was largely a re-enactment of that of 1656; that of 1672 gave power to the county courts to dispose of orphans' estates according to the best judgment of the justices, if they could not find persons to take the estates according to the regulations of previous acts; that of 1679 made justices who failed to take sufficient security for orphans' estates chargeable for all losses due to such failure (*ibid.*, II, 92–94, 295, and 444). These three acts were repealed by the act of 1705, but the main provisions were re-enacted and appear in the Virginia codes of the eighteenth century and hence were in force throughout the colonial period. See also *A Collection of all the Acts of Assembly, now in force*, etc. (Williamsburg, 1733), pp. 186–187; *The Acts of Assembly, now in force*, etc. (Williamsburg, 1752), pp. 226–228; *The Acts of Assembly, now in force*, etc. (Williamsburg, 1769), pp. 156–59.

[12]Hening, III, 375. This act repealed all previous acts on the subject. It appears in the code of 1733, pp. 186–87.

[13]*Ibid.*, IV, 286; also in the code of 1733, pp. 447–48.

[14]*Ibid.*, V, l00–101. The substance of this act was included in that of 1748.

[15]Hening, V 450–52, chap. vi. This act is in the code of 1752, pp. 226–28, and also appears in the code of 1769, pp. 156–59.

[16]See *School Review*, May, 1919.

a laborer, or an artisan, and the negro slave. Out of the last class there developed two more, the free negro and the mulatto servant; the latter, born of a free white mother or white servant, after a long period of service becoming a free man or woman. There was therefore a large element of the population from which poor children might arise. Moreover, many of the white servants were of poor stock, ignorant, lazy, and with low moral standards. Some were convict servants, those liberated from the English jails and sold as servants, or given a sentence by English judges of servitude in the colonies in lieu of a jail sentence in England[17] The moral standards of this last class were very low, and of course there is no need to comment on the lack of moral standards of the negro slaves. There was complaint from an early date of "vagrant idle, and dissolute persons," largely recruited from the white servants. They frequently became the fathers of illegitimate children, by both free white and white servant women. They ran away, with the result that their children were often thrown on the parish for support. White men servants after their term of service might become vagabonds or dissolute persons, or, if married, desert their wives and children, who would then be thrown on the parish. Some white servant women also gave birth to illegitimate mulatto children, which by the law[18] of Virginia were free after their term of service.

The problem then for Virginia, and for other colonies, was much the same as that which had confronted Old and New England, only it was a more serious and pressing one. That problem was first economic—how to protect the parish from the burden of maintaining poor children; how to provide for an artisan class skilled in trades and needed in the colony; how to reduce idleness and unemployment, and how to add rapidly to the wealth and property of all the people. The second aspect of the problem was educational. The natural conception of the relation of the state to education was largely *laissez faire,* on the theory that this was a matter to be intrusted to private initiative or the church. But the pressure of a rapidly growing class of poor children, and the consequent expense to the parish, coupled with the difficulty of obtaining the much-needed supply of artisans, forced the state to modify this conception. Poor parents could not educate their children, and some degree of book education was desirable for artisans in order that they might be efficient in their trades. Two influences also promoted this conception. The period from the Reformation to the great Civil War is marked, in England, by the stimulating effect of religion on education—especially the efforts of competing religious denominations and their anxiety to increase their power through instruction in the peculiar tenets of their creed and in their catechism. In states where there was union of Church and State—the Established Church in Virginia—this influence was strong. A second influence was the beginnings of the humanitarian movement, as exhibited in philanthropy, the desire to give poor children some opportunity for education, best illustrated in the work of the Society for the Propagation of the Gospel in Foreign Parts.[19]

All these forces led to the conception that the state was responsible, to some extent at least, for the education of certain classes of children. From an economic, religious, and humanitarian standpoint, it was undesirable that a large body of illiterate laborers, tradesmen, or farmers should be allowed to develop. From a purely selfish standpoint, the money cost, the state was compelled to take some action. As in the New England colonies, and perhaps influenced by their legislation,[20] the system of apprenticeship seemed to be the most effective agency to gain the ends desired, with the least expense, loss of time from labor, and, in the case of the southern colonies, the least interference with their general attitude toward the relation of the state to education.[21]

An examination of the legislation of Virginia reveals the fact that at least eight important laws were passed from 1646 to 1769 having for their purpose religious, industrial, or book education of poor children of various classes; that five of these acts contemplated some form of book education, and that four of them can be properly classed as compulsory laws. There were in addition general laws applying to all children and providing

---

[17]James D. Butler, "British Convicts Shipped to American Colonies," *American Historical Review,* II, 12–33. See also "A Forgotten Slavery of Colonial Days," article by the author in *Harper's Monthly,* October, 1913.

[18]Hening, II, 270. A law of 1662 even complained that "Some dissolute masters have gotten their maides [white servants) with child" (Hening, II, 167).

[19]See W. W. Kemp, *The Support of Schools in Colonial New York by the Society for the Propagation of the Gospel in Foreign Parts,* New York, 1913.

[20]See article by author in *School Review,* December, 1918.

[21]The Virginia Company agreed February 2, 1620, that one hundred children supplied by the city of London to be sent to Virginia and apprenticed should be "Educated and brought upp in some good Craftes, Trades, or Husbandry" (Kingsbury, *Rec. of Va. Co.,* Vol. I, p. 306).

for compulsory religious education. An act of February, 1631/2,[22] provided that all churchwardens should take an oath administered before the commissioner of the monthly court, to the effect that they "present such maysters and mistresses as shall be delinquents in the catechisinge the youth and ignorant persons." Another act[23] of the same session provided that the minister should upon every Sunday "examine, catechise, and instruct the youth and ignorant persons of his parish, in the ten commandments the articles of the beliefe and in the Lord's prayer. . . . And all fathers, mothers, maysters and mistresses shall cause theire children, servants or apprentizes which have not learned the catachisme to come to the church" to learn the same, and if any of the above neglected their duties they should be "censured by the corts in those places holden." By the act of 1644/5[24] ministers failing to catechise every Sunday were to forfeit five hundred pounds of tobacco for the use of the parish. Finally the act of 1645/6[25] provided that all masters and families failing to send their children and servants to be catechised, upon warning given by the minister where they would officiate, were to be subject to a penalty of five hundred pounds of tobacco for the use of the parish "unless sufficient cause be shewn to the contrary."

The increase of children in Virginia was slow for the first thirty years of the settlement, but by 1646[26] "God Almighty, among many his other blessings, hath vouchsafed increase of children to this colony, who now are multiplied to a considerable number, who if instructed in good and lawful trades, may much improve the honor and reputation of the country, and noe lesse their owne good and their parents comfort." This refers, of course, not to children of wealthy planters and well-to-do farmers, but to poor children. The first three acts relating to this class were those of 1646, 1668, and 1672. They did not, strictly speaking, involve compulsory education, since the laws are permissive rather than mandatory, but they require comment in order to show the conditions accounting for the passage of later compulsory laws.

The act of 1646[27] refers to sundry laws and statutes of parliament established "for the better educateing of youth in honest and profitable trades and manufactures, as also to avoyde sloath and idlenesse wherewith such young children are easily corrupted, as also for the reliefe of such parents whose poverty extends not to give them good breeding." Accordingly justices of the peace were given power to bind out poor children to tradesmen or husbandmen "to be brought up in some good and lawful calling." The remainder of the act outlines an ambitious plan for industrial education. Two children from each county, chosen by the commissioners of the counties, were to be sent to public flax houses to be taught in "cording knitting and spinning." Such children were to be taken only from those parents who "by reason of their poverty are disabled to maintaine and educate them." State and county were to provide the funds to defray the cost of buildings, food, clothing, shelter, etc., including "a sow shote of sixe months old, two laying hens," etc. The act of 1668[28] was somewhat similar. It contemplated the promotion of manufactures—wool, flax, and hemp—and the increase of artificers. It gave power to the commissioners of each county court, with the assistance of the vestries of the parishes, to build houses for "educating and instructing poore children in the knowledge of spinning, weaving and other useful occupations and trades," with power to take poor children from indigent parents to place them to work in such houses. In 1672,[29] because of the increase of "vagabonds idle and desolute persons," justices of the peace and county courts were empowered to place out all children whose parents were not able to bring them up apprentices to tradesmen,

---

[22]Hening, I, 156.

[23]*Ibid.*, p. 157; see also *ibid.*, p. 181, for re-enactment of this law in 1632.

[24]Hening, I, 290.

[25]*Ibid.*, pp. 311–12. None of these four acts appears in the revisal of 1661/2, to be found in *ibid.*, II, 41–162, nor in later codes.

[26]*Ibid.*, I pp. 336–37.

[27]*Ibid.*, This act was omitted in the revisal of 1661/2, and later was replaced by that of 1668.

[28]Hening, II, 266–67. This act remained in force until 1755 (code of 1733, p. 48) and was then superseded by the law of that year, which declared that the number of poor people had greatly increased of late years, and houses for their reception were proposed to help prevent "great mischiefs" arising from such numbers of unemployed poor. Vestries of every parish were given power to provide one or more houses, and provide cotton, hemp, or flax or other material for setting the poor to work. Parishes, if small, might unite to build houses, and were also given power "to levy a reasonable allowance in their parish levies, for the education of such poor children as shall be placed in the said house, or houses, until they shall be bound out according to law." (Hening, VI, 475–76).

[29]Hening, II, 298; also in the code of 1733, p. 57.

males to twenty-one and females "to other necessary employments," to eighteen, and churchwardens of every parish were to be ordered by the county courts to give an account annually at the orphan's court "of all such children within their parish, as they judge to be within the said capacity."

None of these three acts specifies book education, and there is no evidence that the workhouses provided for were ever built. There was no reason, of course, why the justices could not introduce a clause into the indenture providing for book education, if they wished to, and such a practice was not uncommon from 1646 on, but we are here concerned principally with the laws which made this practice *compulsory*. With these permissive acts as a foundation, Virginia opened the eighteenth century with a law providing for compulsory book education of orphan boys, as already stated, and in 1727 this act was made applicable to poor boys apprenticed.

The act of 1727[30] complains that idle and disorderly persons able to work "strole from one county to another, neglecting to labour," and vagabonds "run from their habitations and leave either wives or children, without suitable means for their subsistance." When such parents, because of "idle dissolute and disorderly course of life," were judged by the county court to be incapable of supporting and bringing up such children, or when they neglected to "take due care of the education and instruction of such child or children, in christian principles," the churchwardens, on certificate from the county court, were given power "to bind out or put out to service or apprentice" the children of such parents, for such time and "under such covenants as hath been usual and customary, or the law directs in the case of orphan children." This last clause refers to the act of 1705 which required that in the case of orphan boys apprenticed, "the master of every such orphan shall be obliged to teach him to read and write."[31]

The act of 1748,[32] in force June 10, 1751, was a revision of that of 1727, with important changes respecting the education of poor children. When county courts judged that *any* person or persons were incapable of supporting and bringing up their children "in honest courses," or when it appears to the court "that he, she, or they, neglect to take due care of the education of his, her, or their child or children, and their instruction in the principles of christianity," then on order of the county court churchwardens of parishes could bind such children apprentices "in the same manner, and under such covenants and conditions as the law directs for poor orphan children." This refers to another act of 1748 passed at the same session, providing that the master of an apprenticed orphan should "teach, or cause him or her to be taught to read and write." It will be noticed that this act specifies for the first time as a reason why the court should take a child from a parent the "neglect to take due care of his education." Previous acts had mentioned lack of support, lack of ability to bring up to trades, or lack of instruction in Christian religion. This approaches the ideals of New England in the seventeenth century, and, as we shall see, there is not wanting evidence to show that parents were called to account merely for neglecting the education of their children.

ILLEGITIMATE CHILDREN

Virginia also passed laws for the education of another class of children, those of illegitimate birth. By the end of the seventeenth century there was a large number of indented servants, causing serious problems to arise respecting the maintenance and education of children of this class. Laws were passed as early as 1642/3[33] against the marriage of servants without the consent of their masters, against fornication between servants, and against fornication between freemen and servants. The number of illegitimate children seems to have been considerable, judging from the laws and the recorded cases in the parish records. The first act bearing on the subject was that of 1657/8,[34] requiring the father of an illegitimate child to give security to indemnify the parish against the expense of keeping the child. If the father were an indented servant, he would be unable to obey the act; hence, in 1662, another act[35] provided that the parish should "take care to keepe the child during the time of the reputed father's service by *indenture* or custome, and that after he is free the said reputed father shall make satisfaction

---

[30]Hening, IV, 208–12, also in code of 1733, p. 397.

[31]By the act of 1736 apprentices were to serve full time until they became of age, even if apprenticed in infancy, because "skill in trades, arts and industries. . . . would be very beneficial to such apprentices and increase the number of artificers in the colony," (Hening, IV, 482).

[32]Hening, VI, 32, (chap. xix). This act is also in the code of 1752, pp. 303–5, and that of 1769, pp. 216–18.

[33]Hening, I, 253.

[34]*Ibid.,* I, 438.

[35]*Ibid.,* II, 168.

to the parish." Thus in the indenture there might be provision for teaching the child to read. If the child were not indentured and the father died or ran away, it became a permanent charge on the parish. The only method of relieving the parish of this expense was to bind out the child as an apprentice, as was provided for in the act. The act of 1769[36] complains that the laws in force are insufficient to provide for indemnifying parishes "from the great charges frequently arising from children begotten out of lawful matrimony." It provides specifically for binding out by the churchwardens the illegitimate child of a single free white woman, in language similar to that of 1748, including this phrase: "and the master or mistress of every such apprentice shall find and provide for *him* or *her* diet, cloathes, lodging, and accommodations fit and necessary, and shall teach or cause him or her to be taught to read and write." If the illegitimate child were born of a convict servant woman during the time of her service, because such a servant could not legally give testimony, and hence the reputed father could not be discovered, the master of such servant was obliged to maintain the child until it was twenty-one or eighteen years of age, and was entitled to its service, provided he "find or provide for such child, the like accommodations, education and freedom dues, and shall be compelled to answer his or her complaint, made to the county court, for default therein, or for ill usage, in like manner, as is before directed in the case of other apprentices."[37]

MULATTO CHILDREN

The act of 1691[38] complained that there was need of preventing "that abominable mixture and spurious issue which hereafter may increase in this dominion as well by negroes, mulattoes, and Indians intermarrying with English, or other white women, as by their unlawful accompanying with one another." A free English white woman having an illegitimate child by a negro or mulatto was subject to a fine or was sold for five years. If the woman were a servant, she was sold for the same number of years after her time as a servant had expired, and in each case the child was to be bound out until he or she should be thirty years of age. By the act of 1705[39] this was increased to thirty-one. The law of Virginia had provided as early as 1662[40] that all children "born in this country shall be held bond or free only according to the condition of their mother." A mulatto, then, born of a free white or white servant mother, was not a slave, but after the time of service expired was a free man or woman. The act of 1753[41] continued these provisions for binding out such children, but up to this date no specific provision had been made for their education unless we consider the laws relating to poor children as applicable. The act of 1765[42] reduced the time of service, males to twenty-one and females to eighteen years of age, because the former age was "of unreasonable severity towards such children." Moreover, because mulattoes had been sold as slaves, a penalty of fifty pounds was imposed on the seller to be paid to the purchaser, and an additional penalty of twenty pounds to the informer. For a second offense the service of the servant was forfeited, and the latter was to be bound out to serve to twenty-one years of age "in the same manner as is by law directed for the binding out of orphan children." This would seem to indicate that provision for teaching such a boy or girl to read and write was contemplated. There were actual indentures, to be cited later, which so provided.

CONCLUSION

It is apparent that Virginia considered the education of these unfortunate classes—orphans, poor, illegitimate, and even mulatto children—to be a matter of importance, for no less than ten important laws[43] were passed involving these classes which mention specifically that the guardian or master is responsible for some book education. They provide for direct education by guardians or others for orphans with estates and for poor orphans

[36]*Ibid.,* VIII, 374–77.

[37]Hening, VIII, 377.

[38]*Ibid.,* III, 86–87. The same clause appears in substance in the code of 1769, p. 311, except that the word "Indians" is omitted.

[39]*Ibid.,* p. 457.

[40]*Ibid.,* II, 170. This was in force throughout the colonial period and is found in the code of 1769, p. 308.

[41]*Ibid.,* VI, 361.

[42]Hening., VIII, 133–34. This act is in the code of 1769, p. 450.

[43]This does not include the acts on workhouses, those of 1646, 1668, and 1755, nor several acts relating to orphans involving the security of their estates, part of the purpose of which was to safeguard their education.

and children through the system of apprenticeship; and those acts which do not directly mention education, or such subjects as reading or writing, do not prevent the inclusion of educational clauses in the indenture, as is proved by cases to be cited.[44] The attitude of Virginia toward education was evidently one which recognized that the state was responsible for the education of only those children whose parents were not likely to attend to the matter themselves. There is only one law which would allow the justices to interfere with other children than the poor, for the act of 1748 may be so interpreted. The assumption was that education was a private affair and that capable parents would voluntarily attend to the education of their own children. It will be noticed that during most of the seventeenth century Massachusetts and Connecticut made no such assumption.

It will be observed that the acts concerning orphans provide: first, for education through payment of tuition fees, in the case of those orphans whose estates produced interest on the principal sufficient for the purpose; secondly, for education through the system of apprenticeship, where orphans had a very small estate or none whatever. Although the first law mentioning book education for orphans apprenticed was that of 1705, yet the general acts of 1646 and 1672, giving power to justices of the peace to bind out poor children, would permit them to include a clause in an indenture providing for book education for an orphan bound out. A case of an apprenticed orphan with such a clause included in the indenture is recorded as early as 1648.[45] The fact that a session of the county court was called an "Orphans' Court" at this early date is evidence that the class was of some importance.

It will be noted that there is a progressive increase of orders respecting the administrative features of these laws. The purpose was to provide better methods of discovering whether an orphan was being educated to protect his estate for this purpose, to increase the degree of education, and to provide penalties for negligence. Thus guardians were to make annual reports, provide security, and see that orphans were instructed according to the proportion of their estates. Judges at first merely saw that orphans were provided for; then they were to make yearly inquiry; then they must apprentice the orphan if the estate was small, remove him from the master or guardian in case of neglect, and appoint new masters or guardians. Sheriffs also summoned guardians, and clerks of courts made public record of their accounts. Judges were obliged to see that an educational clause was inserted in the indenture, after 1705 for boys and after 1751 for girls, and could make additional rules for education in 1730. In 1679 they were chargeable for losses for their failure to take sufficient security from guardians, while in 1740 they were subject to a severe penalty for neglect of the laws respecting orphans.

A comparison of the legislation of Virginia with that of the New England colonies with respect to the compulsory education of poor children shows similarities as well as differences. The economic motives appear to be much the same; namely, the effort to avoid pauperism and idleness, and a desire to develop an artisan class. The religious and educational motives are also similar. The laws apply mainly to special, not to all, classes of children, as was the case in New England during most of the seventeenth century, and the purpose of book education is not so specifically stated. There is a failure to mention a specific money penalty, to be imposed on parents or masters or the churchwardens for negligence of the law. The classes of children involved, however, were poor and illegitimate children, and since the desire to relieve the parish of the burden of supporting such children was very strong, a money penalty was perhaps not needed in order to make it certain that they would be apprenticed. It will be remembered that not even Massachusetts imposed a money penalty on officers, except in one instance, after the laws on compulsory education were framed so as to apply only to poor children apprenticed—that is, after the act of 1703. The plan for workhouses for poor children contemplated state, county, and parish support by taxation, though the acts are not compulsory, and only that of 1755 mentioned education directly.

It is apparent that Virginia not only recognized her responsibility for the compulsory education of the classes of children mentioned, but passed a series of notable acts designed to accomplish the purpose. While they are not so elaborate as those of the New England colonies for the seventeenth century, they are in the eighteenth century quite up to the New England standard and in some respects above it. For example, the law required that after

[44]It may also be noted that there was some attention to the Indians. The act of March, 1655, declared that Indian children could be taken as servants, with the consent of their parents, "Provided that due respect and care be had that they the said Indian servants be educated and brought up in the Christian religion and that covenants for such service or services to be confirmed before two justices of the peace as aforesaid" (Hening, I, 410).

[45]*William and Mary College Quarterly*, V, 221.

1751 *all* orphan and poor girls apprenticed should be taught to read and also to write. No New England colony, after 1710, required *all* girls apprenticed to be taught to read and write. The acts cited show that we may fairly assert that Virginia established a compulsory system of education for these special classes of children. The laws are mandatory, indicate the machinery for enforcement, name the responsible officers, provide penalties for negligence of parents, guardians, and masters namely, removal of the child and, in the case of negligent justices, provided a money penalty, or its equivalent in tobacco. The central feature of the system was the county court, composed of the justices of the peace. It was entirely responsible for the workings of the laws respecting orphans. In the case of poor and illegitimate children the churchwardens were about equally responsible with the justices. There is thus the same tendency as in New England, that of making special officers of local units the responsible persons for carrying out the law. There is also the same tendency to increase the amount of education required for boys and girls apprenticed, and to place less emphasis on religious instruction in the eighteenth as compared with the seventeenth century. We shall see from the evidence in court and parish records that these acts were enforced, to some extent at least, but how effectually or universally it is difficult to say. But this observation can be made quite as truly of the legislation of the New England colonies. Later articles will discuss the enforcement of the compulsory education laws cited, in both the New England and the southern colonies.[46]

Date	Class of Children	Education Required
1642/3–1776	Orphans with estates	According to the proportion of their estates and circumstances.
1705–1776	Poor orphan boys and girls apprenticed because of little or no estate.	
	1705–1776, boys	To be taught to read and write
	1751–1776, girls	″ ″ ″ ″ ″ ″ ″
1727–1776	Poor boys and girls apprenticed; children of parents unable to support, or who neglected to instruct them in Christian principles;	
	1727–1776, boys	″ ″ ″ ″ ″ ″ ″
	1751–1776, girls	″ ″ ″ ″ ″ ″ ″
1751–1776	*Any child* apprenticed, because parents neglected his or her education or instruction in the principles of Christianity.	″ ″ ″ ″ ″ ″ ″
1765–1776	Mulatto boy or girl born of a free white or servant woman and apprenticed, because sold as a slave by a master, being his second offense.	″ ″ ″ ″ ″ ″ ″
1769–1776	Illegitimate child apprenticed, born of a single free white woman.	″ ″ ″ ″ ″ ″ ″

[46] A tabular view of the compulsory laws passed by Virginia involving booke ducation [*sic*] follows. This may be compared with the table given for New England in the School *Review, January,* 1919, p. 42.

The Kalamazoo Case

In 1875 a lawsuit was filed in Kalamazoo, Michigan, to collect public funds for the support of a village high school. The town had used taxes to support the school for thirteen years without complaints from the citizens. The defendants in the case, the school officials, felt that a select few out of thousands need not dispute their obligation to pay taxes for the purpose of supporting a high school.

The school officials supported their case with many previous court cases which upheld their position of financial support. They found that the state constitution, at this time, did not have provisions prohibiting the use of tax funds for a publicly supported high school.

The first precedent that was sited in the case was the Code of 1827. This outlined the curriculum as follows:

> 1. Every township in the Michigan territory that had families must have a schoolmaster "of good morals, to teach children to read and write, and to instruct them in the English or French language, as well as in arithmetic, orthography, and decent behavior . . . equivalent to six months for one school in each year."

> 2. All townships that had one hundred families must have a schoolmaster for twelve months for one school in a year with the above curriculum requirements.

> 3. Townships that had two hundred families or more were given a "grammar schoolmaster, of good morals, well instructed in Latin, French and English languages," as well as a schoolmaster to teach the curriculum requirements listed in the first paragraph.

The townships were required by the law to maintain the schools under threat of a large penalty for noncompliance. The Kalamazoo Case used this Code of 1827 establish the precedent of tax supported schools.

They furthered their stance using the papers from the Constitutional Convention of 1850. The people of the Convention declared the necessity for the establishment of a University. The only way to further education beyond grammar school, if high schools were no longer funded, was to travel to a private school. This would limit the educational opportunities to those boys that had money to pay for their education. The lawyers for the Kalamazoo Case defendants inferred that there must be a provision for the public funding of high schools for college prepatory education.

These cases with many smaller precedents were used to establish a basis for the public funding of the Kalamazoo High School and allowed for many townships to follow their historic leadership.

WORKS CITED

Transcripts from the Kalamazoo court case.

Reprinted with permission of Robert N. Barger.

Gary Schools in the Bronx

Superintendent Wirt's Plan Would Seat Thousands of Children at a Saving of Millions in Money.

To the Editor of The New York Times:

The unique feature of the plan now under consideration by the Board of Education for reorganizing a group of twelve schools in the Bronx along the lines worked out in Gary and successfully adapted to New York conditions is that millions of dollars in initial outlay and thousands in annual upkeep and operation can be saved only upon the condition that more playgrounds, shops, and other Jong-desired educational opportunities are afforded the children of the public schools. It removes these opportunities from the realm of things merely to be desired, which they have heretofore occupied, to the realm of things absolutely essential.

It has been customary for the Public Education Association and other civic bodies and citizens interested in the welfare of the public schools to appear annually before the Board of Estimate and Apportionment in support of the requests of the educational authorities for sufficient funds to provide such opportunities. But the enormous initial cost and the expense of subsequent upkeep has rendered them largely prohibitive. It is, therefore, most gratifying that Mr. Writ not merely makes it possible to secure them without additional outlay, but actually makes them the means of saving millions of dollars. Such a proposal, killing two birds with one stone, as it were, should therefore meet with the unqualified approval of educators and taxpayers alike.

The manner in which this is to be accomplished in the twelve Bronx schools is very simple. There are only 25,000 seats in these schools, while there are 36,000 children to occupy them, a situa-tion of extreme congestion, in which a shortage of 10,000 seats forces 20,000 children on part time. To cope with this situation the Board of Education is planning to spend $1,000,000 for two new buildings which will furnish about 4,000 additional seats. If these buildings were completed immediately there would still be 6,000 seats lacking, placing 12,000 children on part time. It would take two years, however, to complete them, by which time the registration would so exceed the additional accommodations that the situation would be even worse than now. The present building policy of the Board of Education in this connection would, therefore, seem to be hopeless.

By expending $750,000, on the other hand, or $250,000 less than the proposed expenditure of the Board of Education for the two new schools, Mr. Wirt would add playgrounds, shops, swimming pools, auditoriums, gymnasiums, libraries and other educational opportunities to the present facilities in the existing schools, which would enable him to put into operation his double school plan and accommodate 46,000 children without erecting a single new building. Several important economies would thereby be effected:

First: The city would be relieved of the necessity of erecting a number of new buildings, at an expenditure of approximately $4,500,000, to care for the additional 20,000 children, as would be required under the old plan of a reserved seat for every child. A seat would be provided immediately for the full period of academic instruction for each of the 36,000 children now on register, which would take care of the 10,000 now unprovided for and eliminate part time completely. "Room would also be provided for 10,000 more, enough to care for the increase in register for the next two years and afford leeway to make provision in advance for the natural growth in population after the maximum facilities of the new plan are exhausted.

Second: Not merely seats but swimming pools, shops, playgrounds, auditoriums and gymnasiums would be available in a short time for 46,000 children, facilities which would have to be provided under the old plan in addition to the reserved seats above referred to, at an additional cost of at least $2,000,000, making a total of at least $0,500,000 for the facilities provided by Mr. Wirt's $750,000. Even if it were possible to spend this enormous sum, however, it is doubtful whether comparable results would be secured because of the lack of flexibility under the old plan.

Third: Many thousands would also be saved annually for heat, light, janitorial service and supervision, since no additional buildings would be erected. Furthermore, it would not be necessary to increase the size of the

From *New York Times, June 17, 1915* by Howard W. Nudd.

teaching force for the additional activities, since only half the staff at present necessary would be needed for purely academic work and the other half would be replaced through transfers and new appointments by teachers skilled in vocational subjects, physical training and special branches. Under the old plan, all such teachers would have to be hired in addition to the present full staff of academic instructors, involving an increase of from 25 to 50 per cent in salaries. This saving in operating expenses and salaries would approximate $400,000 annually.

Briefly stated, then, for $750,000 Mr. Wirt would provide educational facilities which, under the old policy of the Board of Education, would cost at least $6,500,000 to introduce and at least 25 to 50 per cent more to operate!

In view of the fact that the Board of Education is contemplating an immediate expenditure of $1,000,000 to apparently little purpose, it would seem highly desirable that careful consideration be given to the foregoing proposition. When it is further realized that this remarkable economy in reorganizing a single district of only twelve schools can be duplicated in many others, such as the lower and upper east side, the need for such consideration would seem to be imperative. It would lift the entire city out of an intolerable situation in which thousands of its children are at present without even housing accommodations.

It has been pointed out that there are over 132,000 children receiving less than five hours' instruction in the public schools; that is, are on part time. Any plan which would alleviate this condition within the city's present financial ability, and at the same time greatly enrich the school life of every child in the system and enable teachers to teach in the fields they like best should receive the approval of all those who have the welfare of the schools at heart. The long-wished for flexibility in instruction and management would at last become a reality. It is very unlikely that opposition would be raised by the financial authorities to such an economical project. The only question seems to be whether the Board of Education is ready to take this forward step in educational administration.

HOWARD W. NUDD. Director, the Public Education Association.
New York June 16. 1015.

Brown v. Board of Education

ABOUT THE CASE

The 1954 United States Supreme Court decision in *Oliver L. Brown et al. v. the Board of Education of Topeka (KS) et al.* is among the most significant judicial turning points in the development of our country. Originally led by Charles H. Houston, and later Thurgood Marshall and a formidable legal team, it dismantled the legal basis for racial segregation in schools and other public facilities.

By declaring that the discriminatory nature of racial segregation . . . "violates the 14th amendment to the U.S. Constitution, which guarantees all citizens equal protection of the laws," *Brown v. Board of Education* laid the foundation for shaping future national and international policies regarding human rights.

Brown v. Board of Education was not simply about children and education. The laws and policies struck down by this court decision were products of the human tendencies to prejudge, discriminate against, and stereotype other people by their ethnic, religious, physical, or cultural characteristics. Ending this behavior as a legal practice caused far reaching social and ideological implications, which continue to be felt throughout our country. The *Brown* decision inspired and galvanized human rights struggles across the country and around the world.

What this legal challenge represents is at the core of United States history and the freedoms we enjoy. The U.S. Supreme Court decision in *Brown* began a critical chapter in the maturation of our democracy. It reaffirmed the sovereign power of the people of the United States in the protection of their natural rights from arbitrary limits and restrictions imposed by state and local governments. These rights are recognized in the Declaration of Independence and guaranteed by the U.S. Constitution.

While this case was an important historic milestone, it is often misunderstood. Over the years, the facts pertaining to the *Brown* case have been overshadowed by myths and mischaracterizations:

- *Brown v. Board of Education* was not the first challenge to school segregation. As early as 1849, African Americans filed suit against an educational system that mandated racial segregation, in the case of Roberts v. City of Boston.

- Oliver Brown, the case namesake, was just one of the nearly 200 plaintiffs from five states who were part of the NAACP cases brought before the Supreme Court in 1951. The Kansas case was named for Oliver Brown as a legal strategy to have a man head the plaintiff roster.

The *Brown* decision initiated educational and social reform throughout the United States and was a catalyst in launching the modern Civil Rights Movement. Bringing about change in the years since the *Brown* case continues to be difficult. But the *Brown v. Board of Education* victory brought this country one step closer to living up to its democratic ideas.

This document tells the story of *Brown v. Board of Education* and the history makers involved in the case.

THE CASE

The Supreme Court combined five cases under the heading of *Brown v. Board of Education*, because each sought the same legal remedy. The combined cases emanated from Delaware, Kansas, South Carolina, Virginia and Washington, DC. The following describes those cases:

Delaware – Belton v. Gebhart (Bulah v. Gebhart)

First petitioned in 1951, these local cases challenged the inferior conditions of two black schools designated for African American children. In the suburb of Claymont, African American children were prohibited from attending the area's local high school. Instead, they had to ride a school bus for nearly an hour to attend

Howard High School in Wilmington. Located in an industrial area of the state's capital city, Howard High School also suffered from a deficient curriculum, pupil-teacher ratio, teacher training, extra curricular activities program, and physical plant. In the rural community of Hockessin, African American students were forced to attend a dilapidated one-room school house and were not provided transportation to the school, while white children in the area were provided transportation and a better school facility. In both cases, Louis Redding, a local NAACP attorney, represented the plaintiffs, African American parents. Although the State Supreme Court ruled in favor of the plaintiffs, the decision did not apply to all schools in Delaware. These class action cases were named for Ethel Belton and Shirley Bulah.

Kansas – Brown v. Board of Education

In 1950 the Topeka NAACP, led by McKinley Burnett, set out to organize a legal challenge to an 1879 State law that permitted racially segregated elementary schools in certain cities based on population. For Kansas this would become the 12th case filed in the state focused on ending segregation in public schools. The local NAACP assembled a group of 13 parents who agreed to be plaintiffs on behalf of their 20 children. Following direction from legal counsel they attempted to enroll their children in segregated white schools and all were denied. Topeka operated eighteen neighborhood schools for white children, while African American children had access to only four schools. In February of 1951 the Topeka NAACP filed a case on their behalf. Although this was a class action it was named for one of the plaintiffs Oliver Brown.

South Carolina – Briggs v. Elliot

In Claredon County, the State NAACP first attempted, unsuccessfully and with a single plaintiff, to take legal action in 1947 against the inferior conditions African American students experienced under South Carolina's racially segregated school system. By 1951, community activist Rev. J.A. DeLaine, convinced African American parents to join the NAACP efforts to file a class action suit in U.S. District Court. The Court found that the schools designated for African Americans were grossly inadequate in terms of buildings, transportation and teacher's salaries when compared to the schools provided for whites. An order to equalize the facilities was virtually ignored by school officials and the schools were never made equal. This class action case was named for Harry Briggs, Sr.

Virginia – Davis v. County School Board of Prince Edward County

One of the few public high schools available to African Americans in the state was Robert Moton High School in Prince Edward County. Built in 1943, it was never large enough to accommodate its student population. Eventually hastily constructed tar paper covered buildings were added as classrooms. The gross inadequacies of these classrooms sparked a student strike in 1951. Organized by sixteen year old Barbara Johns, the students initially sought to acquire a new building with indoor plumbing. The NAACP soon joined their struggles and challenged the inferior quality of their school facilities in court. Although the U.S. District Court ordered that the plaintiffs be provided with equal school facilities, they were denied access to the white schools in their area. This class action case was named for Dorothy Davis.

Washington, DC – Bolling v. C. Melvin Sharpe

Eleven African American junior High School students were taken on a field trip to the cities [*sic*] new modern John Phillip Sousa school for whites only. Accompanied by local activist Gardner Bishop, who requested admittance for the students and was denied, the African American students were ordered to return to their grossly inadequate school. A suit was filed on their behalf in 1951. After review with the *Brown* case in 1954, the Supreme Court ruled "segregation in the District of Columbia public schools . . . is a denial of the due process of law guaranteed by the Fifth Amendment . . ." This class action case was named for Spottswood Bolling.

SUPREME COURT OF THE UNITED STATES

Brown v. Board of Education,
347 U.S. 483 (1954) (USSC+)

SYLLABUS

Segregation of white and Negro children in the public schools of a State solely on the basis of race, pursuant to state laws permitting or requiring such segregation, denies to Negro children the equal protection of the laws guaranteed by the Fourteenth Amendment—even though the physical facilities and other "tangible" factors of white and Negro schools may be equal.

    a. The history of the Fourteenth Amendment is inconclusive as to its intended effect on public education.

    b. The question presented in these cases must be determined not on the basis of conditions existing when the Fourteenth Amendment was adopted, but in the light of the full development of public education and its present place in American life throughout the Nation.

    c. Where a State has undertaken to provide an opportunity for an education in its public schools, such an opportunity is a right which must be made available to all on equal terms.

    d. Segregation of children in public schools solely on the basis of race deprives children of the minority group of equal educational opportunities, even though the physical facilities and other "tangible" factors may be equal.

    e. The "separate but equal" doctrine adopted in **Plessy v. Ferguson, 163 U.S. 537**, has no place in the field of public education.

    f. The cases are restored to the docket for further argument on specified questions relating to the forms of the decrees.

OPINION WARREN

MR. CHIEF JUSTICE WARREN delivered the opinion of the Court.

These cases come to us from the States of Kansas, South Carolina, Virginia, and Delaware. They are premised on different facts and different local conditions, but a common legal question justifies their consideration together in this consolidated opinion.

In each of the cases, minors of the Negro race, through their legal representatives, seek the aid of the courts in obtaining admission to the public schools of their community on a nonsegregated basis. In each instance, they had been denied admission to schools attended by white children under laws requiring or permitting segregation according to race. This segregation was alleged to deprive the plaintiffs of the equal protection of the laws under the Fourteenth Amendment. In each of the cases other than the Delaware case, a three-judge federal district court denied relief to the plaintiffs on the so-called "separate but equal" doctrine announced by this Court in **Plessy v. Fergson, 163 U.S. 537**. Under that doctrine, equality of treatment is accorded when the races are provided substantially equal facilities, even though these facilities be separate. In the Delaware case, the Supreme Court of Delaware adhered to that doctrine, but ordered that the plaintiffs be admitted to the white schools because of their superiority to the Negro schools.

The plaintiffs contend that segregated public schools are not "equal" and cannot be made "equal," and that hence they are deprived of the equal protection of the laws. Because of the obvious importance of the question presented, the Court took jurisdiction. Argument was heard in the 1952 Term, and reargument was heard this Term on certain questions propounded by the Court.

Reargument was largely devoted to the circumstances surrounding the adoption of the Fourteenth Amendment in 1868. It covered exhaustively consideration of the Amendment in Congress, ratification by the states, then-existing practices in racial segregation, and the views of proponents and opponents of the Amendment. This discussion and our own investigation convince us that, although these sources cast some light, it is not enough to resolve the problem with which we are faced. At best, they are inconclusive. The most avid proponents of the post-War Amendments undoubtedly intended them to remove all legal distinctions among "all persons born or naturalized in the United States." Their opponents, just as certainly, were antagonistic to both the letter and the spirit of the Amendments and wished them to have the most limited effect. What others in Congress and the state legislatures had in mind cannot be determined with any degree of certainty.

An additional reason for the inconclusive nature of the Amendment's history with respect to segregated schools is the status of public education at that time. In the South, the movement toward free common schools, supported by general taxation, had not yet taken hold. Education of white children was largely in the hands of private groups. Education of Negroes was almost nonexistent, and practically all of the race were illiterate. In fact, any education of Negroes was forbidden by law in some states. Today, in contrast, many Negroes have achieved outstanding success in the arts and sciences, as well as in the business and professional world. It is true that public school education at the time of the Amendment had advanced further in the North, but the effect of the Amendment on Northern States was generally ignored in the congressional debates. Even in the North, the conditions of public education did not approximate those existing today. The curriculum was usually rudimentary; ungraded schools were common in rural areas; the school term was but three months a year in many states, and compulsory school attendance was virtually unknown. As a consequence, it is not surprising that there should be so little in the history of the Fourteenth Amendment relating to its intended effect on public education.

In the first cases in this Court construing the Fourteenth Amendment, decided shortly after its adoption, the Court interpreted it as proscribing all state-imposed discriminations against the Negro race. The doctrine of "separate but equal" did not make its appearance in this Court until 1896 in the case of **Plessy v. Ferguson**, supra, involving not education but transportation. American courts have since labored with the doctrine for over half a century. In this Court, there have been six cases involving the "separate but equal" doctrine in the field of public education. In **Cumming v. County Board of Education, 175 U.S. 528**, and **Gong Lum v. Rice, 275 U.S. 78**, the validity of the doctrine itself was not challenged. In more recent cases, all on the graduate school level, inequality was found in that specific benefits enjoyed by white students were denied to Negro students of the same educational qualifications. **Missouri ex rel. Gaines v. Canada, 305 U.S. 337; Sipuel v. Oklahoma, 332 U.S. 631; Sweatt v. Painter, 339 U.S. 629; McLaurin v. Oklahoma State Regents, 339 U.S. 637.** In none of these cases was it necessary to reexamine the doctrine to grant relief to the Negro plaintiff. And in **Sweatt v. Painter**, supra, the Court expressly reserved decision on the question whether **Plessy v. Ferguson** should be held inapplicable to public education.

In the instant cases, that question is directly presented. Here, unlike **Sweatt v. Painter**, there are findings below that the Negro and white schools involved have been equalized, or are being equalized, with respect to buildings, curricula, qualifications and salaries of teachers, and other "tangible" factors. Our decision, therefore, cannot turn on merely a comparison of these tangible factors in the Negro and white schools involved in each of the cases. We must look instead to the effect of segregation itself on public education.

In approaching this problem, we cannot turn the clock back to 1868, when the Amendment was adopted, or even to 1896, when **Plessy v. Ferguson** was written. We must consider public education in the light of its full development and its present place in American life throughout the Nation. Only in this way can it be determined if segregation in public schools deprives these plaintiffs of the equal protection of the laws.

Today, education is perhaps the most important function of state and local governments. Compulsory school attendance laws and the great expenditures for education both demonstrate our recognition of the importance of education to our democratic society. It is required in the performance of our most basic public responsibilities, even service in the armed forces. It is the very foundation of good citizenship. Today it is a principal instrument in awakening the child to cultural values, in preparing him for later professional training, and in helping him to adjust normally to his environment. In these days, it is doubtful that any child may reasonably be expected to succeed in life if he is denied the opportunity of an education. Such an opportunity, where the state has undertaken to provide it, is a right which must be made available to all on equal terms.

We come then to the question presented: Does segregation of children in public schools solely on the basis of race, even though the physical facilities and other "tangible" factors may be equal, deprive the children of the minority group of equal educational opportunities? We believe that it does.

In **Sweatt v. Painter**, supra, in finding that a segregated law school for Negroes could not provide them equal educational opportunities, this Court relied in large part on "those qualities which are incapable of objective measurement but which make for greatness in a law school." In **McLaurin v. Oklahoma State Regents**, supra, the Court, in requiring that a Negro admitted to a white graduate school be treated like all other students, again resorted to intangible considerations: ". . . his ability to study, to engage in discussions and exchange views with other students, and, in general, to learn his profession." Such considerations apply with added force to children in grade and high schools. To separate them from others of similar age and qualifications solely because of their race generates a feeling of inferiority as to their status in the community that may affect their hearts and minds in a way unlikely ever to be undone. The effect of this separation on their educational opportunities was well stated by a finding in the Kansas case by a court which nevertheless felt compelled to rule against the Negro plaintiffs:

Segregation of white and colored children in public schools has a detrimental effect upon the colored children. The impact is greater when it has the sanction of the law, for the policy of separating the races is usually interpreted as denoting the inferiority of the negro group. A sense of inferiority affects the motivation of a child to learn. Segregation with the sanction of law, therefore, has a tendency to [retard] the educational and mental development of negro children and to deprive them of some of the benefits they would receive in a racial[ly] integrated school system.

Whatever may have been the extent of psychological knowledge at the time of **Plessy v. Ferguson**, this finding is amply supported by modern authority. Any language in **Plessy v. Ferguson** contrary to this finding is rejected.

We conclude that, in the field of public education, the doctrine of "separate but equal" has no place. Separate educational facilities are inherently unequal. Therefore, we hold that the plaintiffs and others similarly situated for whom the actions have been brought are, by reason of the segregation complained of, deprived of the equal protection of the laws guaranteed by the Fourteenth Amendment. This disposition makes unnecessary any discussion whether such segregation also violates the Due Process Clause of the Fourteenth Amendment.

Because these are class actions, because of the wide applicability of this decision, and because of the great variety of local conditions, the formulation of decrees in these cases presents problems of considerable complexity. On reargument, the consideration of appropriate relief was necessarily subordinated to the primary question—the constitutionality of segregation in public education. We have now announced that such segregation is a denial of the equal protection of the laws. In order that we may have the full assistance of the parties in formulating decrees, the cases will be restored to the docket, and the parties are requested to present further argument on Questions 4 and 5 previously propounded by the Court for the reargument this Term The Attorney General of the United States is again invited to participate. The Attorneys General of the states requiring or permitting segregation in public education will also be permitted to appear as amici curiae upon request to do so by September 15, 1954, and submission of briefs by October 1, 1954.

It is so ordered.

- Together with **No. 2, Briggs et al. v. Elliott et al.**, on appeal from the United States District Court for the Eastern District of South Carolina, argued December 9–10, 1952, reargued December 7–8, 1953; **No. 4, Davis et al. v. County School Board of Prince Edward County, Virginia, et al.** , on appeal from the United States District Court for the Eastern District of Virginia, argued December 10, 1952, reargued December 7–8, 1953, and **No. 10, Gebhart et al. v. Belton et al.**, on certiorari to the Supreme Court of Delaware, argued December 11, 1952, reargued December 9, 1953.

Annual Message to the Congress on the State of the Union January 8, 1964

—President Lyndon B. Johnson's

[As delivered in person before a joint session]

Mr. Speaker, Mr. President, Members of the House and Senate, my fellow Americans:

I will be brief, for our time is necessarily short and our agenda is already long.

Last year's congressional session was the longest in peacetime history. With that foundation, let us work together to make this year's session the best in the Nation's history.

Let this session of Congress be known as the session which did more for civil rights than the last hundred sessions combined; as the session which enacted the most far-reaching tax cut of our time; as the session which declared all-out war on human poverty and unemployment in these United States; as the session which finally recognized the health needs of all our older citizens; as the session which reformed our tangled transportation and transit policies; as the session which achieved the most effective, efficient foreign aid program ever; and as the session which helped to build more homes, more schools, more libraries, and more hospitals than any single session of Congress in the history of our Republic.

All this and more can and must be done. It can be done by this summer, and it can be done without any increase in spending. In fact, under the budget that I shall shortly submit, it can be done with an actual reduction in Federal expenditures and Federal employment.

We have in 1964 a unique opportunity and obligation—to prove the success of our system; to disprove those cynics and critics at home and abroad who question our purpose and our competence.

If we fail, if we fritter and fumble away our opportunity in needless, senseless quarrels between Democrats and Republicans, or between the House and the Senate, or between the South and North, or between the Congress and the administration, then history will rightfully judge us harshly. But if we succeed, if we can achieve these goals by forging in this country a greater sense of union, then, and only then, can we take full satisfaction in the State of the Union.

II.

Here in the Congress you can demonstrate effective legislative leadership by discharging the public business with clarity and dispatch, voting each important proposal up, or voting it down, but at least bringing it to a fair and a final vote.

Let us carry forward the plans and programs of John Fitzgerald Kennedy-not because of our sorrow or sympathy, but because they are right.

In his memory today, I especially ask all members of my own political faith, in this election year, to put your country ahead of your party, and to always debate principles; never debate personalities.

For my part, I pledge a progressive administration which is efficient, and honest and frugal. The budget to be submitted to the Congress shortly is in full accord with this pledge.

It will cut our deficit in half—from $10 billion to $4,900 million. It will be, in proportion to our national output, the smallest budget since 1951.

It will call for a substantial reduction in Federal employment, a feat accomplished only once before in the last 10 years. While maintaining the full strength of our combat defenses, it will call for the lowest number of civilian personnel in the Department of Defense since 1950.

It will call for total expenditures of $97,900 million-compared to $98,400 million for the current year, a reduction of more than $500 million. It will call for new obligational authority of $103,800 million-a reduction of more than $4 billion below last year's request of $107,900 million.

But it is not a standstill budget, for America cannot afford to stand still. Our population is growing. Our economy is more complex. Our people's needs are expanding.

But by closing down obsolete installations, by curtailing less urgent programs, by cutting back where cutting back seems to be wise, by insisting on a dollar's worth for a dollar spent, I am able to recommend in this reduced budget the most Federal support in history for education, for health, for retraining the unemployed, and for helping the economically and the physically handicapped.

This budget, and this year's legislative program, are designed to help each and every American citizen fulfill his basic hopes—his hopes for a fair chance to make good; his hopes for fair play from the law; his hopes for a full-time job on full-time pay; his hopes for a decent home for his family in a decent community; his hopes for a good school for his children with good teachers; and his hopes for security when faced with sickness or unemployment or old age.

III.

Unfortunately, many Americans live on the outskirts of hope—some because of their poverty, and some because of their color, and all too many because of both. Our task is to help replace their despair with opportunity.

This administration today, here and now, declares unconditional war on poverty in America. I urge this Congress and all Americans to join with me in that effort.

It will not be a short or easy struggle, no single weapon or strategy will suffice, but we shall not rest until that war is won. The richest Nation on earth can afford to win it. We cannot afford to lose it. One thousand dollars invested in salvaging an unemployable youth today can return $40,000 or more in his lifetime.

Poverty is a national problem, requiring improved national organization and support. But this attack, to be effective, must also be organized at the State and the local level and must be supported and directed by State and local efforts.

For the war against poverty will not be won here in Washington. It must be won in the field, in every private home, in every public office, from the courthouse to the White House.

The program I shall propose will emphasize this cooperative approach to help that one-fifth of all American families with incomes too small to even meet their basic needs.

Our chief weapons in a more pinpointed attack will be better schools, and better health, and better homes, and better training, and better job opportunities to help more Americans, especially young Americans, escape from squalor and misery and unemployment rolls where other citizens help to carry them.

Very often a lack of jobs and money is not the cause of poverty, but the symptom. The cause may lie deeper in our failure to give our fellow citizens a fair chance to develop their own capacities, in a lack of education and training, in a lack of medical care and housing, in a lack of decent communities in which to live and bring up their children.

But whatever the cause, our joint Federal-local effort must pursue poverty, pursue it wherever it exists—in city slums and small towns, in sharecropper shacks or in migrant worker camps, on Indian Reservations, among whites as well as Negroes, among the young as well as the aged, in the boom towns and in the depressed areas.

Our aim is not only to relieve the symptom of poverty, but to cure it and, above all, to prevent it. No single piece of legislation, however, is going to suffice.

We will launch a special effort in the chronically distressed areas of Appalachia.

We must expand our small but our successful area redevelopment program.

We must enact youth employment legislation to put jobless, aimless, hopeless youngsters to work on useful projects.

We must distribute more food to the needy through a broader food stamp program.

We must create a National Service Corps to help the economically handicapped of our own country as the Peace Corps now helps those abroad.

We must modernize our unemployment insurance and establish a high-level commission on automation. If we have the brain power to invent these machines, we have the brain power to make certain that they are a boon and not a bane to humanity.

We must extend the coverage of our minimum wage laws to more than 2 million workers now lacking this basic protection of purchasing power.

We must, by including special school aid funds as part of our education program, improve the quality of teaching, training, and counseling in our hardest hit areas.

We must build more libraries in every area and more hospitals and nursing homes under the Hill-Burton Act, and train more nurses to staff them.

We must provide hospital insurance for our older citizens financed by every worker and his employer under Social Security, contributing no more than $1 a month during the employee's working career to protect him in his old age in a dignified manner without cost to the Treasury, against the devastating hardship of prolonged or repeated illness.

We must, as a part of a revised housing and urban renewal program, give more help to those displaced by slum clearance, provide more housing for our poor and our elderly, and seek as our ultimate goal in our free enterprise system a decent home for every American family.

We must help obtain more modern mass transit within our communities as well as low-cost transportation between them.

Above all, we must release $11 billion of tax reduction into the private spending stream to create new jobs and new markets in every area of this land.

IV.

These programs are obviously not for the poor or the underprivileged alone. Every American will benefit by the extension of social security to cover the hospital costs of their aged parents. Every American community will benefit from the construction or modernization of schools, libraries, hospitals, and nursing homes, from the training of more nurses and from the improvement of urban renewal in public transit. And every individual American taxpayer and every corporate taxpayer will benefit from the earliest possible passage of the pending tax bill from both the new investment it will bring and the new jobs that it will create.

That tax bill has been thoroughly discussed for a year. Now we need action. The new budget clearly allows it. Our taxpayers surely deserve it. Our economy strongly demands it. And every month of delay dilutes its benefits in 1964 for consumption, for investment, and for employment.

For until the bill is signed, its investment incentives cannot be deemed certain, and the withholding rate cannot be reduced-and the most damaging and devastating thing you can do to any businessman in America is to keep him in doubt and to keep him guessing on what our tax policy is. And I say that we should now reduce to 14 percent instead of 15 percent our withholding rate.

I therefore urge the Congress to take final action on this bill by the first of February, if at all possible. For however proud we may be of the unprecedented progress of our free enterprise economy over the last 3 years, we should not and we cannot permit it to pause.

In 1963, for the first time in history, we crossed the 70 million job mark, but we will soon need more than 75 million jobs. In 1963 our gross national product reached the $600 billion level-$100 billion higher than when we took office. But it easily could and it should be still $30 billion higher today than it is.

Wages and profits and family income are also at their highest levels in history-but I would remind you that 4 million workers and 13 percent of our industrial capacity are still idle today.

We need a tax cut now to keep this country moving.

V.

For our goal is not merely to spread the work. Our goal is to create more jobs. I believe the enactment of a 35-hour week would sharply increase costs, would invite inflation, would impair our ability to compete, and merely share instead of creating employment. But I am equally opposed to the 45- or 50-hour week in those industries where consistently excessive use of overtime causes increased unemployment.

So, therefore, I recommend legislation authorizing the creation of a tripartite industry committee to determine on an industry-by-industry basis as to where a higher penalty rate for overtime would increase job openings without unduly increasing costs, and authorizing the establishment of such higher rates.

VI.

Let me make one principle of this administration abundantly clear: All of these increased opportunities—in employment, in education, in housing, and in every field—must be open to Americans of every color. As far as the writ of Federal law will run, we must abolish not some, but all racial discrimination. For this is not merely an economic issue, or a social, political, or international issue. It is a moral issue, and it must be met by the passage this session of the bill now pending in the House.

All members of the public should have equal access to facilities open to the public. All members of the public should be equally eligible for Federal benefits that are financed by the public. All members of the public should have an equal chance to vote for public officials and to send their children to good public schools and to contribute their talents to the public good.

Today, Americans of all races stand side by side in Berlin and in Viet Nam. They died side by side in Korea. Surely they can work and eat and travel side by side in their own country.

VII.

We must also lift by legislation the bars of discrimination against those who seek entry into our country, particularly those who have much needed skills and those joining their families.

In establishing preferences, a nation that was built by the immigrants of all lands can ask those who now seek admission: "What can you do for our country?" But we should not be asking: "In what country were you born?"

VIII.

For our ultimate goal is a world without war, a world made safe for diversity, in which all men, goods, and ideas can freely move across every border and every boundary.

We must advance toward this goal in 1964 in at least 10 different ways, not as partisans, but as patriots.

First, wc must maintain—and our reduced defense budget will maintain-that margin of military safety and superiority obtained through 3 years of steadily increasing both the quality and the quantity of our strategic, our conventional, and our antiguerilla forces. In 1964 we will be better prepared than ever before to defend the cause of freedom, whether it is threatened by outright aggression or by the infiltration practiced by those in

Hanoi and Havana, who ship arms and men across international borders to foment insurrection. And we must continue to use that strength as John Kennedy used it in the Cuban crisis and for the test ban treaty—to demonstrate both the futility of nuclear war and the possibilities of lasting peace.

Second, we must take new steps-and we shall make new proposals at Geneva—toward the control and the eventual abolition of arms. Even in the absence of agreement, we must not stockpile arms beyond our needs or seek an excess of military power that could be provocative as well as wasteful.

It is in this spirit that in this fiscal year we are cutting back our production of enriched uranium by 25 percent. We are shutting down four plutonium piles. We are closing many nonessential military installations. And it is in this spirit that we today call on our adversaries to do the same.

Third, we must make increased use of our food as an instrument of peace—making it available by sale or trade or loan or donation-to hungry people in all nations which tell us of their needs and accept proper conditions of distribution.

Fourth, we must assure our pre-eminence in the peaceful exploration of outer space, focusing on an expedition to the moon in this decade—in cooperation with other powers if possible, alone if necessary.

Fifth, we must expand world trade. Having recognized in the Act of 1962 that we must buy as well as sell, we now expect our trading partners to recognize that we must sell as well as buy. We are willing to give them competitive access to our market, asking only that they do the same for us.

Sixth, we must continue, through such measures as the interest equalization tax, as well as the cooperation of other nations, our recent progress toward balancing our international accounts.

This administration must and will preserve the present gold value of the dollar.

Seventh, we must become better neighbors with the free states of the Americas, working with the councils of the OAS, with a stronger Alliance for Progress, and with all the men and women of this hemisphere who really believe in liberty and justice for all.

Eighth, we must strengthen the ability of free nations everywhere to develop their independence and raise their standard of living, and thereby frustrate those who prey on poverty and chaos. To do this, the rich must help the poor—and we must do our part. We must achieve a more rigorous administration of our development assistance, with larger roles for private investors, for other industrialized nations, and for international agencies and for the recipient nations themselves.

Ninth, we must strengthen our Atlantic and Pacific partnerships, maintain our alliances and make the United Nations a more effective instrument for national independence and international order.

Tenth, and finally, we must develop with our allies new means of bridging the gap between the East and the West, facing danger boldly wherever danger exists, but being equally bold in our search for new agreements which can enlarge the hopes of all, while violating the interests of none.

In short, I would say to the Congress that we must be constantly prepared for the worst, and constantly acting for the best. We must be strong enough to win any war, and we must be wise enough to prevent one.

We shall neither act as aggressors nor tolerate acts of aggression. We intend to bury no one, and we do not intend to be buried.

We can fight, if we must, as we have fought before, but we pray that we will never have to fight again.

IX.

My good friends and my fellow Americans: In these last 7 sorrowful weeks, we have learned anew that nothing is so enduring as faith, and nothing is so degrading as hate.

John Kennedy was a victim of hate, but he was also a great builder of faith-faith in our fellow Americans, whatever their creed or their color or their station in life; faith in the future of man, whatever his divisions and differences.

This faith was echoed in all parts of the world. On every continent and in every land to which Mrs. Johnson and I traveled, we found faith and hope and love toward this land of America and toward our people.

So I ask you now in the Congress and in the country to join with me in expressing and fulfilling that faith in working for a nation, a nation that is free from want and a world that is free from hate—a world of peace and justice, and freedom and abundance, for our time and for all time to come.

Source: *Public Papers of the Presidents of the United States: Lyndon B. Johnson, 1963–64. Volume I, entry 91, pp. 112–118. Washington, D. C.:*

http://www.lbjlib.utexas.edu/johnson/archives.hom/speeches.hom/640108.asp

A Nation At Risk

All, regardless of race or class or economic status, are entitled to a fair chance and to the tools for developing their individual powers of mind and spirit to the utmost. This promise means that all children by virtue of their own efforts, competently guided, can hope to attain the mature and informed judgement needed to secure gainful employment, and to manage their own lives, thereby serving not only their own interests but also the progress of society itself.

Our Nation is at risk. Our once unchallenged preeminence in commerce, industry, science, and technological innovation is being overtaken by competitors throughout the world. This report is concerned with only one of the many causes and dimensions of the problem, but it is the one that undergirds American prosperity, security, and civility. We report to the American people that while we can take justifiable pride in what our schools and colleges have historically accomplished and contributed to the United States and the well-being of its people, the educational foundations of our society are presently being eroded by a rising tide of mediocrity that threatens our very future as a Nation and a people. What was unimaginable a generation ago has begun to occur—others are matching and surpassing our educational attainments.

If an unfriendly foreign power had attempted to impose on America the mediocre educational performance that exists today, we might well have viewed it as an act of war. As it stands, we have allowed this to happen to ourselves. We have even squandered the gains in student achievement made in the wake of the Sputnik challenge. Moreover, we have dismantled essential support systems which helped make those gains possible. We have, in effect, been committing an act of unthinking, unilateral educational disarmament.

Our society and its educational institutions seem to have lost sight of the basic purposes of schooling, and of the high expectations and disciplined effort needed to attain them. This report, the result of 18 months of study, seeks to generate reform of our educational system in fundamental ways and to renew the Nation's commitment to schools and colleges of high quality throughout the length and breadth of our land.

That we have compromised this commitment is, upon reflection, hardly surprising, given the multitude of often conflicting demands we have placed on our Nation's schools and colleges. They are routinely called on to provide solutions to personal, social, and political problems that the home and other institutions either will not or cannot resolve. We must understand that these demands on our schools and colleges often exact an educational cost as well as a financial one.

On the occasion of the Commission's first meeting, President Reagan noted the central importance of education in American life when he said: "Certainly there are few areas of American life as important to our society, to our people, and to our families as our schools and colleges." This report, therefore, is as much an open letter to the American people as it is a report to the Secretary of Education. We are confident that the American people, properly informed, will do what is right for their children and for the generations to come.

THE RISK

History is not kind to idlers. The time is long past when American's destiny was assured simply by an abundance of natural resources and inexhaustible human enthusiasm, and by our relative isolation from the malignant problems of older civilizations. The world is indeed one global village. We live among determined, well-educated, and strongly motivated competitors. We compete with them for international standing and markets, not only with products but also with the ideas of our laboratories and neighborhood workshops. America's position in the world may once have been reasonably secure with only a few exceptionally well-trained men and women. It is no longer.

The risk is not only that the Japanese make automobiles more efficiently than Americans and have government subsidies for development and export. It is not just that the South Koreans recently built the world's most efficient steel mill, or that American machine tools, once the pride of the world, are being displaced by German products. It is also that these developments signify a redistribution of trained capability throughout the globe.

"A Nation At Risk: The Imperative For Educational Reform," April 1983, US Dept. of Education.

Knowledge, learning, information, and skilled intelligence are the new raw materials of international commerce and are today spreading throughout the world as vigorously as miracle drugs, synthetic fertilizers, and blue jeans did earlier. If only to keep and improve on the slim competitive edge we still retain in world markets, we must dedicate ourselves to the reform of our educational system for the benefit of all—old and young alike, affluent and poor, majority and minority. Learning is the indispensable investment required for success in the "information age" we are entering.

Our concern, however, goes well beyond matters such as industry and commerce. It also includes the intellectual, moral, and spiritual strengths of our people which knit together the very fabric of our society. The people of the United States need to know that individuals in our society who do not possess the levels of skill, literacy, and training essential to this new era will be effectively disenfranchised, not simply from the material rewards that accompany competent performance, but also from the chance to participate fully in our national life. A high level of shared education is essential to a free, democratic society and to the fostering of a common culture, especially in a country that prides itself on pluralism and individual freedom.

For our country to function, citizens must be able to reach some common understandings on complex issues, often on short notice and on the basis of conflicting or incomplete evidence. Education helps form these common understandings, a point Thomas Jefferson made long ago in his justly famous dictum:

I know no safe depository of the ultimate powers of the society but the people themselves; and if we think them not enlightened enough to exercise their control with a wholesome discretion, the remedy is not to take it from them but to inform their discretion.

Part of what is at risk is the promise first made on this continent: All, regardless of race or class or economic status, are entitled to a fair chance and to the tools for developing their individual powers of mind and spirit to the utmost. This promise means that all children by virtue of their own efforts, competently guided, can hope to attain the mature and informed judgment needed to secure gainful employment, and to manage their own lives, thereby serving not only their own interests but also the progress of society itself.

INDICATORS OF THE RISK

The educational dimensions of the risk before us have been amply documented in testimony received by the Commission. For example:

- International comparisons of student achievement, completed a decade ago, reveal that on 19 academic tests American students were never first or second and, in comparison with other industrialized nations, were last seven times.

- Some 23 million American adults are functionally illiterate by the simplest tests of everyday reading, writing, and comprehension.

- About 13 percent of all 17-year-olds in the United States can be considered functionally illiterate. Functional illiteracy among minority youth may run as high as 40 percent.

- Average achievement of high school students on most standardized tests is now lower than 26 years ago when Sputnik was launched.

- Over half the population of gifted students do not match their tested ability with comparable achievement in school.

- The College Board's Scholastic Aptitude Tests (SAT) demonstrate a virtually unbroken decline from 1963 to 1980. Average verbal scores fell over 50 points and average mathematics scores dropped nearly 40 points.

- College Board achievement tests also reveal consistent declines in recent years in such subjects as physics and English.

- Both the number and proportion of students demonstrating superior achievement on the SATs (i.e., those with scores of 650 or higher) have also dramatically declined.

- Many 17-year-olds do not possess the "higher order" intellectual skills we should expect of them. Nearly 40 percent cannot draw inferences from written material; only one-fifth can write a persuasive essay; and only one-third can solve a mathematics problem requiring several steps.

- There was a steady decline in science achievement scores of U.S. 17-year-olds as measured by national assessments of science in 1969, 1973, and 1977.

- Between 1975 and 1980, remedial mathematics courses in public 4-year colleges increased by 72 percent and now constitute one-quarter of all mathematics courses taught in those institutions.

- Average tested achievement of students graduating from college is also lower.

- Business and military leaders complain that they are required to spend millions of dollars on costly remedial education and training programs in such basic skills as reading, writing, spelling, and computation. The Department of the Navy, for example, reported to the Commission that one-quarter of its recent recruits cannot read at the ninth grade level, the minimum needed simply to understand written safety instructions. Without remedial work they cannot even begin, much less complete, the sophisticated training essential in much of the modern military.

These deficiencies come at a time when the demand for highly skilled workers in new fields is accelerating rapidly. For example:

- Computers and computer-controlled equipment are penetrating every aspect of our lives—homes, factories, and offices.

- One estimate indicates that by the turn of the century millions of jobs will involve laser technology and robotics.

- Technology is radically transforming a host of other occupations. They include health care, medical science, energy production, food processing, construction, and the building, repair, and maintenance of sophisticated scientific, educational, military, and industrial equipment.

Analysts examining these indicators of student performance and the demands for new skills have made some chilling observations. Educational researcher Paul Hurd concluded at the end of a thorough national survey of student achievement that within the context of the modern scientific revolution, "We are raising a new generation of Americans that is scientifically and technologically illiterate." In a similar vein, John Slaughter, a former Director of the National Science Foundation, warned of "a growing chasm between a small scientific and technological elite and a citizenry ill-informed, indeed uninformed, on issues with a science component."

But the problem does not stop there, nor do all observers see it the same way. Some worry that schools may emphasize such rudiments as reading and computation at the expense of other essential skills such as comprehension, analysis, solving problems, and drawing conclusions. Still others are concerned that an over-emphasis on technical and occupational skills will leave little time for studying the arts and humanities that so enrich daily life, help maintain civility, and develop a sense of community. Knowledge of the humanities, they maintain, must be harnessed to science and technology if the latter are to remain creative and humane, just as the humanities need to be informed by science and technology if they are to remain relevant to the human condition. Another analyst, Paul Copperman, has drawn a sobering conclusion. Until now, he has noted:

Each generation of Americans has outstripped its parents in education, in literacy, and in economic attainment. For the first time in the history of our country, the educational skills of one generation will not surpass, will not equal, will not even approach, those of their parents.

It is important, of course, to recognize that *the average citizen* today is better educated and more knowledgeable than the average citizen of a generation ago—more literate, and exposed to more mathematics, literature, and science. The positive impact of this fact on the well-being of our country and the lives of our people cannot be overstated. Nevertheless, *the average graduate* of our schools and colleges today is not as well-educated as the average graduate of 25 or 35 years ago, when a much smaller proportion of our population completed high school and college. The negative impact of this fact likewise cannot be overstated.

HOPE AND FRUSTRATION

Statistics and their interpretation by experts show only the surface dimension of the difficulties we face. Beneath them lies a tension between hope and frustration that characterizes current attitudes about education at every level.

We have heard the voices of high school and college students, school board members, and teachers; of leaders of industry, minority groups, and higher education; of parents and State officials. We could hear the hope evident in their commitment to quality education and in their descriptions of outstanding programs and schools. We could also hear the intensity of their frustration, a growing impatience with shoddiness in many walks of American life, and the complaint that this shoddiness is too often reflected in our schools and colleges. Their frustration threatens to overwhelm their hope.

What lies behind this emerging national sense of frustration can be described as both a dimming of personal expectations and the fear of losing a shared vision for America.

On the personal level the student, the parent, and the caring teacher all perceive that a basic promise is not being kept. More and more young people emerge from high school ready neither for college nor for work. This predicament becomes more acute as the knowledge base continues its rapid expansion, the number of traditional jobs shrinks, and new jobs demand greater sophistication and preparation.

On a broader scale, we sense that this undertone of frustration has significant political implications, for it cuts across ages, generations, races, and political and economic groups. We have come to understand that the public will demand that educational and political leaders act forcefully and effectively on these issues. Indeed, such demands have already appeared and could well become a unifying national preoccupation. This unity, however, can be achieved only if we avoid the unproductive tendency of some to search for scapegoats among the victims, such as the beleaguered teachers.

On the positive side is the significant movement by political and educational leaders to search for solutions—so far centering largely on the nearly desperate need for increased support for the teaching of mathematics and science. This movement is but a start on what we believe is a larger and more educationally encompassing need to improve teaching and learning in fields such as English, history, geography, economics, and foreign languages. We believe this movement must be broadened and directed toward reform and excellence throughout education.

EXCELLENCE IN EDUCATION

We define "excellence" to mean several related things. At the level of the *individual learner*, it means performing on the boundary of individual ability in ways that test and push back personal limits, in school and in the workplace. Excellence characterizes a *school or college* that sets high expectations and goals for all learners, then tries in every way possible to help students reach them. Excellence characterizes a *society* that has adopted these policies, for it will then be prepared through the education and skill of its people to respond to the challenges of a rapidly changing world. Our Nation's people and its schools and colleges must be committed to achieving excellence in all these senses.

We do not believe that a public commitment to excellence and educational reform must be made at the expense of a strong public commitment to the equitable treatment of our diverse population. The twin goals of equity and high-quality schooling have profound and practical meaning for our economy and society, and we cannot permit one to yield to the other either in principle or in practice. To do so would deny young people their chance to learn and live according to their aspirations and abilities. It also would lead to a generalized accommodation to mediocrity in our society on the one hand or the creation of an undemocratic elitism on the other.

Our goal must be to develop the talents of all to their fullest. Attaining that goal requires that we expect and assist all students to work to the limits of their capabilities. We should expect schools to have genuinely high standards rather than minimum ones, and parents to support and encourage their children to make the most of their talents and abilities.

The search for solutions to our educational problems must also include a commitment to life-long learning. The task of rebuilding our system of learning is enormous and must be properly understood and taken seriously: Although a million and a half new workers enter the economy each year from our schools and colleges, the adults working today will still make up about 75 percent of the workforce in the year 2000. These workers, and new entrants into the workforce, will need further education and retraining if they—and we as a Nation—are to thrive and prosper.

THE LEARNING SOCIETY

In a world of ever-accelerating competition and change in the conditions of the workplace, of ever-greater danger, and of ever-larger opportunities for those prepared to meet them, educational reform should focus on the goal of creating a Learning Society. At the heart of such a society is the commitment to a set of values and to a system of education that affords all members the opportunity to stretch their minds to full capacity, from early childhood through adulthood, learning more as the world itself changes. Such a society has as a basic foundation the idea that education is important not only because of what it contributes to one's career goals but also because of the value it adds to the general quality of one's life. Also at the heart of the Learning Society are educational opportunities extending far beyond the traditional institutions of learning, our schools and colleges. They extend into homes and workplaces; into libraries, art galleries, museums, and science centers; indeed, into every place where the individual can develop and mature in work and life. In our view, formal schooling in youth is the essential foundation for learning throughout one's life. But without life-long learning, one's skills will become rapidly dated.

In contrast to the ideal of the Learning Society, however, we find that for too many people education means doing the minimum work necessary for the moment, then coasting through life on what may have been learned in its first quarter. But this should not surprise us because we tend to express our educational standards and expectations largely in terms of "minimum requirements." And where there should be a coherent continuum of learning, we have none, but instead an often incoherent, outdated patchwork quilt. Many individual, sometimes heroic, examples of schools and colleges of great merit do exist. Our findings and testimony confirm the vitality of a number of notable schools and programs, but their very distinction stands out against a vast mass shaped by tensions and pressures that inhibit systematic academic and vocational achievement for the majority of students. In some metropolitan areas basic literacy has become the goal rather than the starting point. In some colleges maintaining enrollments is of greater day-to-day concern than maintaining rigorous academic standards. And the ideal of academic excellence as the primary goal of schooling seems to be fading across the board in American education.

Thus, we issue this call to all who care about America and its future: to parents and students; to teachers, administrators, and school board members; to colleges and industry; to union members and military leaders; to governors and State legislators; to the President; to members of Congress and other public officials; to members of learned and scientific societies; to the print and electronic media; to concerned citizens everywhere. America is at risk.

We are confident that America can address this risk. If the tasks we set forth are initiated now and our recommendations are fully realized over the next several years, we can expect reform of our Nation's schools, colleges, and universities. This would also reverse the current declining trend—a trend that stems more from weakness of purpose, confusion of vision, underuse of talent, and lack of leadership, than from conditions beyond our control.

THE TOOLS AT HAND

It is our conviction that the essential raw materials needed to reform our educational system are waiting to be mobilized through effective leadership:

- the natural abilities of the young that cry out to be developed and the undiminished concern of parents for the well-being of their children;

- the commitment of the Nation to high retention rates in schools and colleges and to full access to education for all;

- the persistent and authentic American dream that superior performance can raise one's state in life and shape one's own future;

- the dedication, against all odds, that keeps teachers serving in schools and colleges, even as the rewards diminish;

- our better understanding of learning and teaching and the implications of this knowledge for school practice, and the numerous examples of local success as a result of superior effort and effective dissemination;

- the ingenuity of our policymakers, scientists, State and local educators, and scholars in formulating solutions once problems are better understood;

- the traditional belief that paying for education is an investment in ever-renewable human resources that are more durable and flexible than capital plant and equipment, and the availability in this country of sufficient financial means to invest in education;

- the equally sound tradition, from the Northwest Ordinance of 1787 until today, that the Federal Government should supplement State, local, and other resources to foster key national educational goals; and

- the voluntary efforts of individuals, businesses, and parent and civic groups to cooperate in strengthening educational programs.

These raw materials, combined with the unparalleled array of educational organizations in America, offer us the possibility to create a Learning Society, in which public, private, and parochial schools; colleges and universities; vocational and technical schools and institutes; libraries; science centers, museums, and other cultural institutions; and corporate training and retraining programs offer opportunities and choices for all to learn throughout life.

THE PUBLIC'S COMMITMENT

Of all the tools at hand, the public's support for education is the most powerful. In a message to a National Academy of Sciences meeting in May 1982, President Reagan commented on this fact when he said:

This public awareness—and I hope public action—is long overdue. . . . This country was built on American respect for education. . . Our challenge now is to create a resurgence of that thirst for education that typifies our Nation's history.

The most recent (1982) Gallup Poll of the *Public's Attitudes Toward the Public Schools* strongly supported a theme heard during our hearings: People are steadfast in their belief that education is the major foundation for the future strength of this country. They even considered education more important than developing the best industrial system or the strongest military force, perhaps because they understood education as the cornerstone of both. They also held that education is "extremely important" to one's future success, and that public education should be the top priority for additional Federal funds. Education occupied first place among 12 funding categories considered in the survey—above health care, welfare, and military defense, with 55 percent selecting public education as one of their first three choices. Very clearly, the public understands the primary importance of education as the foundation for a satisfying life, an enlightened and civil society, a strong economy, and a secure Nation.

At the same time, the public has no patience with undemanding and superfluous high school offerings. In another survey, more than 75 percent of all those questioned believed every student planning to go to college should take 4 years of mathematics, English, history/U.S. government, and science, with more than 50 percent adding 2 years each of a foreign language and economics or business. The public even supports requiring much of this curriculum for students who do not plan to go to college. These standards far exceed the strictest high school graduation requirements of any State today, and they also exceed the admission standards of all but a handful of our most selective colleges and universities.

Another dimension of the public's support offers the prospect of constructive reform. The best term to characterize it may simply be the honorable word "patriotism." Citizens know intuitively what some of the best economists have shown in their research, that education is one of the chief engines of a society's material well-being. They know, too, that education is the common bond of a pluralistic society and helps tie us to other cultures around the globe. Citizens also know in their bones that the safety of the United States depends principally on the wit, skill, and spirit of a self-confident people, today and tomorrow. It is, therefore, essential—especially in a period of long-term decline in educational achievement—for government at all levels to affirm its responsibility for nurturing the Nation's intellectual capital.

And perhaps most important, citizens know and believe that the meaning of America to the rest of the world must be something better than it seems to many today. Americans like to think of this Nation as the preeminent country for generating the great ideas and material benefits for all mankind. The citizen is dismayed at a steady 15-year decline in industrial productivity, as one great American industry after another falls to world competition. The citizen wants the country to act on the belief, expressed in our hearings and by the large majority in the Gallup Poll, that education should be at the top of the Nation's agenda.

Findings

We conclude that declines in educational performance are in large part the result of disturbing inadequacies in the way the educational process itself is often conducted. The findings that follow, culled from a much more extensive list, reflect four important aspects of the educational process: content, expectations, time, and teaching.

FINDINGS REGARDING CONTENT

By content we mean the very "stuff" of education, the curriculum. Because of our concern about the curriculum, the Commission examined patterns of courses high school students took in 1964–69 compared with course patterns in 1976–81. On the basis of these analyses we conclude:

- Secondary school curricula have been homogenized, diluted, and diffused to the point that they no longer have a central purpose. In effect, we have a cafeteria style curriculum in which the appetizers and desserts can easily be mistaken for the main courses. Students have migrated from vocational and college preparatory programs to "general track" courses in large numbers. The proportion of students taking a general program of study has increased from 12 percent in 1964 to 42 percent in 1979.

- This curricular smorgasbord, combined with extensive student choice, explains a great deal about where we find ourselves today. We offer intermediate algebra, but only 31 percent of our recent high school graduates complete it; we offer French I, but only 13 percent complete it; and we offer geography, but only 16 percent complete it. Calculus is available in schools enrolling about 60 percent of all students, but only 6 percent of all students complete it.

- Twenty-five percent of the credits earned by general track high school students are in physical and health education, work experience outside the school, remedial English and mathematics, and personal service and development courses, such as training for adulthood and marriage.

FINDINGS REGARDING EXPECTATIONS

We define expectations in terms of the level of knowledge, abilities, and skills school and college graduates should possess. They also refer to the time, hard work, behavior, self-discipline, and motivation that are essential for high student achievement. Such expectations are expressed to students in several different ways:

- by grades, which reflect the degree to which students demonstrate their mastery of subject matter;

- through high school and college graduation requirements, which tell students which subjects are most important;

- by the presence or absence of rigorous examinations requiring students to demonstrate their mastery of content and skill before receiving a diploma or a degree;

- by college admissions requirements, which reinforce high school standards; and

- by the difficulty of the subject matter students confront in their texts and assigned readings.

Our analyses in each of these areas indicate notable deficiencies:

- The amount of homework for high school seniors has decreased (two-thirds report less than 1 hour a night) and grades have risen as average student achievement has been declining.

- In many other industrialized nations, courses in mathematics (other than arithmetic or general mathematics), biology, chemistry, physics, and geography start in grade 6 and are required of *all* students. The time spent on these subjects, based on class hours, is about three times that spent by even the most science-oriented U.S. students, i.e., those who select 4 years of science and mathematics in secondary school.

- A 1980 State-by-State survey of high school diploma requirements reveals that only eight States require high schools to offer foreign language instruction, but none requires students to take the courses. Thirty-five States require only 1 year of mathematics, and 36 require only 1 year of science for a diploma.

- In 13 States, 50 percent or more of the units required for high school graduation may be electives chosen by the student. Given this freedom to choose the substance of half or more of their education, many students opt for less demanding personal service courses, such as bachelor living.

- "Minimum competency" examinations (now required in 37 States) fall short of what is needed, as the "minimum" tends to become the "maximum," thus lowering educational standards for all.

- One-fifth of all 4-year public colleges in the United States must accept every high school graduate within the State regardless of program followed or grades, thereby serving notice to high school students that they can expect to attend college even if they do not follow a demanding course of study in high school or perform well.

- About 23 percent of our more selective colleges and universities reported that their general level of selectivity declined during the 1970s, and 29 percent reported reducing the number of specific high school courses required for admission (usually by dropping foreign language requirements, which are now specified as a condition for admission by only one-fifth of our institutions of higher education).

- Too few experienced teachers and scholars are involved in writing textbooks. During the past decade or so a large number of texts have been "written down" by their publishers to ever-lower reading levels in response to perceived market demands.

- A recent study by Education Products Information Exchange revealed that a majority of students were able to master 80 percent of the material in some of their subject-matter texts before they had even opened the books. Many books do not challenge the students to whom they are assigned.

- Expenditures for textbooks and other instructional materials have declined by 50 percent over the past 17 years. While some recommend a level of spending on texts of between 5 and 10 percent of the operating costs of schools, the budgets for basal texts and related materials have been dropping during the past decade and a half to only 0.7 percent today.

FINDINGS REGARDING TIME

Evidence presented to the Commission demonstrates three disturbing facts about the use that American schools and students make of time: (1) compared to other nations, American students spend much less time on school work; (2) time spent in the classroom and on homework is often used ineffectively; and (3) schools are not doing enough to help students develop either the study skills required to use time well or the willingness to spend more time on school work.

- In England and other industrialized countries, it is not unusual for academic high school students to spend 8 hours a day at school, 220 days per year. In the United States, by contrast, the typical school day lasts 6 hours and the school year is 180 days.

- In many schools, the time spent learning how to cook and drive counts as much toward a high school diploma as the time spent studying mathematics, English, chemistry, U.S. history, or biology.

- A study of the school week in the United States found that some schools provided students only 17 hours of academic instruction during the week, and the average school provided about 22.

- A California study of individual classrooms found that because of poor management of classroom time, some elementary students received only one-fifth of the instruction others received in reading comprehension.

- In most schools, the teaching of study skills is haphazard and unplanned. Consequently, many students complete high school and enter college without disciplined and systematic study habits.

FINDINGS REGARDING TEACHING

The Commission found that not enough of the academically able students are being attracted to teaching; that teacher preparation programs need substantial improvement; that the professional working life of teachers is on the whole unacceptable; and that a serious shortage of teachers exists in key fields.

- Too many teachers are being drawn from the bottom quarter of graduating high school and college students.

- The teacher preparation curriculum is weighted heavily with courses in "educational methods" at the expense of courses in subjects to be taught. A survey of 1,350 institutions training teachers indicated that 41 percent of the time of elementary school teacher candidates is spent in education courses, which reduces the amount of time available for subject matter courses.

- The average salary after 12 years of teaching is only $17,000 per year, and many teachers are required to supplement their income with part-time and summer employment. In addition, individual teachers have little influence in such critical professional decisions as, for example, textbook selection.

- Despite widespread publicity about an overpopulation of teachers, severe shortages of certain kinds of teachers exist: in the fields of mathematics, science, and foreign languages; and among specialists in education for gifted and talented, language minority, and handicapped students.

- The shortage of teachers in mathematics and science is particularly severe. A 1981 survey of 45 States revealed shortages of mathematics teachers in 43 States, critical shortages of earth sciences teachers in 33 States, and of physics teachers everywhere.

- Half of the newly employed mathematics, science, and English teachers are not qualified to teach these subjects; fewer than one-third of U.S. high schools offer physics taught by qualified teachers.

Part 3

Sociology of Education

Introduction to Sociology of Education

This section on the sociology of education looks at what has happened to groupings of individuals as they have been influenced by American educational practice throughout the years.

Here we get a flavor of and perhaps some insight into the results of the ideas and ideals of those who have had the power to influence educational practice. We will be able to better understand some of the thinking in the mid-1860s about the place of education in the lives of women. We will also see from that same time period what role education was to play for African Americans and Native Americans. We will be able to ponder the influence of a child's social class on his or her opportunities or lack of opportunities to be educated in America's schools. We may better understand "tracking," the separation of the bluebirds from the redbirds, sometimes for the reason of "ability" and other times for the reason of class or color or gender.

Lastly, in this section we look at some contemporary problems (often under the guise of solutions) of the groupings of individuals when we study a bit about the role of vouchers and magnet schools in American education.

The Education of Women

In most of the discussions in relation to the improvement of female education, the objectors have shown themselves unable to rise above the utilitarian, or rather the purely material, argument, and have assumed that those who ask a higher intellectual training for woman are as incapable as themselves of regarding the question from a loftier point of view. The range of woman's powers and duties, say they, is confined, by her physical and her mental nature alike, to a narrow and a humble sphere. Of what use is it for her to pursue studies or cultivate arts, which for her can have no practical application? Why should she concern herself about the political history, the constitution, or the jurisprudence of her country, seeing that she is deprived of the political franchise, and ineligible to legislative or judicial office? Why should she know anything of theology, except as a body of positive dogmas, inasmuch as she can neither preach nor perform any priestly function? Why should she study the rules of aesthetical criticism or the fundamental principles of any art, when it is notorious that she can neither invent a character, paint a historical picture, model a group, nor compose an anthem?

Now this reasoning is objectionable, not merely as assuming much that is disputable, much even that this generation has seen dispelled, but because it raises a false issue, while, at the same time, it places a low and degrading estimate on the uses of knowledge, and virtually denies that it is, in and of itself, a good. Our intellectual training, our discernment of good and evil, of the true and the false, of the beautiful and the base—these are as much constituents of that complex entity which we call *self*, as our physical appetites and sensations. Discipline, self-culture, soundness of judgment, positive attainment, all which are implied in *knowledge*, are equally necessary for the discharge of our duties to our Maker, to ourselves, and to our brother. Knowledge, then, helps us alike *to be* and *to do*, and the obscurantists, in refusing a better education to woman, are denying her the choicest of jewels as a possession, the most efficient of instrumentalities as a means of action.

The present question is not, as is perversely insisted, What shall women *do*? Shall they command fleets and armies? Shall they preside in the councils of the nation? Shall they defend criminals at the bar of justice? Shall they expound Scripture and enforce religious and moral obligation in the pulpit? Shall they administer potions and perform capital operations? Shall they be allowed publicly to buy and sell and get gain? But it is: Shall woman be encouraged, or at least permitted freely, to cultivate such humble faculties as she is admitted to enjoy, and develop those intellectual powers which, in common with what grammarians call the "sexus dignior," the worthier sex—though, as a half-reasoning animal, in an inferior degree—she appears to possess; may she receive a mental training which will raise her in her own self-respect, contribute to her rational enjoyment, and render her a more useful and less tiresome companion to the Solomon who is destined to lord it over her?

There are, certainly, persons who propose to put women forthwith upon a footing of absolute, social, civil, legal, and political parity with men, and suppose the fifteen hundred British maids and matrons who are demanding the exercise of political franchises in England, will have many sympathizers in and out of their own sex, many powerful advocates in Parliament, in society, and in literature. But, after all, we do not know or believe that, as a general rule, women now want, or ever will want, to exercise many of those functions of which generous man reserves to himself the monopoly. Physical reasons, and the appetites and repugnances naturally resulting from the physical constitution of women, will secure man, to a very great extent, from the dangerous competition, the apprehension of which is throwing universal fogydom into such a fever; and the law of supply and demand will, in the long run, when the market is fairly thrown open, bring the custom to the right shop, whether Adam or Eve stand behind the counter. As we have already said, we have no sound experimental knowledge in regard to the capacities and aptitudes of women, but, so far as the evidence goes, it is, as in all cases of the extension of human liberty, entirely favorable to the enlargement of woman's sphere of action. Women, we all know, once voted in New Jersey. The world was then by no means as well prepared for such an anomaly as it now is; but history does not tell us that New Jersey gained very much in wisdom of internal administration, or in respect abroad, by their exclusion from the polls. Had women continued to vote in that State, or rather *station*, we believe New Jersey would have been sooner redeemed from thraldom to the slave-driver; and had

This article appeared in the August 30, 1866 edition of *The Nation*.

she still, for a time, worshipped some Juggernaut as the god of her idolatry, she would have placed him on a nobler chariot than a snorting locomotive, and the lesser divinities of her pantheon would have been something better than deified stokers.

The opponents of the social and intellectual elevation of woman may be divided into two categories—the hierarchies, which fear or rather foresee that their own usurped powers and privileges will be reduced in proportion as rights shall be recovered by classes which have hitherto been deprived of them, and the vast body of men and women who honestly believe that woman is, upon the whole, an inferior creature.

The love of power is the strongest of human passions, and it is a remarkable proof of the intensity of the social feeling in man that aggregate bodies cling more tenaciously than individuals to the exceptional privileges they have become possessed of. Kings have voluntarily abdicated their thrones, but never did an *order* resign its prerogatives except upon compulsion. This is especially true of all hierarchies, lay or ecclesiastical, which, by incorporation or otherwise, have or claim perpetual existence by continuous succession, the transmission of a *virus*, as Dr. Rice called it. Happily the inviolability of corporate rights of all sorts is now becoming matter of frequent question. The reverence with which associate bodies were regarded is greatly diminished. The old Whig superstition of the immaculate conception of the United States Bank is now pretty much exploded, and it is very doubtful whether every point of the judgment in the famous Dartmouth College case would be affirmed upon a rehearing to-day. Although financial, and especially railroad, corporations have been the great springs of pecuniary, and too often of political, corruption in our time, yet their social influence is far less dangerous than that of bodies which rest their claims to power on the higher basis of religion. Ancient oppressions were sanctioned by appeals to vaguely conceived divinities, speaking, as in a great part of Europe they do to this day, only through the priests. In nations which have shaken off some part of their mediaeval superstitions— royalty, hereditary aristocracy, consecrated priesthoods—advocates of the slavery of man and the degradation of woman fortify every proposition by quotations from Holy Writ—the joint authority of "Peter and Paul." When it was a penitentiary offence in South Carolina to teach the negro to read, when generous Georgia condemned missionaries to penal servitude for preaching Christianity to the Indians, the pious, the learned, the wise, and even the philanthropists of those enlightened communities had no doubt that the sentences were just. Reason and experience proved the inferiority of the black skin and the red just as logically as they establish the inferiority of woman now, and devout gospellers appealed to Scripture in the former case as triumphantly as they still do in the latter. It was clear from Holy Writ that "Ham's sons was gi'n to us in charge;" slavery was their natural, divinely ordained condition, their earthly school and paradise; and though the "nigger" was a "useful institution" to his owner, yet it was more as a matter of duty than of interest that the magnanimous Southron held him in perpetual bondage. In fact, the Southern States constituted a great Society for the Propagation of the Gospel, the slaveholders and priesthood; and when a religious congregation in Charleston sold a few "communicants" further "down South" to raise money to repair their church, they had the comfortable reflection that they were sending out catechists and missionaries to teach the way of truth to their yet but half-converted brother on the sugar plantations. As to the Indian, his name did not appear in the biblical genealogies—he was not the son of anybody; they "'spected he growed." Of course he inherited no share in the "covenant promises," and the taking of his lands and his goods and appropriating them to better uses was a praiseworthy spoiling of the Egyptians. All this was conscientiously believed five years ago by seven or eight millions of men, women, and children. Does anybody but a Copperhead believe, it now?

Is it not possible that the all but universal belief in the inferior nature of woman rests on a not less sandy foundation? We look back with astonishment at the solemn decision of Southern judicial tribunals, that, unless restrained by local statute, the master's power over his slave was as unlimited as over his ox; that at common law no indictment would lie against the owner for torturing or even killing his "servant"—that, in short, he had all the rights over his bondman which the volunteer gladiator's oath and the laws of Rome conferred upon the *ludimagister*, "to bind, burn, scourge, slay with the sword, or whatsoever else the master should please." Justice Buller declared that, by the law of England, beating a wife with a stick not thicker than his lordship's thumb was not to be considered as anything more than that "moderate chastisement" which the husband might rightfully administer. Shall we not by and by grow wise enough and humane enough to try to get a mitigation of this judgment and reduce the size of the stick to perhaps the measure of a judge's little finger?

Dr. Johnson, whose strong sense helped him, in spite of the tenacity of his prejudices, to see the hollowness of many of the social shams of his time, said that woman was not made subject to man because she was his inferior, but because, "when two ride on one horse, one of them must ride behind." In our day everybody travels in the East, and the Western world is becoming familiar with the fact that, by the use of a pannier-saddle, which the Orientals call a *kajaxa*, two persons may travel on one camel and yet ride side by side.

Some time since a European lady expressed to us the regret she felt, in visiting a school which her husband had been instrumental in establishing for the purpose of so far educating peasant girls as to make them useful domestic servants, to find that the girls were not content with the little their instructors were willing to teach them, but that they desired to acquire knowledge enough to qualify them for teachers in higher female schools. When we said that we thought this was a creditable feeling, which ought to be encouraged rather than repressed, she replied, "*Mais, Monsieur, elles aspirent à se déclasser!*" They want to rive above their caste. "Well," said we, "this answer of yours points to a fundamental distinction between your Old World institutions and those of which we Americans are so proud. The very thing we aim at is to '*déclasser*' our people, to relieve them from the servitude and the tyranny of caste, to 'exalt the humble' majority, even at the cost of 'depressing the proud' minority. True, we strive to lengthen upwards the ladder on which all alike stand, that all may climb higher than the highest has yet ascended, but we do not allow the occupant of the topmost round any possessory right to exclude from a place beside him the aspirant who is rising from the lowest."

The European traditions, which reduce woman to the condition of an inferior caste, are in conflict with the whole tone and purport of American institutions. They constitute what lawyers call a "discrepancy," an irreconcilable discord, in our whole social life. Let us begin with recognizing true and liberal principles, and trust to the logic of society to work out legitimate and beneficent results. Let us not dispute whether women shall, if special vocation call them, walk in hitherto untrodden paths, or still be confined to such rude "small chores" as lofty manhood scorns to stoop to; let us not, like the bee, feed one human larva to be a worker, one a mother, and another a drone; but let us administer to both sexes, in every condition of life, that generous intellectual, moral, and physical nutriment which will enable each to develop most perfectly the powers and faculties of its material and moral organization.

No person has discussed this general question with greater ability, none with more of that sage moderation which is the sure token of an elevated and an enlightened spirit, than the noble woman whose essays we take as the text of this article.* We do not know how much her works have yet been read in the United States, but no writer of our time, male or female, better deserves to be listened to by Americans who seek the true solution of the greatest social problem which it remains for Americans to determine.

---

*"*Essays on the Pursuits of Women. By Frances Power Cobbe.*" London, 1863.

AFT

—Margaret Haley, Florence Rood, and Mary Barker

At the turn of this century teachers routinely suffered intolerable working conditions, and women who taught the youngest children were among the most exploited. Facing poor wages, little political or community support, and no national forum sensitive to the needs of classroom teachers, three women who taught urban grade school children helped create, shape, and lead the American Federation of Teachers (AFT) through its early years: Margaret Haley of Chicago, Florence Rood of St. Paul, and Mary Barker of Atlanta.

The American educational system from which these three leaders emerged had undergone dramatic changes in the last quarter of the nineteenth century. Emphasis on the need for widespread public education for all children, coupled with a decline in the economy's dependence on child labor, had led many states to pass compulsory education laws and to lengthen the duration of school terms. Required education demanded more teachers, but the high costs associated with expanding public education systems and inadequate funding from state legislatures led local education officials to offer meager wages.

Women teachers disproportionally filled the ranks of these low paying jobs. In 1870, about 65 percent of all classroom teachers were female; by 1900 the number reached 75 percent; and in 1920 it peaked at 86 percent. (1) The highest percent of women teachers always occurred at the grade school level. In 1870, the average male classroom teacher received $35 a week while female teachers earned only $12. Fifty years later, in 1920, the average weekly pay for women teachers reached $36, only a dollar more than men's 1870 wages, while men in the 1920s earned an average $61 a week. (2)

Low pay was not the only reason that school systems recruited women. As early as 1841, women classroom teachers were characterized as "unambitious, frugal and filial." (3) Lacking many of the legal rights of men, women at the turn of the century often had extra restrictions placed on them as a condition of employment. Many school districts refused to hire married women, resulting in a profession where only 10 percent of female teachers had spouses. (4) Although considered more nurturing of young children than men, women teachers were perceived to be second-class workers, cheaper and more malleable than their male counterparts.

Nowhere was this second-class status more evident than at the grade school level. Few college-educated women chose public education as a profession and almost none taught the youngest children. Although many grade school teachers attended "normal schools" that had been established to train elementary school teachers and, in some cases, provide a year or two of training beyond secondary school, a large number did not have a high school diploma. Most often the youngest teachers were perceived as undereducated and unimportant; grade school instructors had little influence in the profession.

For all classroom teachers, both male and female, working conditions in the nation's schools at the turn of the century could be physically harsh and politically demoralizing. This was especially true in rural areas, which as late as 1910 composed 58 percent of the school population. Teachers often worked in log cabins and sod houses heated with a fireplace facing a crude door supported by leather hinges. Windows were small slits and rarely glazed; they were covered with paper in the winter. In some places, there were no student desks; children sat on benches. Textbooks were sparse and frequently old. Sanitary conditions were rudimentary. Urban teachers faced many of the same primitive conditions; the schools were often crowded, boxlike structures that were cold in winter and hot in summer. (5)

In addition to teaching in physically demanding environments, classroom teachers faced a hierarchical and bureaucratic educational structure aimed more at economic efficiency than quality education. Schools had rigid rules and, in many places, teachers worked under constant supervision. Usually, teachers could be fired at a principal's will or whim. (6) Among the critics of this system was John Dewey, philosopher and educational reformer, who pointed out the hypocrisy of the "teacher's obligation to give lessons about democracy, and her obligation to take orders and remain silent at her workplace." (7)

From *Labor's Heritage, Vol. 7, No. 2* by Paula O'Connor. Copyright © 1995 by The George Meany Memorial Archives. Reprinted by permission.

Many teachers were dissatisfied with this situation. They formed local teachers' associations in their cities, but these functioned as forums for complaints, with little or no power. The National Education Association (NEA), a nationwide professional organization founded in 1857, provided meagre support for classroom teachers. In the 1890s, school administrators comprised 50 percent of the membership while classroom teachers were only 11 percent. Supervision and higher education dominated the agenda of the NEA's board, headed by school superintendents and college presidents.(8)

Starting in the late 1890s, Chicago teachers began the fight for classroom rights, increased wages, and guaranteed pensions. Foremost among them was Margaret Haley, a Chicago sixth grade school teacher who became a leader of the movement to unionize teachers. Born in 1861, Haley learned to read from her mother, an Irish immigrant who used the Bible and a pictorial history of Ireland to educate her daughter. Haley's father, also Irish, was born in Canada and immigrated to Illinois as a child. He operated a stone quarry and construction firm but was active in the Knights of Labor as well as the Joliet Illinois Trade and Labor Council. (9) In her autobiography, Haley gave an example of her father's fair-mindedness. She recalled that he led her out of a hall when a speaker criticized women's rights advocate Susan B. Anthony, telling his daughter, "I don't know Susan B. Anthony and I suppose that I never shall, but she's a woman who is working for a cause, a just cause, and I will not allow my children to continue to listen to any half-baked nincompoop who sneers at her." (10)

Trained at a nearby "normal school," Haley began teaching even before she graduated. (11) After she gained experience, she delivered an ultimatum to the school superintendent that she must have a $5.00 raise, and if she did not hear from him by noon of the first day of the fall term, she would quit. Receiving no response, she set out for Chicago to teach.

In Chicago, Haley met Catharine Goggin, a like-minded grade school teacher, who shared a dissatisfaction with the Chicago Teachers Federation (CTF). Founded in 1897 and composed of elementary school teachers, the CTF was unable to obtain a needed pay increase for city teachers, who had not had a raise for twenty years. With Haley as her campaign manager, Goggin successfully ran for president of the CTF, receiving 1,701 of 2,243 votes.

The next step was to educate the CTF membership about the benefits of affiliation with the 200,000-member Chicago Federation of Labor (CFL). In early 1902, the CTF voted to join the CFL, becoming the first group of teachers in the country to join with organized labor. (12) "We realized," Haley explained, that we had "to fight the devil with fire and, if we were to preserve not only our own self-respect but the basic independence of the public schools, we must make [a] powerful political alliance." (13)

Haley resigned her teaching post in 1901, becoming a business agent for the CTF. She took over the full-time leadership of the organization in 1916 when Goggin was killed in a traffic accident. Haley evoked strong reactions from everyone, including her fellow teachers. Opponents referred to her as a "lady labor slugger."(14) She travelled across the country, speaking about her positive experience with organized labor in Chicago and trying to convince other teachers' organizations to join the labor movement. In 1916, she sent Ida Fursman to represent the CTF at the founding meeting of the American Federation of Teachers. A movement to make Haley the AFT's first president was weakened by concern that she had been overly entangled in Chicago politics. Ironically, her involvement centered on the fight to defeat legislation to prohibit Chicago teachers from joining a labor union.

The AFT elected Charles Stillman, a Chicago vocational high school teacher, as its first president. He had the support of male and female high school teachers who predominated at the meeting. The AFT did, however, elect Haley as its national organizer, an unpaid position. (15)

The following year, Haley made two far-reaching decisions. She pulled the CTF out of both the CFL and the AFT. She reluctantly withdrew from the city labor federation, forced to do so by a court decision upholding a ban on teacher unions. She did this only after securing passage of a state tenure law for teachers. Removal from the AFT was ideological, mainly due to her differences with Stillman. The immediate cause was that Stillman, without consulting the AFT board, had joined with AFL President Samuel Gompers in support of America's involvement in World War I. This angered Haley, who along with many of her grade school colleagues, had strong anti-war beliefs. The CTF also considered Stillman too conservative on issues such as his backing of Gompers' support of a no-strike pledge for public employees. (16)

Although separated from the AFT, Haley continued her efforts to spark teacher interest in joining the labor movement. She led the CTF until her death in 1939, crusading from every podium she could find on behalf of better teaching conditions. Perhaps Chicago poet Carl Sandburg best summed up her accomplishments: "this one little woman has flung her clenched fists into the faces of contractors, school land leaseholders, tax dodgers and their politicians, fixers, go-betweens and stool pigeons .... manipulators who hate Margaret Haley have not been able to smutch her in the eyes of decent men and women of this town who do their own thinking." (17)

The influence of the elementary school teacher in the AFT did not end when the CTF left the organization. Six years after Haley's departure, the AFT elected kindergarten teacher Florence Rood as its president. Born in 1873, Rood could trace her ancestors back to the Mayflower. She was from a family that prized education and learning. Following her lifelong ambition to be a teacher, Rood attended St. Paul City Normal, known as The Teachers' Training School. In 1894, after she earned her two-year diploma, she began teaching kindergarten-aged children. (18)

According to Rood's associates, Frances Biskup and Elizabeth Newton, "Miss Rood had an unusual insight into child nature and introduced innovations in educational method long before the new approach to this education was recognized by all educators." (19) Her kindergarten room and her teaching style drew visits from educators as well as students from teacher training schools in Minneapolis and St. Paul, and she became a demonstration teacher and a critic teacher at the St. Paul Normal School in 1913. (20) When the normal school closed in 1916, she was appointed assistant supervisor in charge of kindergartens in the St. Paul school system.

Rood believed in "democratic supervision," regarding teachers and supervisors as co-workers, cooperating to improve the classroom teaching. She helped form the Grade Teachers Organization (GTO). (21) At first, the superintendent of schools outlawed the organization. When that did not deter the women, the superintendent formed "Loyalty Clubs" made up of teachers who were rewarded for reporting the names of those who belonged to the GTO. The state education commissioner, business groups, and the press all attacked the GTO. (22) These attacks were a reflection of the anti-union activity occurring across the country—spurred by fear of workers uniting and managers losing their near-absolute control.

Soon, almost every grade school teacher in St. Paul belonged to the GTO. In 1909 and again in 1917, Rood, as a GTO lobbyist, fought against the so-called "merit pay" plan, helping to win the cooperation of other teacher groups in the state and civic organizations including Minnesota Farmer Labor groups and the Farmer Labor Women's Club. Helen Conway, one of her biographers, noted that Rood's strongest trait was the "ability to select real leaders and to inspire confidence in her coworkers." Conway reports one of Rood's colleagues as saying, "We worked harder than we ever thought we could, and loved doing it with Miss Rood." (23)

In the GTO, Rood began her lifelong work on pensions for teachers. Before the expansion of the public school system in the last quarter of the nineteenth century, teaching had been seen as a temporary occupation and career teachers were an anomaly. In the twentieth century, the situation changed. Single women, like Rood, who were entering the profession in growing numbers, knew that they were primary bread winners who had to be self-sufficient; they needed the assurance of a pension for their retirement years. (24)

Rood led a group of fellow teachers, both women and men, to take advantage of an enabling act on pensions passed by the Minnesota legislature. The pension plan devised by Rood's group was simple and workable and involved contributions from both the city and the teachers. It went into operation in 1910, and Rood managed the pension system for St. Paul's teachers until 1939. (25)

Rood joined the NEA and in 1913 headed its newly formed Department of Classroom Teachers. Margaret Haley and others had fought to create this department because they believed the NEA neglected this segment of the teaching profession. After her election, Rood drew up an ambitious agenda that dealt with salary and tax issues for the NEA to consider. She particularly wanted the NEA to understand the problems of administrator favoritism inherent in "merit pay," and spoke out about the need for tenure for teachers. Due to her work for teacher pensions, she learned a good deal about state and local taxing systems and was eager to share her expertise. Through the NEA's National Council, however, college presidents and school superintendents controlled the finances of the NEA as well as its priorities. Among them, there was a strong sentiment that teacher welfare issues were not "professional." The National Council never gave Rood's new department a budget or empowered it to tax its own members. Rood felt that the department only served as a place to air grievances without actually compelling recognition of the needs of teachers. Accordingly, she turned to other organizations. (26)

Rood and her associates began to receive support from the St. Paul Trades and Labor Assembly. The Grade Teachers Organization issued a series of "Letters to the Public," protesting merit pay and other problems facing teachers, but were unable to get them published in the local newspapers. According to the historian of the St. Paul local, "The only organization that recognized teachers' problems, having similar problems themselves, was labor." (27) The St. Paul Trades and Labor Assembly published the teachers' letters and publicized their causes. The campaign defeated merit pay and resulted in a salary increase for teachers.

In 1918 Rood led the St. Paul grade school teachers into the AFT. Rood's name was on the top line of the St. Paul charter, and she was the group's key leader. The new 400-member St. Paul Federation of Women Teachers, AFT Local 28, was entirely female; a year later, fifty male teachers in the city formed the St. Paul Men Teachers' Union, AFT Local 43. No publications mention why the men did not join the women teachers, but the decision to remain separate seems to have been mutual. They did, however, form a coordinating committee to work together on various issues, and Rood served on it. The two locals did not merge until 1957. Rood never became president of the St. Paul Federation of Women Teachers, but she was always active in the leadership of the group, chairing committees and working behind the scenes.

The St. Paul union was one of the largest in the AFT; from 1922, Rood was a member of the AFT executive council. In 1923, Charles Stillman, with an empty union treasury and faced with opposition to his conservative policies, resigned the AFT presidency. Rood was elected president. According to the convention's proceedings, "Miss Rood modestly tried to bring before the convention necessary pressure through her remarks and suggestions to sway the convention to the negative as regards her name on the ballot. Miss Rood did not attempt to withdraw her name from the ballot but suggested that she be not so elected." (28)

In Rood's first presidential report, delivered extemporaneously, she did not hesitate to criticize the problems she saw in the AFT. From a high of 10,000 members in 1920, the union's membership had plunged to 3,600 in 1923. (29) One mistake the AFT continued to make, Rood believed, was to charter a local and give it insufficient support. Under Stillman, the AFT had tried to organize as many locals as possible, but many floundering locals had disbanded. Rood argued that if the AFT could not support a local, it should not charter it. To strengthen existing locals, Rood encouraged each to share their successes and failures by writing about them for the AFT semimonthly bulletin. (30) She wrote to AFT local leaders and offered advice and encouragement. She continued to stress the importance of tenure and pensions throughout her term of office, and encouraged locals to campaign for these benefits. She was also able to offer advice from her experience about how to lobby for these goals.

Preferring to work behind the scenes, Rood had been a reluctant candidate for the AFT presidency, and within a year was contemplating who might succeed her in office. In 1924, Mary Barker, AFT vice-president and president of the Atlanta Public School Teachers' Association, invited Rood to Atlanta to speak to her members. The event solidified their friendship. (31) In 1925, Barker succeeded Rood as president of the AFT. Rood remained on the AFT executive council and was an active vice-president. Later, Rood stepped down from the AFT executive council but continued to work for her local and for the national AFT, until shortly before her death in 1944 at age seventy-one.

Barker was born in 1879. Both of her parents were teachers and she and her two sisters followed their parents' vocation. Barker trained to be an elementary school teacher at Agnes Scott Institute in Decatur, Georgia, and then began her teaching career in small Georgia communities. In 1904, she moved to Atlanta, where her career in the public grade schools spanned the next forty-four years. Although she was promoted to school principal by 1921, her writing and actions show that she always thought of herself as a classroom teacher, not a manager. She continued to teach at her school and had very little autonomy as a principal. (32)

As the school population in Atlanta continued to grow and school funding did not, working conditions deteriorated. By 1910, salaries had been dropping for three decades.(33) The school board required teachers to furnish their own desk copies of textbooks, and the threat loomed constantly that the schools might have to close for lack of money. To take care of the crowding, Atlanta initiated summer school, paying teachers only $10 a week. Merit pay also went into effect, and when teachers examined the wage levels under merit pay, they found that more salaries decreased than increased.(34) Atlanta also adopted a system of paying teachers on a twelve-month basis, instead of the usual nine months.

In her second year of teaching in Atlanta, Barker helped found the Atlanta Public School Teachers' Association (APSTA), a broad-based, city-wide, white teachers' organization. It became a substantial organization in the 1920s. Unlike the teachers in Chicago and St. Paul, who formed multiple associations in their cities that were separated by grade level and gender, 90 percent of the white Atlanta teachers soon belonged to the APSTA.

Shortly after the APSTA was formed, the Atlanta Federation of Trades sought its affiliation. Some of the teachers, including Barker, resisted, feeling the connection to labor would lower their status as professionals or, as Barker recalled, "for fear of being drawn into other people's strikes." (35) In 1918, however, the Atlanta firemen formed a union, and in 1919, when the teachers were denied a raise because of lack of funds, the city found the money to give the firemen a raise. (36) A committee of APSTA that included Barker then recommend affiliation with the labor movement. As Barker recalled:

"The suggestion that teachers affiliate with organized industrial workers once seemed to me an absurd proposition. Their work was so different. Organized association on the basis of their work appeared incongruous. How little I knew about organized labor and what it was all about! The organizers of the American Federation of Teachers gave us the common denominator. We are all employees, they said. As such we have common problems. We pool our resources the more effectively to solve those problems." (37)

The APSTA became Local 89 of the AFT in 1919 and affiliated with the Atlanta Federation of Trades. Barker became reading secretary of the latter.

The dire financial position of the Atlanta school system was exacerbated by the continued failure of city tax and bond issues that would have helped fund the schools. A well-organized African-American community showed that it could use its power at the polls to defeat bond issues as a way of protesting the inadequacies of the segregated school system. Barker was atypical in her concern for of the problems of African-American teachers. She belonged to the League of Women Voters, the Urban League, the Atlanta Commission of Interracial Cooperation, and the American Civil Liberties Union. Barker encouraged a group of African-American teachers to organize and apply for an American Federation of Teachers charter in 1920. The AFT asked APSTA for its endorsement of the African-American teachers' local, but despite Barker's motion to support this new local, the APSTA refused. The AFT nevertheless granted the charter without Local 89's approval. (38)There were also divisions between grade school teachers, who believed they deserved a raise because they had such low pay, and the principals and high school teachers, who argued that their extra training and, in the principals' case, extra work, deserved more pay.

Despite her liberalism, Barker was elected president of the APSTA in 1921. Membership in the APSTA grew under Barker's leadership and, during her two years in office, teachers won a tenure law. This had been Barker's top priority. Early in her presidency, she had had to cope with the firing of Julia Riordan, a teacher with thirty years of teaching experience, an APSTA founding member, and an activist who was targeted because she was a Catholic. The Ku Klux Klan decided to make an example of Riordan and, through their members on the school board, had her fired. Though the Atlanta Federation of Trades supported her, Riordan was not rehired.

Barker used the Riordan firing and the surrounding publicity to work successfully for the new tenure law. At that time, teachers worked on a one-year contract, and they could be ousted from the system by the superintendent. Rood worked with the APSTA's legislative committee, presenting a tenure proposal to the school board. She also worked through the Georgia Education Association and the Atlanta Federation of Trades to garner support. She had an attorney draft a proposal for statewide teacher tenure; that proposal lost, but focused statewide attention on the tenure proposal in Atlanta, and contributed to its passage. Under the new law, after three years in the school system, a teacher could not be dismissed except for cause, after presentation of charges at a formal hearing. (39)

Barker stepped down from the APSTA presidency in 1923, after two years in office, but remained first vice-president. In the 1920s, she devoted much of her energy to the national teacher's organization. Barker had been elected to the AFT executive council in 1922, and served three years before taking over the presidency from Florence Rood in 1925.

During Barker's presidency, the AFT became outspoken on racial issues. At earlier conventions, the New York City local, led by Abraham Lefkovitz and Henry Linville, had supported unsuccessful resolutions calling for a more balanced view of African-American history in textbooks and calling for a "more tolerant attitude between races that constitute the nation." (40) These passed in 1928, and that convention also attacked the intolerance of the Ku Klux Klan and of the Daughters of the American Revolution.

The AFT's support of liberal causes sometimes caused problems. Its support for left-of-center Brookwood Labor College led to a souring of relations with AFL leaders during Barker's term. AFL President William Green was concerned with the radicalism of the faculty at Brookwood, an institution that the AFL's more liberal unions helped finance. In 1927, Green further strained relations with the union when he declined an invitation to speak at the AFT convention but did accept one to address the NEA gathering. An outraged Baker wrote to the AFT's secretary-treasurer Florence Hanson about the episode: "The affinity between the AFL and the NEA has finally dawned on me. As much alike as two peas in a pod. Autocratic, complaisant, monopolistic-antisocial, fear ridden, illiberal inherently." (41) Barker never, however, considered leaving the AFL. In 1950, she wrote an article about her long association with the labor movement, acknowledging that there are always people in it who fall short of its goals. Nevertheless, she believed that "Association promotes understanding . . . and provides opportunity for assembling the forces that project forward steps in human progress." (42)

Barker stepped down as AFT president in 1931, in favor of Henry Linville. She continued as an AFT vice-president until 1934. That year, her local finally withdrew its support of her because of her liberal statements and votes on racial issues.

Haley, Rood, and Barker are representative of a generation of women teaching in the primary grades in the expanding school systems of the early twentieth century. The AFT provided a vehicle for such women to grapple with issues central to the reality that they were career women, not secondary workers, and to tackle some of the most important educational and social issues of their day. In return, their talents benefited to the leadership of the AFT in its formative years.

This article was prepared by Paula O'Connor, former director of information services at the AFT. It originally appeared in *Labor's Heritage*, Vol. 7, No. 2, Fall 1995.

REFERENCE NOTES

(1) Donald Warren, ed., American Teachers: Histories of a Professional at Work (New York, 1989), p. 29.

(2) David Tyack, The One Best System: A History of American Urban Education (Cambridge, Mass., 1974), p. 62.

(3) Ibid. p. 60.

(4) Local school districts varied in their regulations concerning the marital status of their female teachers. Before the Depression, surveys showed that 60% of urban districts had regulations against hiring or retaining married women. In 1914 in New York City, a married woman could be hired only if she had been separated from her husband for three years. See Donald Warren, ed. American Teachers: Histories of a Profession at Work (New York, 1989), pp. 322–323.

(5) Ibid., pp. 98–100.

(6) Ibid., p. 123.

(7) Ibid. p. 127.

(8) Marjorie Murphy, Blackboard Unions: The AFT and the NEA, 1900–1980 (Ithaca, N.Y., 1990), p. 50.

(9) Robert Reid, ed., Battleground: The Autobiography of Margaret A. Haley (Urbana, 1982), p. 7.

(10) Ibid., p. 13.

(11) The term "normal school" originated in France and meant that teachers should be trained to perform according to "norms" or high standards.

(12) The CTF did not join the AFL until they came into the AFT, since Haley felt more comfortable with John Fitzpatrick, head of the Chicago Federation of Labor, than with Samuel Gompers, AFL president. Haley thought Gompers was pro-British. The San Antonio, Texas teachers were granted a directly affiliated local charter from the AFL later in 1902.

(13) Reid, Battleground, p. 90.

(14) Ibid.

(15) Ibid., p. 84.

(16) Murphy, Blackboard Unions, pp. 85–89.

(17) Carl Sanburg, The Day Book, (Chicago, 1918), p. ? [*sic*]

(18) All biographical information is from Flora Smalley, ed., Florence Rood: An Appreciation, (n.p., n.d.) published by the local union after Rood's death. Rood left no papers or archives.

(19) Smalley, Florence Rood, p. 12.

(20) Rood demonstrated improved teaching methods.

(21) At that time, only women taught in elementary school, so the Grade Teachers Organization was all women.

(22) Michael McDonough, St. Paul Federation of Teachers: Fifty Years of Service, 1918–1968, (St. Paul, 1968), p. 4 & 7.

(23) Smalley, Florence Rood, p. 27.

(24) Warren, American Teachers, pp. 321–22.

(25) Ibid. Gene Waschbusch, the present-day administrator of the fund, calls Rood's pension stewardship "very progressive," because she made sure the fund was audited, not a common practice at the time. He commends her for being alert to attacks on the fund by the legislature or anyone with questionable motives. He is impressed by the extensive minutes that detail the extra work she put into administering the fund for the teachers. She contacted relatives about problems facing infirm teachers and made herself available on a regular basis to meet with teachers and advise them. Author interview with Gene Wasehbusch, April 9, 1990, St. Paul.

(26) Eaton, The AFT, p. 11 and Murphy, Blackboard Unions, pp. 77–78.

(27) McDonough, "St. Paul Federation of Teachers", p. 4.

(28) American Federation of Teachers, Convention Proceedings, (Chicago, 1923), p. 36.

(29) "AFT Membership May 31st Each Year," AFT internal publication, n.d.

(30) AFT President Stillman stopped publication of American Teacher in 1921. Money may not have been in the only reason for its demise. Stillman had many arguments with its editor, Henry Linville.

(31) "American Federation of Teachers Semi-Monthly Bulletin," 4 (Mar. 20, 1924): 4.

(32) William Scott, "Mary Cornelia Barker, 1879–1963," adopted by the Atlanta Public School Teachers Association, December 16, 1963, Barker Collection, Box 8, Emory University Archives (EU). Biographical material is from this paper, and from Joseph W. Newman, "Mary C. Barker and the Atlanta Teachers' Union," in Southern Workers and Their Unions, 1880–1975: Selected papers, The Second Southern Labor History Conference, 1978, Merle Reed, Leslie S. Hough and Gary M. Fink, eds. (Westport, Conn., 1981), pp. 61–77.

(33) Commission on Education Reconstruction, Organizing the Teaching Profession: The Story of the AFT (Glencoe, Ill., 1955), p. 29.

(34) Joseph Whitworth Newman, "A History of the Atlanta Public School Teachers' Association [APSTA], Local 89 of the American Federation of Teachers, 1919–1956," (Ph.D. diss., Georgia State University, 1978), p. 10.

(35) Ibid., p. 39.

(36) Ibid., p. 25.

(37) Mary Barker, "Identification of Teachers with Other Workers in the Community," Barker Collection, Box 3, EU.

(38) Scott, "Barker: 1879–1963," p. 3, Barker Collection, Box 8, EU.

(39) Newman, "A History of APSTA," p. 90.

(40) Ibid, p. 124.

(41) Mary Barker to Florence Hanson, June 23, 1927, AFT Collection, Series 1, Box 1, Wayne State Archives.

(42) Mary Barker, "Identification of Teachers with Other Workers in the Community," Barker Collection, Box 3, item 1, EU.

Traditional Indian Education

The traditional way through which Native American children were educated for the responsibilities that they would assume as adults was by working with and imitating their elders. There was no "school" as it was understood by nineteenth century Europeans. Rather, children were allowed to roam freely throughout the community stopping and asking questions when and where they pleased. Children would work companionably alongside their parents or other adults, helping in small ways and gaining confidence and ability in various skills. Children often engaged in what the Dakota referred to as "small play," impersonating adults and mimicking their activities, conversations, and manners.

Grandparents played a very important role in the education of children. Grandmothers, for example, bore responsibility for making girls "well behaved women." A grandmother would take it upon herself to tutor her granddaughter in the subtleties of daily life, such as how to move, how to interact with elders, where to sit at ceremonial occasions. In the evening it was common to send a daughter to her grandmother bearing a gift of food or tobacco. The gift was an invitation to the grandmother to instruct the child in the tribe's traditions that would help the girl understand both her place in the tribe and her people's place in the world.

As children aged their spiritual development was nurtured. Chippewa girls of four or five years of age, for example, undertook their first vision quests in the forest. As the child grew older the length of the quests gradually lengthened. Eventually an older child might spend several days in the forest fasting and seeking a vision that would define his or her spirituality and relationship with the supernatural. Upon returning from such a quest a child would be ritually greeted by relatives, feasted for his or her accomplishment, and listened to respectfully as the child reported on the dreams experienced during the quest.

From a very young age children were treated with considerable dignity and respect. When a child required discipline it usually came in the form of a scolding or a threat that an animal might kidnap the misbehaving child. Physical punishment was rare and modest, usually involving a twig applied to the hands or knees.

THE WHITE PERSPECTIVE

Changing Federal Policy

After the Civil War trans-Mississippi settlement of whites on the southern plains spurred large-scale military conflict with many Indian tribes. For over a decade the United States army fought various combinations of tribes. Although Indian wars were not a new phenomena, the scope of the conflict led a reform-minded group of Euro-Americans began to call for a new Indian policy. Over time many reformers, or the "Friends of the American Indians" as this group eventually called itself, came to believe that the only answer to the "Indian problem" was to assimilate Native Americans into Euro-American society. Education was quickly identified as the a critical tool in accomplishing this goal.

Specifically, the Friends argued for abolition of the reservation system and the creation of government-run Indian schools that would emphasize vocational skills. The Friends hoped that the schools would teach Native American marketable skills so that an Indian could be self-supporting in white American society. The idea of educating Indians into white ways was not a new one. By the 1850's treaties signed with Indian tribes routinely included a "six to sixteen clause," promising a school house and school teacher for Indian children between the ages of six and sixteen. For most of the nineteenth century Congress had also routinely appropriate money for a "Civilization Fund," that was very pointedly created to transform Indians into the model of white pioneer settlers. But the treaty agreements and the Civilization Fund had assumed a voluntary transformation of Indians. The assimilation policy advocated by the Friends was comprehensive and compulsory.

Richard Pratt and Indian Boarding Schools

In Richard H. Pratt both the Friends and the government found the person to create a new education policy. In April 1875 Pratt was placed in charge of a group of seventy-two Indian prisoners from several tribes who he was to transport from the plains to Fort Marion, near St. Augustine, Florida. There the Indians were to be imprisoned. Pratt was a veteran of the Indian wars who had twice commanded Indian scouts. Because of his experience with the Indian scouts, Pratt held the somewhat unusual view among contemporary Euro-Americans that Indians were trustworthy and could learn white ways. Pratt did not accept Indian culture as the equal of his. Rather, he believed that through education Indians could be "elevated" to white standards. This opinion served as the starting point for an experiment in Indian education that would become federal policy.

At Fort Marion Pratt developed a "prison school" to acculture his prisoners into white society. Pratt immersed the prisoners in white culture, giving them European clothing, creating daily work routines to develop in them an appreciation for the European sense of time and labor, and giving the prisoners an opportunity to learn marketable vocational skills and use those skills to make money. Christianity, Pratt believed, was an important element in becoming part of the European community. Pratt held weekly Christian services for the prisoners and eventually encouraged them to attend denominational services in nearby St. Augustine. Finally, Pratt believed that the elimination of native language was critical to the success of his efforts. Thus, prisoners were taught the English language as well as the rudiments of reading and writing. Once the prisoners had obtained a basic competency in English all further instruction was in that language.

In 1878 the Fort Marion school came to an abrupt end when the War Department determined that conditions on the plains were such that the prisoners could be allowed to return west. Pratt believed that the now freed Indian prisoners would benefit from continued education. He persuaded the Hampton Normal and Agricultural Institute in Virginia to accept them. Hampton had been founded in 1867 to supply mechanical training to newly freed African-Americans. Twenty-two of Pratt's former prisoners voluntarily agreed to continue their education; seventeen at Hampton and five at other Eastern schools. Pratt himself was also assigned to Hampton.

Pratt's days at Hampton were few. Tireless in his advocacy, in 1879 Pratt convinced the Secretary of War to allow him to establish an independent Indian school at an abandoned military post in Carlisle, Pennsylvania.

Pratt opened Carlisle Industrial Training school on November 1, 1879. At Carlisle Pratt founded a multi-tribal, co-educational school that isolated the students from their tribal cultures and attempted to fully assimilate the students into a European lifestyle. In its now nearly perfected form the school employed military, cadet-like training to teach the English language, basic academics, industrial training focused largely on agricultural skills, the importance of hard manual labor, and the need for remunerative employment. To further reinforce the value of the work ethic Pratt adopted the "outing system," in which student labor was contracted out to local farmers and other businesses, with the student receiving at least some of the wages earned. Native languages were banned and Christianity was strongly encouraged.

Government officials, who saw Carlisle as a potentially useful alternative to the expensive and bloody Indian campaigns in the West, and humanitarian reformers, who sought to assimilate Indians into European society, both rallied to the support of the educational policies employed at the new school. Carlisle became the model for a vision of Indian education that built upon military subjugation to achieve cultural assimilation. Pratt would remain at the school until his removal in 1904, and continue to argue vigorously for his vision of Indian education until his death in 1924. The General Allotment Act of 1887, more commonly referred to as the Dawes Act, incorporated the Carlisle model into government policy.

Thomas Morgan as Commissioner of Indian Affairs

Thomas Jefferson Morgan, appointed commissioner of Indian Affairs in 1889, vigorously supported the educational agenda created through the Dawes Act. Upon appointment as commissioner of Indian Affairs, he announced:

> "When we speak of education of the Indians, we mean that comprehensive system of training and instruction which will convert them into American citizens, put within their reach the blessings which the rest of us enjoy, and enable them to compete successfully with the white man on his own ground and with his own methods."

He saw his task in missionary terms, writing, "We must either fight Indians, feed them, or else educate them. To fight them is cruel, to feed them is wasteful, while to educate them is humane, economic, and Christian."

To accomplish his goals, Morgan expanded the number of off-reservation Indian boarding schools from seven to nineteen. Morgan controlled activities within these schools through a detailed volume of rules. The 1890, Rules for Indian Schools, explicitly established "preparation of Indian youth for assimilation into the national life" as the schools' overall objective. Over the course of eight years Morgan assumed Indians would receive two years of intensive English language training and the equivalent of a sixth grade education. An 1892 revision of the Rules added a ninth year of study and opened the door for kindergarten classes. The revision also specifically included efforts to promote Christianity by including in the curriculum memorization and recitation of the Lord's Prayer as well as the Beatitudes, the Psalms, and the ten commandments.

Although Morgan had created a primary school system, he consistently argued for more advanced courses. Like Pratt, Morgan disagreed with the day's popular wisdom regarding the ability of Indians to learn. Morgan believed Indians capable of significant intellectual achievement and argued that simply training Indians to be good farmers was insufficient.

When Indians resisted Morgan's program, he responded quickly and harshly. In 1892 he wrote to the Secretary of the Interior, to whom he reported, that while he preferred reasoning with Indian parents, he had also, "wherever it seemed wise, resorted to mild punishment by the withholding of rations or supplies, and where necessary, . . . directed Agents to use their Indian police as truant officers in compelling attendance." Further explaining himself Morgan wrote:

> *"I do not believe that Indians . . . people who for the most part speak no English, live in squalor and degradation, make little progress from year to year, who are a perpetual source of expense to the government and a constant menace to thousands of their white neighbors, a hindrance to civilization and a clog on our progress have any right to forcibly keep their children out of school to grow up like themselves, a race of barbarians and semi-savages."*

Like Pratt, Morgan saw no value in Indian culture.

Vocational Education

In 1901 Estelle Reel, who now headed Indian education, concluded that her predecessors efforts had failed in accomplishing the basic goal of assimilation. To accomplish this objective Reel favored vocational education over academics. The goal, in Reel's words, was to make Indians "self-supporting as speedily as possible." Given this goal, Reel believed that "literary instruction should be secondary, and industrial training of primary importance in the system of Indian education." The 1901 curriculum sent forth by Reel focused attention on teaching agricultural skills. It was fairly explicit in stating the assumption that Indians would never advance beyond the lower economic stratas of American society and brutally pragmatic in observing that, whatever talents an Indian child might have, more advanced education had little demonstrable impact on the assimilation of Native youth.

The 1901 curriculum, in contrast to those found in earlier editions of the Rules, did allow for the teaching of Native American art forms, particularly basket making. The motive for these courses, however, was economic rather than cultural. Reel acknowledged that there was both a practical and collectible market for these products. Thus basket weaving skills could help Indians be self-supporting. Reel also acknowledged that in places where farming was impractical, such as the desert southwest, baskets and other art work was a more viable source of income.

Reel's adoption of a curriculum that lowered expectations for Indian students did not go unchallenged. Former Indian Commissioner Morgan was outraged. In 1902 he wrote,

> *"Every child born into the Republic is entitled to claim as his birthright such kind and degree of education as will fit him for good citizenship. The Indian child has a right to demand of the government, which has assumed responsibility for his training, that he shall not be hopelessly handicapped by such an inferior training as from the very beginning dooms him to failure. . ."*

Despite criticism, Reel continued in her post until 1910, pursuing with vigor her new curriculum.

Long after Reel left her post, her views continued to strongly influence education at the Indian boarding schools. A 1915 revision of the Rules further limited the academic curriculum. As early as the first grade Indian girls were taught sewing, weaving, and lace work, at the expense of basic English language and reading skills. In fact, the 1915 Rules went so far in the direction of a prescriptive vocational education that they were criticized by white public school reformers.

Criticism By Euro-Americans

By the mid-1920's discontent over the state of Indian education was high. Sharp public criticism led Secretary of the Interior Hubert Work to request the Washington-based Brookings Institute investigate Indian education. In 1928 the Institute published a then definitive study, The Problem of Indian Administration, more commonly referred to as Meriam Report after its principal author Lewis Meriam.

The Meriam report criticized the physical plant of the schools, the care given the students, and the core ideas behind education in Indian schools. It found overcentralized government-run schools employing a rigid and largely discredited curriculum. The report concluded that despite the official rhetoric regarding the centrality of vocational education, in practice students seeking vocational training were poorly served.

> *"Very little of the work provided in Indian boarding schools is directly vocational in the sense that it is aimed at a specific vocation which the youngster is to pursue, or based upon a study of known industrial opportunities, and vocational direction in the form of proper guidance, placement, and follow-up hardly exists at all."*

Although the Report criticized as ineffective the government's implementation of vocational education, it went much further and called upon the government to completely change the nature of education in Indian schools. Indian schools should abandon their single minded quest for assimilation and replace it with a child-centered educational approach that would maximize the vocational and academic achievements of each student. To accomplish this most effectively the report called for the inclusion of key elements of Indian life and culture into the curriculum. Although never using the word, the Meriam report in practice endorsed a multi-cultural education for Indian children that allowed each child to retain significant elements of their tribal culture while at the same time develop fully his or her Euro-American defined academic potential.

The Meriam report was a significant checkpoint in Indian education. Its findings and recommendations became widely distributed and very influential when the popular magazine Good Housekeeping ran a series of articles drawn largely from the report. Embarrassed into action by public outrage over the poor treatment given to Indian children, the Hoover administration almost doubled spending on Indian schools between 1928 and 1933.

Most of this money was spent on improving the schools' physical plant as well as improving the diet and medical attention received by the children. The administration also placed greater emphasis in on-reservation education, at the expense of the already hard pressed off-reservation boarding schools. Indeed, to save money, many off-reservation schools, including the one at Mount Pleasant, were closed in this era. Although overall living conditions improved, the curricular changes recommended in the report were largely ignored. At least until World War II government run Indian schools continued to offer students a vocational education program largely defined by Estelle Reel at the beginning of the twentieth century.

THE INDIAN EXPERIENCE

A Parent's Dilemma

The federal government's Indian education policy created tremendous tension among America's Indian population. Traditionalists strongly opposed sending children to distant schools to learn the "white man's" ways. They rightly understood that the objective of the schools was completely antithetical to the traditional way of Indian life, learning, and custom. Shrewd parents told their children that owls, bears, and white men would harm them, leading the children to flee at the sight of a white man. Women seemed particularly reluctant to release their daughters, perhaps reflecting the particularly close mother-daughter relationships that existed in tribal society.

However the grinding poverty and seeming hopelessness of reservation life caused many Indian parents to consider the possibility of sending their children to learn the white man's ways, and hopefully find a more prosperous life, albeit not a traditional one. Children who were orphans or had lost a parent were particularly likely to be sent away. Alice Littlefield, who has studied the Mount Pleasant Indian School extensively, has written that "by the 1920s Mt. Pleasant was in large part an institution emphasizing care for orphans and the children of the poor." Almost two-thirds of the students in the Mount Pleasant Indian School came from homes were one or both parents were missing. Although both contemporary documents and Littlefield's writing acknowledge that Mount Pleasant's school had a particularly high percentage of orphaned children, Brenda J. Child, who has researched attendance at boarding schools by Chippewa living in Wisconsin and Minnesota, echoes Littlefield's finding in that many children from the Red Lake Reservation were sent to Indian Boarding schools due to the death of one or both parents.

Indian agents anxious to comply with Washington's desire to send children to the distant boarding schools also pressured parents to allow their children to leave. Sometimes the agents simply resorted to force. Brenda J. Child recounts how at the beginning of the twentieth century police used a compulsory school attendance law passed in 1898 to round up "students" on the Red Lake Reservation to be sent to boarding schools.

Indian families bitterly resented the control white officials exercised over their children. Not only could the officials round up their children and send them away but they also controlled if and when the children would return home for visits. Child notes the frustration of one mother who wrote to a boarding school superintendent, "It seems it would be much easier to get her out of prison than out of your school." It was not until 1933, when assimilation was waning as an educational goal, that off-reservation boarding school students were routinely allowed to go home for summer vacation.

The decision to send a child away was extraordinarily difficult. Indian parents understood the painful effects separation would have on a child and the impact of the school's military-like lifestyle. "You will cry for me, but they will not even soothe you." one mother warned her departing child. Other parents drew a comparison between a child's going to a boarding school and death itself. After receiving a letter from her daughter, one mother said, "the place has become full of ghosts." The parents understood that even if the school's officials and teachers cared appropriately for their children's physical well being, a point about which they had good reason to worry, a child's cultural and spiritual development would likely be changed forever.

In many cases, even if the parents voluntarily agreed to send a child to a boarding school, the child resisted, fleeing home and hiding in the woods or with sympathetic relatives. Because of this the child was often not told in advance of the decision. One student who attended a boarding school in the southwest recalled that on the day that he left, his mother had simply handed him a lunch and sent him off to a day school he was attending. When he arrived for his day's lessons, he was informed he was to leave immediately. He and several other students were placed in a truck equipped with a wire cage, to keep them from fleeing, and driven to the nearest railroad station. The trauma of such a parting, on both parent and child, can only be imagined.

A Student's First Days

An Indian student's first days at an off reservation boarding school were extraordinarily difficult. Suddenly thrust into an institution that their previous experience had given them no way of comprehending they were often in shock. One woman later wrote of the experience,

> "My long travel and the bewildering sights had exhausted me. I fell asleep, heaving deep, tired sobs. My tears were left to dry themselves in streaks, because neither my aunt nor my mother was near to wipe them away."

Procedures which were of little consequence to the school authorities could induce tremendous trauma among the students. One girl, for example, had to be pulled from under her bed and held in order for her hair to be cut. She later explained,

"Our mother's had taught us that only unskilled warriors who were captured had their hair shingled by the enemy. Among our people, short hair was worn by mourners, and shingled hair by cowards."

Another student wrote, many years after the experience, that

It is almost impossible to explain to a sympathetic white person what a typical old Indian boarding school was like; how it affected the Indian child suddenly dumped into it like a small creature from another world, helpless, defenseless, bewildered, trying desperately and instinctively to survive it all."

Some students never came to terms with life in a boarding school. Other children did adjust, at least marginally, to this strange new world. Some flourished and did assimilate white values. An example of how Indian Boarding schools affected the pupils who stayed in them can be found by looking at authors who have studied Boarding schools to which Chippewa children were sent. One of these boarding schools operated in Mount Pleasant Michigan, from 1893 until 1933.

The Use of English

English was the official language of all Indian schools. Until the 1920's use of Native American languages would be punished. An Indian caught speaking a native tongue might have his or her mouth washed out with soap or might suffer some other, more severe, penalty. Some children who spent several years at school found that when they returned home to the reservation they had difficulty communicating with their Ojibway-speaking parents.

Many students resisted the loss of their Native tongue. These students employed a variety of ways to maintain fluency in their mother tongue. Child tells the story of one young woman who retained her fluency by silently praying in Ojibway at the compulsory church services. In Mount Pleasant, by the 1920's punishment for the use of Ojibway had become relatively infrequent. Child also notes that in some Indian schools the children were also strongly encouraged to accept a "Christian" name in place of their Indian name. School officials considered Indian names an unpronounceable remnant of a "pagan" past. A student who translated his or her Indian name into English was often mocked by instructors.

Daily Routine

Daily life at the Mount Pleasant school was similar to that at all the Indian Boarding schools. As defined in the "Rules," students lived a quasi-military life-style. They rose and went to bed upon a signal. The wore uniforms, were organized into "companies" under the command of student captains and majors, and were expected to marched from activity to activity.

The student's day was divided roughly in half. A half day was spent in class, the balance of the day was spent in "vocational" education, which could consist either of formal study or "work details" that performed routine cleaning and maintenance activities around the school. Given the curriculum's emphasis on agricultural education the students engaged in a wide variety of agriculturally-related tasks. In Mount Pleasant the students grew potatoes, corn, wheat, and hay, kept vegetable gardens, apple orchards, and vineyards, and also cared for chickens, pigs, dairy cows, and draft horses. In addition the "outing" system was employed in Mount Pleasant, particularly during the summer. Many students worked in sugar beet fields, a crop requiring a great deal of hand cultivation. Male students served as seasonal laborers on area farms while female students often found summer employment as domestic help.

Living Conditions

Living conditions were usually spartan, however, because so many of the children came from backgrounds of extreme poverty school conditions were often better than those at home. By the twentieth century school buildings were often run down and crowded. Children usually slept in dormitories that placed thirty or forty students in a large room. Students bathed once or twice weekly, otherwise washing in community troughs. Soap, in the words of the Meriam report, "was rarely immediately accessible." Indoor toilets were usually provided, however the Meriam report found them in poor repair and in at least half of the toilets visited by report staff lacking in toilet paper due to budgetary shortfalls.

Students had very little privacy. The slept and ate in communal facilities. After bathing or showering students used communal dressing rooms equipped with long wooden benches to dry and dress. Correspondence either sent to or written by the student was routinely read by school staff.

Food

The quality of food given the students was a point of considerable contention. Many students recall the food as being at least adequate. The Meriam report, however, was quite critical of the food. The report suggested widespread malnutrition among students and in some cases actual food shortages. The diet at the schools usually focused on meat and starches, with fresh vegetables or fruit rarely served. A typical supper might include bread, stew, or meat with gravy. This problem particularly irked many reformers because most of the schools emphasized the learning of agricultural skills and maintained substantial farming operations. It had become customary, however, to produce cash crops to supplement the schools budget rather than raise crops to feed the students.

The Meriam report estimated that to adequately feed children in the schools the government should allow thirty-five cents per day per student. The report's staff calculated that the government actually spent eleven cents per day per student on food. Students expressed their concern over food somewhat differently. Littlefield records the following ditty, told to her by two former students from the Mount Pleasant School:

Six o'clock in the morning,
Our breakfast comes around.
A bowl of mush and molasses,
Was enough to knock you down.
Our coffee's like tobacco juice,
Our bread is hard and stale,
and that's the way they treat you
At Mt. Pleasant Indian Jail.

Health

In part because of the inadequate sanitary conditions and marginal diet, students' health was often poor. Health conditions were made worse, however, by the conscious decision to enroll sick children and allow them to freely mingle with healthy students. Despite rules to the contrary this practice was commonplace at Indian schools. As a results epidemics of trachoma, tuberculosis, and other diseases were endemic. In 1912 children with active cases of tuberculosis were officially banned from enrolling in Indian schools, but as late as 1924 Child documents the presence of children with active cases of tuberculosis in boarding schools.

In the first years of the twentieth century over one-half of all children in off-reservation boarding schools suffered from trachoma, an eye disease which if left untreated causes blindness in approximately one percent of its victims. Trachoma is easily caught and is usually associated with unsanitary conditions and poor living standards. Until the development of an effective treatment in 1937 the disease was very difficult to cure. Congress in 1909 voted some funds to help deal with the disease but very little effective work was accomplished.

Deaths among students were not uncommon. A policy to not share information with parents about "minor" illnesses could lead to stunning consequences. One can only imagine the reaction of the father who, unaware that his daughter was ill, received in the mail this letter:

Dear Sir:

It is with a feeling of sorrow that I write you telling of the death of your daughter Lizzie. She was not sick but a short time and we did not think her so near her end. On the evening of March 30th, I was at the girls building and the matron informed me that Lizzie had gone to bed not feeling well. I went up to her room and with the matron and found her in bed with what seemed a bad cold. . . . She had quite a fever for several days and then seemed to improve, but did not rally as she ought to have done, and the doctor made a careful examination and said that she was without doubt going into quick consumption. . . . Last

Wednesday I was called away to Minneapolis and . . . I was very much surprised upon my return Saturday evening to find she was dad [sic], as the doctor had given us no information except she might live for a number of months."

The superintendent closed his letter by expressing his sympathy and noting,

"Had we known that she was not going to live but so short a time, we would have made a great effort to have gotten you here before she died. . ."

Merely being diagnosed as dying was insufficient in itself to justify a letter to Lizzie's parents. Her death needed to be imminent.

Punishments

Infractions of the many rules usually resulted in the withdrawal of privileges or the assignment of extra work details. However more severe punishments also occurred. Students might be deprived of a meal. Girls were often forced to kneel for an extended period on a hard surface and boys and girls were occasionally beaten with a strap or rubber hose. Particularly in the nineteenth century flogging with a whip was also allowed. Flogging and other extreme forms of punishment were not banned formally until 1929. Even then rules regarding extreme punishments remained muddy because of a 1930 statement that may might be allowed in "emergency situations."

Run-Aways

Students did run away. A few from the Mount Pleasant school made it back to Michigan's upper peninsula by hitching rides on freight trains and sneaking aboard ferries. However the most common reason cited for fleeing a boarding school was homesickness rather than poor treatment.

BIBLIOGRAPHIC NOTE

Much of the material used in writing this section came from Jeffrey Louis Hamley, "Cultural Genocide in the Classroom: A History of the Federal Boarding School Movement in American Indian Education, 1875–1920," unpublished Ph.D. dissertation, Harvard University, 1994 and Francis Paul Prucha, The Great Father: The United State Government and the American Indians (Lincoln: University of Nebraska Press, 1984). Carol Devens, "'If We Get the Girls, We Get the Race': Missionary Education of Native American Girls," Journal of World History 3 (1992): 219–237 was used to help document the reaction of Indian parents and children to boarding schools, although Green's article discusses boarding schools run by religious missionaries rather than the federal government. Discussion of the Mount Pleasant School was taken from Alice Littlefield, "Indian Education and the World of Work in Michigan, 1893–1933," published in Alice Littlefield and Martha C. Knack, eds. Native Americans and Wage Labor (Norman: University of Oklahoma Press, 1996); Alice Littlefield, "The BIA Boarding School," Humanity & Society 13 (1989): 428–441; Alice Littlefield, "Learning to Labor: Native American Education in the United States, 1880–1930," in John H. Moore, Ed., The Political Economy of North American Indians (Norman: University of Oklahoma Press, 1993), 43–59. Discussion of school life also came from Brenda J. Child, Boarding School Seasons: American Indian Families, 1900–1940 (Lincoln: University of Nebraska Press, 1998) and Robert A. Trennert, Jr., The Phoenix Indian School: Forced Assimilation in Arizona, 1891–1935 (Norman: University of Oklahoma Press, 1988).

Against Schooling: Education and Social Class

—*Stanley Aronowitz*

". . the crisis in American education, on the one hand, announces the bankruptcyof progressive education and, on the other hand, presents a problem of immense difficulty because it has arisen under the conditions and in response to the demands of a mass society" Hannah Arendt, 1961)

INTRODUCTION

Americans have great expectations of their schools. We tend to invest them with the primary responsibility for providing our children with the means by which they may succeed in an increasingly uncertain work world. More, if the child "fails" to be inducted, through academic discipline, into the rituals of labor—we blame teachers and school administrators. Indirectly schools have been burdened with addressing many of the world's ills. Along with two world wars, and revolutions, the 20th century witnessed great hopes for democracy but experienced its demise in the wake of the rise of the dictatorships. We knew that education was the key to technological transformation which became the main engine of economic growth. Schooling was a bulwark of secularism but has buckled under the onslaught produced by the revival of religious fundamentalism. And in almost every economically "developed" country we count on schools to smooth the transition of huge populations from rural to urban habitats, from "foreign" languages and cultures to English and Americanism.

At the dawn of the new century no American institution is invested with a greater role to bring the young and their parents into the modernist regime than public schools. The common school is charged with the task of preparing children and youth for their dual responsibilities to the social order: citizenship and, perhaps its primary task, learning to labor. On the one hand, in the older curriculum on the road to citizenship in a democratic, secular society schools are supposed to transmit the jewels of the enlightenment, especially literature and science. On the other, students are to be prepared for work world by means of a loose, but definite stress on the redemptive value of work, the importance of family and, of course, the imperative of love and loyalty to one's country. As to the enlightenment's concept of citizenship students are, at least putatively, encouraged to engage in independent, critical thinking.

But the socializing functions of schooling play to the opposite idea: children of the working and professional and middle classes are to be molded to the industrial and technological imperatives of contemporary society. Students learn science and mathematics, not as a discourse of liberation from myth and religious superstition, but as a series of algorithms the mastery of which are presumed to improve the student's logical capacities, or with no aim other than fulfilling academic requirements . In most places the social studies do not emphasize the choices between authoritarian and democratic forms of social organization, or democratic values, particularly criticism and renewal, but as bits of information that have little significance for the conduct of life. Perhaps the teaching and learning of world literature where some students are inspired by the power of the story to, in John Dewey's terms "reconstruct" experience is a partial exception to the rule that for most students high school is endured rather than experienced as a series of exciting explorations of self and society. (Dewey, 1980)

In the wake of these awesome tasks fiscal exigency as well as a changing mission have combined to leave public education in the United States in a chronic state of crisis. For some the main issue is whether schools are failing to transmit the general intellectual culture, even to the most able students. What is at stake in this critique is the fate of America as a civilization, particularly the condition of its democratic institutions and the citizens who are, in the final analysis, responsible for maintaining them. Hannah Arendt goes so far as to ask whether we "love the world" and our children enough to devise an educational system capable of transmitting to them the salient cultural traditions. Other critics complain schools are failing working class students, black, Latino and white, to fulfill the promise of equality of opportunity for good jobs. While they are concerned to address the class bias of schooling they unwittingly reinforce it by ignoring its content.

The two positions, both with respect to their goals and to their implied educational philosophies, may not necessarily be contradictory but their simultaneous enunciation produces considerable tension for, with exceptions to be discussed below, the American workplace has virtually no room for dissent and individual or collective initiative not sanctioned by management. The corporate factory, which includes sites of goods and symbolic production alike, is perhaps the nation's most authoritarian institution. But any reasonable concept of democratic citizenship requires an individual who is able to discern knowledge from propaganda, is competent to choose among conflictual claims and programs and is capable of actively participating in the affairs of the polity. Yet the political system offers few opportunities, beyond the ritual of voting, for active citizen participation. (Arendt,1961)

Even identifying the problem of why and how schools fail has proven to be controversial. For those who would define mass education as a form of training for the contemporary workplace, the problem can be traced to the crisis of authority, particularly school authority. That some of the same educational analysts favor a curriculum that stresses critical thinking for a small number of students in a restricted number of sites is consistent with the dominant trends of schooling since the turn of the 21st century. In their quest to restore authority conservative educational policy has forcefully caused schools to abandon, both rhetorically and practically, the so-called "child-centered" curriculum and pedagogy in favor of a series of measures that not only hold students accountable for passing standardized tests and for a definite quantity of school knowledge on penalty of being left back from promotion or expelled, but also impose performance-based criteria on administrators and teachers. For example in New York City the schools chancellor has issued "report cards" to principals and has threatened to fire those whose schools do not meet standards established by high stakes tests. These tests are the antithesis of critical thought. Their precise object is to evaluate the student's ability to imbibe and regurgitate information and to solve problems according to prescribed algorithms.

On the other side the progressives, who misread John Dewey's educational philosophy to mean that the past need not be studied too seriously, have offered little resistance to the gradual vocationalizing, and dumbing down of the mass education curriculum. In fact, historically they were advocates of making the curriculum less formal, reducing requirements and, on the basis of a degraded argument that children learn best by "doing", promoted practical, work-oriented programs for high school students. Curricular deformalization was often justified on interdisciplinary criteria, which resulted in watering-down of course content and de-emphasizing writing. Most American high school students, in the affluent as well as the "inner city" districts, may write short papers which amount to book reviews and autobiographical essays, but most graduate without ever having to perform research and write a paper of considerable length. Moreover, in an attempt to make the study of history more "relevant" to students' lives, since the late 1960s the student is no longer required to memorize dates; he may have learned the narratives but was often unable to place them in a specific chronological context. Similarly economics has been eliminated in many schools or taught as a "unit" of a general social studies course. And if philosophy is taught at all, it is construed in terms of "values clarification", a kind of ethics in which the student is assisted to discover and examine her own values.

That after more than a century of universal schooling the relationship between education and class has once more been thrust to the forefront is just one more signal of the crisis in American education. The educational left, never strong on promoting intellectual knowledge as a substantive demand, clings to one of the crucial precepts of progressive educational philosophy: under the sign of egalitarianism, the idea that class deficits can be overcome by equalizing access to school opportunities without questioning what those opportunities have to do with genuine education. The access question has been in the forefront of higher education debates since the early 1970s; even conservatives who favor vouchers and other forms of public funding for private and parochial schools have justified privatizing instruction on access grounds.

The structure of schooling already embodies the class system of society and, for this reason, the access debate is mired in a web of misplaced concreteness. To gain entrance into schools always entails placement into that system. "Equality of Opportunity" for class mobility is the system's tacit recognition that inequality in normative. In the system of mass education schools are no longer constituted to transmit the enlightenment intellectual traditions or the fundamental prerequisites of participatory citizenship, even for a substantial minority. While acquiring credentials that are conferred by schools remains an important prerequisite for many occupations, the conflation of schooling with education is mistaken. Schooling is surely a source of training both by its disciplinary regime and its credentialing system. But schools transmit not a "love for the world" or "for our children" as Arendt suggests and, contrary to their democratic pretensions, teach conformity to the social, cultural and occupational hierarchy. In our contemporary world they are not constituted to foster independent thought, let alone encourage independence of thought and action. School knowledge is not the only source of education for students, perhaps not even the most important source.

On the contrary, in black and Latino working class districts, schools are, for many students, way stations to the military or to prison even more to the civilian paid labor force. As Michelle Fine observes: "visit a South Bronx high school these days and you'll find yourself surrounded by propaganda from the army/navy and marines. . . look at the "stats" and you'll see that 70% of the men and women in prison have neither a GED or a diploma; go to Ocean Hill–Brownsville 40ish years later, and you "see a juvenile justice facility on the very site that they wanted to a build their own schools".(personal communication with the author). In the current fiscal crisis afflicting education and other social services there is an outstanding exception: prisons continue to be well-funded and despite the decline of violent crimes in the cities, drug busts keep prisons full and rural communities working.

Young people learn, for ill as well as good, from popular culture, especially music, from parents and family structure, and perhaps most important, from their peers. Schools are the stand in for "society", the aggregation of individuals who, by contract or by coercion, are subject to governing authorities in return for which they may be admitted into the world albeit on the basis of different degrees of reward. To the extent they signify solidarity and embody common dreams popular culture, parents, and peers are the worlds of quasi-communities which are more powerful influences on their members.

ACCESS TO WHAT?

In the main the critique of education has been directed to the question of access its entailments particularly the credentials that presumably open up the gates to the higher learning or to better jobs. Generally speaking, critical education analysis focuses on the degree to which schools are willing and able to open their doors to working class students, because through their mechanisms of differential access, schools are viewed as, perhaps, the principal reproductive institutions of economically and technologically advanced capitalist societies. With some exceptions most critics of schooling have paid scant attention to school authority, the conditions for the accumulation of social capital—the intricate network of personal relations that articulate with occupational access—, and to cultural capital—the accumulation of the signs, if not the substance, of kinds of knowledge that are markers of distinction.

The progressives assume that the heart of the class question is whether schooling provides working class kids equality of opportunity to acquire legitimate knowledge and marketable academic credentials. They have adduced overwhelming evidence that contradicts schooling's reigning doctrine: that despite class, race, or gender hierarchies in the economic and political system, public education provides every individual with the tools to overcome conditions of birth. In reality only about a quarter of people of working class origin attain professional, technical and managerial careers through the credentialing system. They find occupational niches, but not at the top of their respective domains. Typically graduating from third tier, non-research colleges and universities their training does not entail acquiring knowledge connected with substantial intellectual work: theory, extensive writing and independent research. Students leaving these institutions find jobs as line supervisors, computer technicians, teachers, nurses, social workers and other niches in the social service professions.

A small number may join their better educated colleagues in getting no collar jobs, where "no collar"—Andrew Ross's term—designates occupations which afford considerable work autonomy, such as computer design, which, although salaried, cannot be comfortably folded into the conventional division of manual and intellectual labor. That so-called social mobility, was a product of the specific conditions of American economic development at a particular time—the first quarter of the 20th century—and was due, principally, to the absence of an indigenous peasantry during its industrial revolution and the forced confinement of millions of blacks to southern agricultural lands—is conveniently forgotten or ignored by consensus opinion. Nor were the labor shortages provoked by World War Two and the subsequent US dominance of world capitalism until 1973 taken into account by the celebrants of mobility. Economic stagnation has afflicted the United States economy for more than three decades and, despite the well-known high-tech bubble of the 1990s, its position has deteriorated in the world market.

Yet, the mythology of mobility retains a powerful grip over the popular mind. That schooling makes credentials available to anyone regardless of rank or status, forms one of the sturdy pillars of American ideology. (Ross 2003)

In recent years the constitutional and legal assignment to the states and local communities of responsibility for public education has been undermined by what has been termed the "standards" movement which is today the prevailing national educational policy, enforced not so much by federal law as by political and ideological coercion. At the state and district levels the invocation to "tough love" has attained widespread support. We are witnessing the abrogation, both in practice and in rhetoric, of the tradition of social promotion whereby students moved through the system without acquiring academic skills. Having proven unable to provide to most working class kids the necessary educational experiences that qualify them for academic promotion, after more than decade after its installation, the standards movement reveals its underlying content: it is the latest means of exclusion whose success depends on placing the onus for failure to achieve academic credentials on the individual rather than the system. Although state departments of education frequently mandate certain subjects be taught in every school and have established standards based on high stakes tests applicable to all districts, everyone knows that districts with working-class majorities provide neither a curriculum and pedagogy nor facilities which meet these standards because, among other problems, they are chronically underfunded. But there is no shortage of money for the private corporations who are making huge profits on school systems High stakes testing, a form of privatization, transfers huge amounts of public money to publishers, testing organizations and large consulting companies. The state aid formulae which, since the advent of conservative policy hegemony, reward those districts whose students perform well on high stakes standardized tests, tend to be unequal. Performance based aid policies means that school districts where the affluent live get more than their share, and make up for state budget deficits by raising local property taxes and soliciting annual subventions from parents, measures not affordable by even the top layer of wage-workers, and low-level salaried employees. The result is overcrowded classrooms, poor facilities, especially libraries, and underpaid, often poorly prepared teachers, an outcome of financially- starved education schools in public universities.

Standards presuppose students' prior possession of cultural capital, —an acquisition which almost invariably entails having been reared in a professional or otherwise upper class family. That, in the main, even the most privileged elementary and secondary schools are ill-equipped to compensate for home backgrounds in which reading and writing are virtually absent, has become a matter of indifference for school authorities. In this era of social Darwinism poor school performance is likely to be coded as genetic deficit rather than being ascribed to social policy. Of course the idea that working-class kids, whatever their gender, race or ethnic backgrounds, were selected by evolution or by God, to perform material rather than immaterial labor is not new; this view is as old as class divided societies. But in an epoch in which the chances of obtaining a good working class job have sharply diminished, most kids face dire consequences if they don't acquire the skills needed in the world of immaterial labor. Not only are 75% assigned to working class jobs but in the absence of a shrinking pool of unionized industrial jobs, which often pay more than some professions such as teaching and social work, they must accept low-paying service sector employment, enter the informal economy, or join the ranks of the chronically unemployed.

From 1890–1920, the greatest period of social protest in American history before the industrial union upsurge of the 1930s John Dewey, the leading educational philosopher of the progressive era, decisively transformed class discourse about education into a discourse of class-leveling. Dewey's philosophy of education is a brilliant piece of bricolage: it combines an acute sensitivity to the prevailing inequalities in society with a pluralist theory which, by definition, excludes class struggles as a strategy for achieving democracy. It was a feat that could have been achieved only by tapping into the prevailing radical critique of the limits of American democracy. But Dewey's aim was far from founding a new educational or political radicalism. True to the pragmatist tradition of "tinkering" rather than transforming institutions, Dewey sought to heal the breach between labor and capital through schooling. To the extent schools afforded workers' children access to genuine education, American democracy—and the Americanization of waves of new immigrants—would be secure.

Dewey was not only America's pre-eminent philosopher, he was a major intellectual spokesperson of the progressive movement at a time when social reform had achieved high visibility and had enormous influence over both legislation and public opinion, principally among wide sections of the middle class as well as in the higher circles of power. Not only did his writings help bring education into the center of intellectual and political discourse by arguing that a society that wished to overcome the stigma of class distinction associated with industrial capitalism had to fervently embrace universal schooling. He was able to elaborate the doctrine that schooling was the heart of education, the core institution for the reproduction of liberal-democratic society, and the basis for the objective of class leveling . In the end "democracy in education" signifies that by means of universal schooling all children, regardless of class origins, could have access to social mobility. Which is not egalitarian at all.

Democracy and Education (1916), Dewey's main philosophical statement on education may be viewed in the context of the turn of the 20th century emergence of mass public education which, among other goals, was designed to address a multitude of problems that accompanied the advent of industrial society and the emergence of the United States as a world power: the enormous task of "Americanizing"—ideological education—millions of immigrants' children, most of whom were of the working class; the rise of scientifically-based industrial and commercial technologies that, in the service of capital, required a certain level of verbal, scientific, and mathematical literacy of a substantial portion of the wage-labor force; and the hard-won recognition by economic and political authorities as well as the labor movement that child labor had deleterious consequences for the future of the capitalist system and, in an era of rapid technological change, the fact that industrial labor had become relatively expendable. In this context the high school became an important ageing vat or warehouse, whether adolescents learned anything or not. As Mchael B. Katz has shown this latter concern was the basis of the public education movement in the 19th century the question for educators, law enforcement officials and political and economic leaders was what to do with unemployed youth during the day. The day-prison was one solution but Horace Mann prevailed upon his colleagues to establish public schools as a more "productive" way of containing unruly youngsters. Later the institution was expanded from six to twelve grades and the minimum age for leaving rose from twelve to sixteen. After a century of compulsory secondary schooling, the educational value of high schools is still in doubt (Katz, 1970).

At the outset, Dewey specifies the purposes of education: through adult transmission and communication to assist the young to direct their own lives. Dewey cautions adults that, since the young hold in their hands society's future, the nature of their transmissions inevitably have serious consequences. Yet, having recognized, briefly, the role of "informal" education in the self-formation of the young, Dewey establishes the rule for virtually all subsequent educational philosophy. Consistent with a liberal democratic society educators are admonished to devise a formal method for directing the future: by organization of a common school that provides the necessary discipline, array of learnings and methods by which learning that reproduces the social order, may occur. While transmitting and communicating knowledge are intended to provide "meaning to experience", and Dewey invokes "democratic criteria" as the basis for his concept of the "reconstruction of experience", the objective of "control and growth" in order to achieve "social continuity" occupies an equally important place in any educational enterprise to the creative possibilities of education. (Dewey,1980, 331).

Dewey walks a tightrope between the creative side of education as a playful and imaginative reflection on experience and the necessary task of reproducing the social order in which work, albeit as much as possible creative, remains the key educational goal. But he also endorses the role of the school for training the labor force. Dewey advocated for the ability of children to obtain the knowledge that could aid in their quest for an autonomous future even as he approached the problem of moral education (character building, values) from the perspective of society's need to reproduce itself on the basis of the criteria inherited from the past. He deplores the separation of labor and leisure, the cleavage of liberal arts and vocational education in which the former is regarded as activity to be tolerated but not enjoyed. Labor should not be viewed as a "job" but as much as possible, a "calling". Without addressing the nature of the rationalized labor to which wage workers, including most professional and technical workers are subjected, Dewey's educational philosophy is directed mostly to the ideal of educational humanism. Class distinctions are not denied but are assumed to be blurred, if not eliminated, by democratic education.

In both its critical and celebratory variants of his philosophy Dewey's intellectual children have not, with few exceptions, addressed the issue of whether, given its conflictual [sic] purposes and hierarchical organization, schools can fulfill its liberal democratic, let alone egalitarian promise. Having narrowly confined itself to school practices, post-Deweyan progressive educational thought has recoded his philosophy by invoking phrases such as "self-realization" and "child centered" to describe education's goals. Or worse, Dewey has been used to justify a relentless instrumentalism in curriculum design: in the name of anti-traditionalism and nationalism high schools do not teach philosophy, social history—principally the role of social movements in making history—or treat world literature as a legitimate object of academic study. Needless to say few, if any, critics have challenged the curricular exclusions of working class history, let alone the histories of women and of blacks. Nor have curricular critics addressed the exclusion of philosophy and social theory.

In recent years the philosophy of education has waned and been replaced by a series of policy-oriented empirical research projects that conflate democracy with access, and openly subordinate school knowledge to the priorities of the state and the corporations. Educational thought has lost, even renounced, Dewey's program directed to the reconstruction of experience. In fact, after the early grades student experience is viewed by many educators and administrators with suspicion, even hostility. Recent educational policy has veered towards delineating pre-school and kindergarten as sites for academic and vocational preparation. If the child is to grow to become a productive member of society—where productive is equated with work-ready—, play must be directed, free time severely constrained. The message emanating from school authorities is to "forget" all other forms and sites of learning. Academic and technical knowledge become the only legitimate forms, and the school is the only reliable site. Whatever its defects, in contrast to the penchant of modern educational researchers to focus on "policy" to the detriment of historical and theoretical analysis, Dewey's ideas demonstrate a passion for citizenship and ambivalence about the subordination of education to the imperatives of the system: he deplored the subordination of knowledge to the priorities of the state while, at the same time, extolling the virtues of the liberal state; he subjected vocational education to the scrutiny of the enlightenment prescription that education be critical of the existing state of affairs, while approving the reproductive function of schools.

The rise of higher education since world war two has been seen by many as a repudiation of academic elitism. Do not the booming higher education enrollments validate the propositions of social mobility and democratic education? Not at all. Rather than constituting a sign of rising qualifications and widening opportunity, burgeoning college and university enrollments signify changing economic and political trends. The scientific and technical nature of our production and service sectors increasing require qualified and credentialed workers (it would be a mistake to regard them as identical). Students who would have sought good factory jobs in the past now believe, with reason, they need credentials to qualify for a good-paying job. On the other hand even as politicians and educators decry social promotion, and most high schools with working-class constituencies remain ageing vats, mass higher education is, to a great extent, a holding pen by effectively masking unemployment and underemployment Which may account for its rapid expansion over the last thirty five years of chronic economic stagnation, deindustrialization and the proliferation of part-time and temporary jobs, largely in the low-paid service sectors. Consequently working-class students are able, even encouraged, to enter universities and colleges at the bottom of the academic hierarchy—community colleges but also public four year colleges—thus fulfilling the formal pledge of equal opportunity for class mobility even as most of these institutions suppress its content. But grade-point averages which, in the standards era depend as much as the Scholastic Aptitude Test on high stakes testing, measure the student's acquired knowledge, and restrict her access to elite institutions of higher learning, the obligatory training grounds for professional and managerial occupations. Since all credentials are not equal graduating from third and fourth tier institutions does not confer on the successful candidate the prerequisites for entering a leading graduate school—the preparatory institution for professional/managerial occupations, or the most desirable entry level service jobs which require only a bachelor's degree. (Aronowitz, 2000)

Pierre Bourdieu argues that schools reproduce class relations by reinforcing rather than reducing class-based differential access to social and cultural capital, key markers of class affiliation and mobility. These forms of capital, he argues, are always already possessed by children of the wealthy, professionals, and the intelligentsia.

Far from making possible a rich intellectual education, or providing the chance to affiliate with networks of students and faculty who have handles on better jobs, through mechanisms of discipline and punishment, schooling habituates working-class students to the bottom rungs of the work world, or the academic world, by subordinating or expelling them. (Bourdieu and Passeron 1979) Poorly prepared for academic work by their primary and secondary schools, and having few alternatives to acquiring some kind of credential, many who stay the course and graduate high school and third and fourth tier college, inevitably confront a series of severely limited occupational choices—or none at all. Their life chances are just a cut above those who do not complete high school or college. Their school performances seem to validate what commonsense has always suspected: given equal opportunity to attain school knowledge, the cream always rises to the top and those stuck at the bottom must be biologically impaired or victimized by the infamous "culture of poverty". That most working class high school and college students are obliged to hold full or part-time jobs in order to stay in school fails to temper this judgement for as is well known, preconceptions usually trump facts. (cicourel, 1963). Nor does the fact that children of the recent 20 million immigrants from Latin America and Asia, speak their native languages at home, in the neighborhood and to each other in school evoke more than hand-ringing from educational leaders; in this era of tight school budgets English as a second language funds have been cut or eliminated at every level of schooling.

But Paul Willis insists that working class kids get working class jobs by means of their refusal to accept the discipline entailed in curricular mastery and by their rebellion against school authority. Challenging the familiar "socialization" thesis, of which Bourdieu's is perhaps the most sophisticated version, according to which working class kids "fail" because they are culturally deprived or, in the American critical version, are assaulted by the hidden curriculum and school pedagogy which subsumes kids under the prevailing order, Willis recodes kids' failure as refusal of [school] work. (Willis 1981). Which lands them in the factory or low level service jobs. Willis offers no alternative educational model to schooling: his discovery functions as critique. Indeed, as Willis himself acknowledges the school remains, in Louis Althusser's famous phrase, the main "ideological state apparatus", but working class kids are not victims. Implicitly rejecting Sennett and Cobb's notion that school failure is a "hidden injury" of class insofar as working class kids internalize poor school performance as a sign of personal deficit, he argues that most early school leavers are active agents in the production of their own class position (Althusser, 1971); (Sennett and Cobb, 1973) While students' antipathy to school authority is enacted at the site of the school, its origins are the working class culture from which they spring. Workers do not like bosses and kids do not like school bosses, the deans and principals, but often as well the teachers, whose main job in the urban centers is to keep order. The source of working class kids' education is not the school but the shop-floor, where their parents work, the home and the neighborhood. About this more below.

In the past half century the class question has been inflected by race and gender discrimination and, in the American way, the "race, gender, class" phrase implies that these domains are ontologically distinct, if not entirely separate. Nor have they theorized the race and gender question as a class issue, but as an attribute of bio-identities. In fact in the era of identity politics class itself stands alongside race and gender as just another identity. Having made the easy, inaccurate, judgement that white students, regardless of their class or gender stand in a qualitatively different relation to school-related opportunities than blacks, class is often suppressed as a sign of exclusion. In privileging issues of access, not only is the curriculum presupposed, in which case Bourdieu's insistence on the concept of cultural capital is ignored, but also the entire question is elided of whether schooling may be conflated with education. Only rarely do writers examine other forms of education. In both the Marxist and liberal traditions schooling is presumed to remain, over a vast spectrum of spatial and temporal situations, the theatre within which life chances are determined.

EDUCATION AND IMMATERIAL LABOR

Education may be defined as the collective and individual reflection on the totality of life experiences: what we learn from peers, parents and the socially situated cultures of which they are a part, media, and schools. By reflection I mean the transformation of experience into a multitude of concepts that constitute the abstractions we call "knowledge". Which of the forms of learning predominate are always configured historically. The exclusive focus by theorists and researchers on school knowledge—indeed the implication that school is the principal site of what we mean by education—reflects the degree to which they have, themselves, internalized the equation of education with school knowledge and its preconditions. The key learning is they (we) have been habituated to a specific regime of intellectual labor which entails a high level of self-discipline, the acquisition of the skills of reading and writing, and the career expectations associated with professionalization.

To say this constitutes the self-reflection by intellectuals—in the broadest sense of the term—of their own relation to schooling. In the age of the decline of critical intelligence and the proliferation of technical intelligence "intellectual" in its current connotation, designates immaterial labor, not primarily those engaged in traditional intellectual pursuits such as literature, philosophy and art. Immaterial labor describes those who work not with objects or administration of things and people, but with ideas, symbols and signs. Some of the occupations grouped under immaterial labor have an affective dimension, particularly people who, in one way or another, care for each other. The work demands the complete subordination of brain, emotion and body to the task, while requiring the worker to exercise considerable judgement and imagination in its performance. At sites such as "new economy" private-sector software workplaces, some law firms that deal with questions of intellectual property, public interest, constitutional and international law, research universities and independent research institutes and small, innovative design, architectural and engineering firms, the informality of the labor process, close collaborative relationships among members of task-oriented teams, the overflow of the space of the shop floor with the spaces of home and play, evoke, at times, a high level of exhilaration, even giddiness among members. (Ross 2003) But these relationships are present in such work as teaching, child care, care for seniors and the whole array of therapeutic services, including psychotherapy.

To be an immaterial worker means, in the interest of having self-generated work, surrendering much of her unfettered time. They are obliged to sunder the conventional separation of work and leisure, to adopt the view that time devoted to creative, albeit commodified labor, is actually "free". Or, to be more exact, even play must be engaged in as serious business. For many the golf course, the bar, the weekend at the beach are work places, where dreams are shared, plans formulated, and deals are made. Just as time becomes unified around work, so work losses its geographic specificity. As Andrew Ross shows in his pathbreaking ethnography of a New York new economy workplace during, and after the dot.com boom, the headiness for the pioneers of this new work world was, tacitly, a function of the halcyon period of the computer software industry when everyone felt the sky was no longer the limit. When the economic crunch descended on thousands of workplaces, people were laid off and those who remained experienced a heavy dose of market reality.

It may be argued that among elite students and institutions schooling not only prepares immaterial labor by transmitting a bundle of legitimate knowledge; the diligent, academically successful student internalizes the blur between the classroom, play and the home by spending a great deal of time in the library or ostensibly playing at the computer. Thus the price of the promise of autonomy, a situation that is intrinsic to professional ideology, if not always its practice in the context of bureaucratic and hierarchical corporate systems, is to accept work as a mode of life; one lives to work, rather than the reverse. The hopes and expectations of these strata are formed in the process of schooling; indeed they have most completely assimilated the ideologies linked to school knowledge and to the credentials conferred by the system. Thus whether professional school people, educational researchers or not, they tend to evaluate people by the criteria to which they, themselves, were subjected. If the child has not fully embraced work as life, he is consigned to the educational netherland. Even the egalitarians (better read populists) accept this regime: their object is to afford those for whom work is a necessary evil into the social world where work is the mission.

MEDIA AND POPULAR CULTURE

Most educators and critics acknowledge the enormous role of media in contemporary life. The ubiquity and penetration of the visual media such as tv, vcr, dvd, and electronic oral equipment like cd and tape players into the home has called into question the separation of the public and private spheres, and challenged the notion that autonomous private life any longer exists. Which has prompted writers such as Hannah Arendt to insist on the importance of maintaining their separation.(Arendt, 1958) When taken together with the advent, in the technical as well as metaphoric sense, of "big brother" where the government now announces openly its intention to subject every telephone and computer to surveillance, it is difficult to avoid the conclusion that media are a crucial source of education and may, in comparison to schools, exercise a greater influence on children and youth. Many claim that television for example, is the prime source of political education, certainly the major source of news for perhaps a majority of the population. And there is a growing academic discourse of the importance of popular culture, especially music and film in shaping the values, but more to the point the cultural imaginary of children and adolescents. Many writers have noted the influence of media images on the dream work, on children's aspirations, on their measurement of self-worth, both physically and emotionally. Of course debate rages as to what is learned, for example, the implied frameworks that are masked by the face of objectivity presented by television news, and by fiction which, as everybody knows, is suffused with ethical perspective on everyday relations. (Horkheimer and Adorno 2002, Macdonald 1962, Mcluhan 1964).

Nor does every critic accept the conventional wisdom that, in the wake of the dominance of visual media in everyday life, we are, in the phrase of a leading commentator, "amusing ourselves to death", or that the ideological messages of popular music, sitcoms and other TV fare are simply conformist. (Postman 1986) But it must be admitted that since the 1920 and 1930s when critics argued that the possibility of a radical democracy in which ordinary people participated in the great and small decisions affecting their lives was undermined by the advent of the culture industry, popular culture has, to a large degree, become a weapon against, as well as for, the people. As a general rule, in periods of upsurge, when social movements succeed in transforming aspects of everyday life as well as the political landscape art, in its "high" as well as popular genres, has expressed popular yearning for a better world In this vein a vast literature, written largely by participants in the popular culture since the 1960s, rejects the sharp divide between high and low art. While many contemporary cultural critics such as Griel Marcus and Robert Christgau, acknowledge their debt to the work of the Critical Theory of the Frankfurt School, particularly that of Herbert Marcuse and Theodor Adorno, both by dint of their independent judgement, and the influence of Walter Benjamin—who, despite his elective affinity to critical theory welcomed, with some trepidation, the eclipse of high art—they find a subversive dimension in rock and roll music. (Marcus 1975; Christgau 2002) It may be that the 1960s phrase, "sex, drugs and rock n' roll" no longer resonates as a universal sign of rebellion. Yet, when evaluated from the perspective of a society still obsessed with drug use among kids, pre-marital sex and "blames" the music for this non-conformity, the competition between school and popular culture still rages. From anthems of rebellion to musical expressions of youth rejection of conventional sexual and political morality, critics have detected signs of resistance to official mores.

Of course even as punk signalled the conclusion of a sort of "golden age" of rock n' roll and the succeeding genres—heavy metal, alternative, techno among others—were confined to market niches, hip-hop took on some of the trapping of a universal oppositional cultural form which, by the 1990s, had captured the imagination of white as well as black kids. Out of the "bonfires" of the Bronx came a new generation of artists whose music and poetry enflamed the embers of discontent Figures such as Ice-T, Tupac, Biggie Small and many others articulated the still vibrant rebellion against what George Bernard Shaw had once called "middle class morality", and the smug, suburban confidence that the cities could be safely consigned to the margins. Like Dylan, some of the hip-hop artists were superb poets; Tupac had many imitators and, eventually the genre became fully absorbed by the culture industry, a development which, like the advent of the Velvets, the Who and other avant-garde rock groups of the early 1970s gave rise to an underground. And just as rock n' roll was accused of leading young people astray into the dungeons of drugs and illicit sex, the proponents of hip hop suffered a similar fate. Some record producers succumbed to demands they censor artistic material, radio stations refused to air some hip-hop, and record stores, especially in suburban malls, were advised to restrict sales of certain artists and records.

What white kids learn from successive waves of rock n' roll and hip-hop music is chiefly their right to defy ordinary conventions. After the mid-1950s, the varied genres of rock, rhythm and blues and hip-hop steadily challenged the class, racial and sexual constructs of this ostensibly egalitarian, but puritanical culture. Bored and dissatisfied with middle class morality and its cultural values, teenagers flooded the concerts of rock and hip-hop stars, smoked dope and violated the precepts of conventional sexual morality, to the best of their abilities. Many adopt black rhetoric, language and disdain for mainstream values. Of course, middle class kids are obliged to lead a double life: since their preferred artistic and cultural forms are accorded absolutely no recognition in the worlds of legitimate school knowledge and, for reasons we have already stated, they are in a double bind:. Since the 1960s their shared music and the messages of rebellion against a racist, conventional suburban, middle class culture has constituted a quasi-counter community. Yet on penalty of proscription they must absorb school knowledge without, invoking the counter-knowledge of popular culture.

The products of visual culture, particularly film and television, are no less powerful sources of knowledge. Since movies became a leading form of recreation early in the 20th century, critics have distinguished schlock from "films", produced both by the Hollywood system and by a beleaguered corps of independent filmmakers. In the 1920s, elaborating the dynamic film technique pioneered by D.W. Griffith the Soviet filmmakers, notably, Sergei Eisenstein and Zhiga Vertov and the great cultural critic, Siegfried Kracauer, fully comprehended the power of visual culture in its ornamental, aesthetic sense, and gave pride of place to film as a source of mass education. Vertov's *Man With a Movie Camera* and Eisenstein's *October* were not only great works of art they possessed enormous didactic power. (Kracauer 1995) Vertov evoked the romance of industrial reconstruction in the new Soviet regime and the imperative of popular participation in building a new technologically—directed social reality. And in most of his films Eisenstein was the master of revolutionary memory. The people should not forget the how brutal was the ancient regime and that the future was in their hands and he would produce the images that created a new "memory" even among those who had never experienced the heady days of the revolution. Of course Griffith conveyed a different kind of memory: in his classic *Birth of a* Nation he deconstructed the nobility and romance of the American Civil War and the Reconstruction period by depicting them a corrupt alliance of blacks and northern carpetbaggers, the epitaph applied to the staff of the Freemens Bureau and the military which had been dispatched to guarantee the newly won civil rights of millions of African Americans.

In 1950 anthropologist Hortense Powdermaker termed Hollywood "the dream factory". While we were entertained by the movies she argued, a whole world of hopes and dreams was being manufactured that had profound effects on our collective unconscious. Rather than coding these experiences as "illusion" she accorded them genuine social influence. With the later writings of Andre Bazin, Francois Truffault, Christian Metz, Stephen Heath, Laura Mulvey and Pauline Kael, movies as an art form, but also a massive influence on what we know and how we learn, came into its own. Film, which was for Critical Theory, just another product of the Culture Industry, is now taken seriously by several generations of critics and enthusiasts as a many-sided cultural force. At the same time film criticism has evolved from reviews in the daily and weekly press and television, whose main function is to advise the public whether to choose a particular film to spend an evening, or to hire a baby-sitter to attend a movie, into a historical and critical discipline worthy of academic departments and programs, and whose practitioners are eligible for academic rank (Powdermaker, 1950; Bazin 1961; Metz 1990; Kael 1994) Despite their ubiquity and vast influence, the kinds of knowledge derived from mass media and popular music remain largely unexamined by the secondary school curriculum. In this respect, public education may be regarded as one of the last bastions of high cultural convention, and of the book. Perhaps more to the point by consistently refusing to treat popular culture—television, film, music and video games—as objects of legitimate intellectual knowledge schools deny the validity of student experiences, even if the objective would be to deconstruct them. Thus, a century after mass- mediated music and visual arts captured our collective imagination, notwithstanding its undeniable commodification, popular culture remains subversive, regardless of its content, because it continues to be outlaw in official precincts . By failing to address this epochal phenomenon, even as its forms are overwhelmingly influential in everyday life, school knowledge loses its capacity to capture the hearts and minds of its main constituents. And if schools cannot enter the students' collective imagination other forms of knowledge are destined fill the vacuum.

Of course the power of television in shaping the political culture is far less well understood. If the overwhelming majority of the population receive their news and viewpoints from television sources then, absent counterweights such as those that may be provided by social movements, counterhegemonic intellectuals, and independent media, the people are inevitably subjected to the ruling common sense, in which alternatives to the official stories lack legitimacy, even when they are reported in the back pages or by a thirty second spot on the 11 O'Clock news. Even journalists have discovered that the integration of the major news organizations with the ruling circles, inhibits their ability to accurately report the news. For example, on October 26, 2002 more than 100,000 people descended on Washington, DC to protest the Bush administration's plan to wage war against Iraq. *The New York Times* reporter on the scene estimated the crowd in the "thousands" and stated that the turnout had disappointed organizers who had expected more than 100,000 demonstrators to show up. Since the *Times* functions as a guide to the rest of the American news media, including television and radio news, the coverage of the demonstration throughout the nation was scant, in part because other media relied on the *Times*'s understated numbers. For the majority of Americans, the original report, and its numerous re-capitulations, left the impression that the demonstration was a bust. But the *Washington Post*, perhaps the *Times*'s only competitor in daily print journalism, estimated the number of demonstrators more or less accurately, and by the evening of the event a wealth of information and furious condemnation of the *Times*'s biased coverage swarmed over the internet. Days later in an obscure little piece the paper's editors issued a correction without referring the readers to the previous report.

But more importantly the relation of education and class is indicated by the way issues are framed by experts, opinion surveys and the media, which faithfully feature them. That Iraq's president, Saddam Hussein and his government, constitutes an imminent threat to US security—a judgement that, neither for the media nor for the Bush administration seems to require proof—is the starting point of virtually all of the media's coverage of US foreign policy. On the nightly news, PBS's (The Public Broadcasting System) many programs of talking expert heads, no less that than Sunday morning talk shows on commercial networks where experts mingle with the political directorate to discuss world and national events, the question is almost never posed whether there is warrant for this evaluation, but revolves instead around the issue, not of whether the US should go to war to disarm the regime, but when it inevitably will occur. The taken-for-granted assumption is that Saddam has viable "weapons of mass destruction" in his possession, whether or not the United Nations inspectors dispatched by the Security Council to investigate this allegation can affirm this US government-manufactured "fact". Since the Bush administration knows that there nothing as efficient as a war to unify the underlying population behind its policies, and the media is complicit, citizens are deprived of countervailing assessments unless they emanate from within the establishment. And even then, there is only a small chance that these views will play prominently.

Thus when Brent Shocroft, the national security advisor in the first Bush administration, and retiring Republican conservative US Representative Dick Armey expressed reservations about the current administration's war plans, neither received the notice such an ideological breach might deserve. Only the tiny fraction of the population that reads a handful of liberal newspapers and magazines of opinion were likely to know about their objections. From the perspective of the leading media Americans are in virtual unanimous agreement that we should and will go to war against Iraq. Yet, by the results of some polls, which are poorly reported in most media, we know that support for the war is not only soft, but is qualified; while few are opposed to a war on any terms, many Americans would object to a unilateral attack by US forces. But there are ample indications the administration may proceed *as if* public opinion was unified around its policy. In this mode of governance absent massive protest that may be manifested directly or electorally, silence is tantamount to consent. Without visible dissent, a visibility routinely denied by the media to protestors, the administration interpreted the Republican victory in the 2002 mid-term elections as a retrospective mandate for its war policies.

The pattern of government vetting and censorship of war news was established during World War Two, but the first Bush administration elevated it to an art form. During the 1991 Gulf War the administration took pains to shield reporters from the battlefield and insisted they be quartered in Saudi hotels, miles away from the action. They received all of the war news from government sources, including video footage and photographs shown to them in special briefings. By the contemporary and subsequent testimony of some journalists who had been assigned to cover the events, the Bush administration was intent on not repeating the mistakes of the Vietnam war when the Johnson administration permitted the press full access to American and enemy troops and to the battle scenes. Historians and political observers agree that this policy may have had a major impact on building the anti-war movement, especially the images of body bags being loaded on airplanes and the human gore associated with any close combat, supplied by staff photographers. Americans never got the chance to view the physical and human destruction visited by US bombs and missiles on Baghdad or the extent of US casualties. The war was short-lived so the political damage at home was relatively light. Needless to say, that of the 700,000 troops who entered the combat area some 150,000 have since reported psychological or physical injuries, barely makes it to the back pages of most newspapers, let alone the visual media.

Note well, at its inception, some educators and producers touted the educational value of television. Indeed perhaps the major impact of the dominance of visual culture on our everyday knowledge is that to be, is to be seen. Celebrity is a word that is reserved for people whose names become "household" words. Celebrity is produced by the repetition of appearances of an individual on the multitude of television talk shows —Oprah, Today, Leno, Letterman, and others—in which personalities constitute the substance of the event. The point of the typical interview between the anchor and her or his subject is not what is said, or even that the guest in currently appearing in a film or television show, the ostensible purpose of the segment. The interview is a statement of who exists, and by implication, who doesn't. The event has little to do with economic or high-level political power, for these people are largely invisible, or on occasion may appear on the *Charlie Rose* show on PBS or, formerly, on ABC's *Nightline*. The making of sports, entertainment, political or literary celebrities defines the boundary of popular hope or aspiration. The leading television celebrity talk shows are instances of the American credo that, however high the barrier, anyone can become a star. For this is not an instance of having charisma or exuding aura: the celebs are not larger than life, but are shown to be ordinary in an almost banal sense. Fix your nose, cap your teeth, lose weight, take acting lessons and, with a little luck, the person on the screen could be me.

THE LABOR AND RADICAL MOVEMENTS AS EDUCATIONAL SITES

The working class intellectual as a social type precedes and parallels the emergence of universal public education. At the dawn of the public school movement in the 1830s, the antebellum labor movement, that consisted largely of literate skilled workers, favored six years of schooling in order to transmit to their children the basics of reading and writing, but opposed compulsory attendance in secondary schools. The reasons were bound up with their congenital suspicion of the state which they believed never exhibited sympathy for the workers' cause. Although opposed to child labor, the early the workers' movements were convinced that the substance of education—literature, history, philosophy—should be supplied by the movement itself. Consequently in both the oral and the written tradition workers organizations often constituted an alternate university to that of public schools. The active program of many workers and radical movements until world war two consisted largely in education through newspapers, literacy classes for immigrants where the reading materials were drawn from labor and socialist classics, and world literature. These were supplemented by lectures offered by independent scholars who toured the country in the employ of lecture organizations commissioned by the unions and radical organizations. (Tannenbaum 1995)

But the shop floor was also a site of education. Skilled workers were usually literate in their own language and in English, and many were voracious readers and writers. Union and radical newspapers often ran poetry and stories written by workers. Socialist-led unions such as those in the needle trades, machinists, breweries, and bakeries sponsored educational programs; in the era when the union contract was still a rarity, the union was not so much an agency of contract negotiation and enforcement as an educational, political and social association. In his autobiography Samuel Gompers, the founding AFL president, remembers his fellow cigar makers hiring a "reader" in the 1870s, who sat at the center of the work-floor and read from literary and historical classics as well as more contemporary works of political and economic analysis such as the writings of Marx and Engels. Reading groups met in the back of a bar, in the union hall, or in the local affiliate of the socialist wing of the nationality federations. Often these groups were ostensibly devoted to preparing immigrants to pass the obligatory language test for citizenship status. But the content of the reading was, in addition to labor and socialist newspapers and magazines, often supplemented by works of fiction by Shakespeare, the great 19th century novelists and poets, and of Marx and Karl Kautsky. In its anarchist inflection, Kropotkin, Moses Hess and Bakunin were the required texts. (Gompers 1924)

In New York, Chicago, San Francisco and other large cities where the Socialist and Communist movements had considerable membership and a fairly substantial periphery of sympathizers, the parties established adult schools that not only offered courses pertaining to political and ideological knowledge, but were vehicles for many working and middle class students to gain a general education. Among them, in New York, the socialist-oriented Rand School and the Communist sponsored Jefferson School (formerly the Workers' School) lasted until the early 1950s when, due to the decline of a left intellectual culture among workers as much the contemporary repressive political environment, they closed. But in their respective heydays, from the 1920s to the late 1940s, for tens of thousands of working class people—, many of them high school students and industrial workers—, these schools were alternate universities; they not only offered courses that promoted the party's ideology an program. Many courses concerned history, literature and philosophy and, at least at the Jefferson school the student could study art, drama and music, and could their children. The tradition was revived, briefly, by the 1960s New Left which, in similar sites, sponsored free universities where the term "free" designated not an absence of tuition fees but signaled they were ideologically and intellectually unbound to either the traditional left parties or to the conventional school system. I participated in organizing New York's Free University and two of its successors While not affiliated to the labor movement or socialist parties, it succeeded in attracting more than a thousand students in each of its semesters—mostly young— and offered a broad range of courses which were taught by people of divergent intellectual and political orientations, including some free market libertarians who were attracted to the school's non-sectarianism.

When I worked in a steel mill in the late 1950s some of us formed a group that read current literature, labor history and economics. I discussed books and magazine articles with some of my fellow workers in bars as well as on breaks. Tony Mazzocchi, who was at the same time a worker and union officer of a Long Island local of the Oil, Chemical and Atomic Workers, organized a similar group and I knew of several other cases where young workers did the same. Some of these groups evolved into rank and file caucuses that eventually contested the leadership of their local unions; others were mainly for the self-edification of the participants and had no particular political goals.

But beyond formal programs since industrializing era the working class intellectual, although by no means visible in the United States, has been part of shop-floor culture. In almost every workplace there is a person or persons to whom other workers turn for information about the law, the union contract, contemporary politics or, equally important, as a source of general education. This individual(s) may or may not be schooled but, until the late 1950s, had rarely any college. For schools were not the primary source of their knowledge. They were, and are, largely self-educated. In my own case, having left Brooklyn College after less than a year, I worked in a variety of industrial production jobs. When I worked the midnight shift, I got off at 8:00 in the morning, ate breakfast, and spent four hours in the library before going home. Mostly I read American and European history and political economy, particularly the physiocrats, Adam Smith, David Ricardo, John Maynard Keynes and Joseph Schumpeter. Marx's Capital I read in high school and owned the three volumes.

My friend Russell Rommele, who worked in a nearby mill, was also an autodidact. His father was a first generation German-American brewery worker, with no particular literary interests. But Russell had been exposed to reading a wide range of historical and philosophical works as a high school student at Saint Benedict's Prep, a Jesuit institution. The priests singled out Russell for the priesthood and mentored him in theology and social theory. The experience radicalized him and he decided not to answer the call but to enter the industrial working class instead. Like me he was active in the union and Newark Democratic party politics. Working as an educator with a local union in the auto industry recently, I have met several active unionists who are intellectuals. The major difference between them and those of my generation is that they are college graduates, although none claims to have acquired their love of learning or their analytic perspective from schools. One is a former member of a radical organization and another learned his politics from participation in a shop-based study group/union caucus organized by a member of a socialist grouplet which dissolved in the mid-1990s when the group lost a crucial union election. In both instances, with the demise of their organizational affiliations, they remain habituated to reading, writing and union activity.

PARENTS, NEIGHBORHOOD, CLASS CULTURE

John Locke observes that, consistent with his rejection of innate ideas, even if conceptions of good and evil are present in divine or civil law, morality is constituted by reference to our parents, relatives and especially the "club" of peers to which we belong: "he who imagines commendation and disgrace not to be strong motives to men to accommodate themselves to the opinions and rules of those with whom they converse seems little skilled in the nature or the history of mankind: the greatest part whereof we shall find govern themselves, chiefly, if not solely by this law of *fashion* (emphasis in the original);and so they do what keeps them in reputation with their company, little regard for the laws of God or the magistrate." (Locke 1959 book one chapter 28, #12, p. 478) William James put the manner equally succinctly:

"A man's social self is the recognition which he gets from his mates. We are not only gregarious animals, liking to be in the sight if our fellows, but we have an innate propensity to get ourselves noticed, and noticed favorably, by our kind. No more fiendish punishment could be devised, were such a thing physically possible, that that should be turned loose in society and remain absolutely unnoticed by all the members thereof." (James 1890, 351)

That the social worlds of peers and family are the chief referents for the formation of the social self, neither philosopher had a doubt. Each in his own fashion situates the individual in social context, which provides a "common measure of virtue and vice"(Locke 1959) even as they acknowledge the ultimate choice resides with the individual self. These, and not the institutions, even those that have the force of law, are the primary sources of authority.

Hannah Arendt argues that education "by its very nature cannot forego either authority or tradition". Nor can it base itself on the presumption that children share an autonomous existence from adults. (Arendt 1961, 180–81) Yet schooling ignores the reality of the society of kids at the cost of undermining its own authority. The society of kids is in virtually all classes an alternative and opposition site of knowledge and of moral valuation. We have already seen how working class kids get working class jobs by means of their rebellion against school authority. Since refusal and resistance is a hallmark of the moral order, the few who will not obey the invocation to fail or to perform indifferently in school often find themselves marginalized or expelled from the community of kids While they adopt a rationality that can be justified on eminently practical grounds the long tradition of rejection of academic culture has proven hard to break, even in the wake of evidence that those working class jobs to which they were oriented no longer exist. For what is at stake in adolescent resistance is their perception that the blandishments of the adult world are vastly inferior the pleasures of their own. In the first place the new service economy offers few inducements: wages are low, the job is boring and the future bleak. And since the schools now openly present themselves as a link in the general system of control it may appear some students that cooperation is a form of self-deception.

If not invariably, then in many households parents provide to the young a wealth of knowledge: the family mythologies which feature an uncle or aunt, a grandparent or an absent parent. These are the stories, loosely based on some actual event(s) in which the family member has distinguished her or himself in various ways that(usually)illustrate a moral virtue or defect the telling of which constitutes a kind of didactic message. Even when not attached to an overt narrative, parable, or myth we learn from our parents by their actions in relation to us and others: how do they deal with adversity? How do they address ordinary, everyday problems? What do they learn from their own trials and tribulations and what do they say to us? What are our parents attitudes towards money, joblessness, everyday life disruptions such as sudden, acute illness or accidents? What do they learn from the endless conflicts with their parent(s) over issues of sex, money and household responsibilities?

The relative weight of parental to peer authority is an empirical question that cannot be decided in advance; what both have in common is their location within everyday life. The parents are likely to be more susceptible to the authority of law and of its magistrates and, 21 in a world of increasing uncertainty, will worry that if their children choose badly they may be left behind. But the associations with our peers we make in everyday life provide the recognition that we crave, define what is worthy of praise or blame, and confer approbation or disapproval on our decisions. But having made a choice that runs counter to that of "their company" or club the individual must form, or join, a new "company" to confer the judgement of virtue on her or his action. This company must, of necessity, consist of "peers", the definition of which has proven fungible.

Religion, the law and, among kids, school authorities face the obstacles erected by the powerful rewards and punishments meted out by the "clubs" to which people are affiliated. At a historical conjunction when, beneath the relentless pressure imposed by capital to transform all labor into wage labor, thereby forcing every adult into the paid labor force, the society of kids increasing occupies the space of civil society. The neighborhood, once dominated by women and small shopkeepers, has all but disappeared save for the presence of children and youth. As parents toil for endless hours to pay the ever mounting debts incurred by home ownership, perpetual car and appliance payments, and the costs of health care, kids are increasingly on their own and these relationships have consequences for their conceptions of education and life.

Some recent studies and teacher observations have discovered a not inconsiderable reluctance among black students in elite universities to perform well in school, even those of professional/managerial family backgrounds. Many seem indifferent to arguments that show that school performance is a central prerequisite to better jobs and higher status in the larger work world. Among the more acute speculations is the conclusion that black students resistance reflects an anti-intellectual bias, and a hesitation, if not refusal, to enter the mainstream corporate world. Perhaps the charge of anti-intellectualism is better understood as healthy skepticism about the chance that a corporate career will provide the well-publicized satisfactions There are similar indications among some relatively affluent white students as well. Although by no means a majority some students are less enamored by the work world to which they, presumably, have been habituated by school, especially by the prospect of perpetual work In the third tier universities, state and private alike, apparently forced by their parents to enroll, many students wonder out loud why they are there. Skepticism about schooling still abounds even as they graduate high school and enroll in post-secondary schools in record numbers. According to one colleague of mine who teaches in a third tier private university in the New York Metropolitan area, many of these mostly suburban students "sleepwalk" through their classes, do not participate in class discussions and are lucky to get a "C" grade.

In the working class neighborhoods—white, black and Latino—the word is out: given the absence of viable alternatives, you must try to obtain that degree, but this defines the limit of loyalty to the enterprise. Based on testimonies of high school and community college teachers for every student who takes school knowledge seriously there are twenty or more who are time-servers. Most are ill-prepared to perform academic work and, since the community colleges and state four year colleges and "teaching" universities simply lack the resources to provide the means by which their school performance can improve, beyond the credential there is little motivation among students to try to get an education.

In some instances those who break from their club and enter the regime of school knowledge is a decision that risks being drummed out of a lifetime of relationships with their peers. What has euphemistically been described as "peer pressure" bears, among other moral structures, on the degree to which kids are permitted to cross over the line into the precincts of adult authority. While being a success in school is not equivalent to squealing on a friend or to the cops, or transgressing some sacred moral code of the society of kids, it comes close to committing an act of betrayal. This is comprehensible only if the reader is willing to suspend prejudice that schooling is tantamount to education and is an unqualified "good" as compared to the presumed evil of school failure, or the decision of the slacker to rebel by refusing to succeed.

To invoke the concept of "class" in either educational debates or any other politically charged discourse generally refers to the white working class. Educational theory and practice treats Blacks and Latinos, regardless of their economic positions, as unified, bioidentities.

That blacks [sic] kids from professional, managerial and business backgrounds share more with their white counterparts than with working class blacks is generally ignored by most educational writers Just as, in race discourse "whites" are undifferentiated, since the war "race"—which refers in slightly different registers to people of African origin and those who migrated from Latin countries of South America and the Caribbean—, are treated as a unified category. The narrowing of the concept limits our ability to discern class at all. I want to suggest that, although we must stipulate ethnic, gender, race and occupational distinction among differentiated strata of wage labor, with the exception of children of salaried professional and technical groups, where the culture of schooling plays a decisive role, class education transcends these distinctions. No doubt there are gradations among the strata that comprise this social formation, But the most privileged professional strata (physicians, attorneys, scientists, professors), and the high-level managers are self-reproducing, not principally through schooling but through social networks. These include: private schools, some of which are residential; clubs and associations; and, in suburban public schools the self-selection of students on the basis of distinctions. Show me a school friendship between the son or daughter of a corporate manager and the child of a janitor or factory worker and I will show you a community service project to get into one of the "select" colleges or universities such as Brown, Oberlin and Wesleyan.

Schooling selects a fairly small number of children of the class of wage labor for genuine class mobility. In the first half of the 20th century, having lost its appeal among middle class youth, the Catholic Church turned to working class students as a source of cadre recruitment. In my neighborhood of the East Bronx two close childhood friends, both of Italian background, entered the priesthood. As sons of construction workers the Church provided their best chance to escape the hardships and economic uncertainties of manual labor. Another kid became a pharmacist because the local Catholic college, Fordham University, offered scholarships. A fourth was among the tiny coterie of students who passed the test for one of the city's special schools, Bronx Science, and became a science teacher. Otherwise almost everybody else remained a worker or, like my best friend, Kenny, went to prison.

Despite the well publicized claim that anyone can escape their condition of social and economic birth—a claim reproduced by schools and by the media with numbing regularity—most working class students, many of whom have some college credits, but often do not graduate—end up in low and middle-level service jobs that do not pay a decent working class wage. Owing to the steep decline of unionized industrial production jobs those who enter factories increasingly draw wages that are substantially below union standards. Those who do graduate find work in computers, although rarely at the professional levels. The relatively low paid become k-12 teachers and health care professionals, mostly nurses and technicians, or enter the social service field as case workers, medical social workers or line social welfare workers. The question I want to pose is whether these "professional" occupations represent genuine mobility.

During the post-war economic boom which made possible a significant expansion of spending for schools, the social services, and administration of public goods, the public sector workplace became a favored site of black and Latino recruitment, mainly for clerical, maintenance and entry-level patient care jobs in hospitals and other health care facilities. Within several decades a good number advanced to middle and registered nursing, but not in all sections of the country. As unionization spread to the non-profit private sector as well as public employment in the 1960s and 1970s, these jobs paid enough to enable many enjoy became known as a "middle class" living standard but also a measure of job security offered by union security and civil service status. While it is true that "job security" has often been observed in its breach the traditional deal made by teachers, nurses and social workers was that they traded higher incomes for job security. But after about 1960 spurred by the resurgent civil rights movement, these "second-level" professionals—white and black—began to see themselves as workers more than professionals: they formed unions, struck for higher pay and shorter hours, and assumed a very unprofessional adversarial stance towards institutional authority. Contracts stipulated higher salaries, definite hours— a sharp departure from professional ideology— on seniority as a basis for layoffs, just like any industrial contract, and demand substantial vacation and sick leave.

Their assertion of working-class values and social position may have been strategic, indeed it inspired the largest wave of union organizing since the 1930s. But, together with the entrance of huge numbers of women and blacks into the public and quasi-public sector workforces it was as well a symptom of the proletarianization of the second-tier professions. Several decades later salaried physicians made a similar discovery; they formed unions and struck against high malpractice insurance costs as much as the onerous conditions imposed on their autonomy by Health Maintenance Organizations and government authorities bent on cost containment, often at their expense. More to the point, the steep rise of public employees' salaries and benefits posed the question of how to maintain services in times of fiscal austerity which might be due to economic downturn or to pro-business tax policies. The answer has been that the political and public officials told employees that the temporary respite from the classical trade union trade-off was over. All public employees have suffered relative deterioration in their salaries and benefits. Since the mid-1970s fiscal crises, begun in New York City, they have experienced layoffs for the first time since the depression. And their unions have been on a continuous concessionary bargaining mode for decades. In the politically and ideologically repressive environment of the last twenty five years the class divide has sharpened. Ironically, in the wake of the attacks by legislatures and business against their hard-won gains in the early 1980s the teachers unions abandoned their militant, class posture and reverted to professionalism and to a center-right political strategy.

In truth schools are learning sites, even if only for a handful, of intellectual knowledge. In the main they transmit the instrumental logic of credentialism, together with their transformation from institutions of discipline to those of control, especially in working class districts. Even talented, dedicated teachers have more difficulty reaching kids and convincing them that the life of the mind may hold unexpected rewards, even if the career implications of critical thought are not apparent. The breakdown of the mission of public schools has produced varied forms of disaffection; if school violence has abated in some places, it does not signify the decline of gangs and other "clubs" that signify the autonomous world of youth. The society of kids is more autonomous because, in contrast to 1960s, official authorities no longer offer hope; instead, in concert with the doctrine of control they threaten punishment which includes, but is not necessarily associated with, incarceration. Although I note that the large number of drug busts of young black and Latino men should not be minimized. With over a million blacks, more than 3% of the African American population—most of them young—within the purview of the criminal justice system, the law may be viewed as a more or less concerted effort to counter by force of the power of peers. This may be regarded in the context of the failure schools. Of course, more than three hundred years ago John Locke knew the limits of the magistrates indeed, of any adult authority to overcome the power of the society of kids. (Giroux)

CONCLUSION

What are the requisite changes that would transform schools from credentials mills and institutions of control to a site of education that prepares young people to see themselves as active participants in the world?. As my analysis implies the fundamental condition is to abolish high stakes standardized tests that dominate the curriculum and subordinate teachers to the role of drill masters and subject students to stringent controls. By this proposal I do not mean to eliminate the need for evaluative tools. The essay is a fine measure of both writing ability and of the student's grasp of literature, social science and history. While it must be admitted that math and science as much as language proficiency require considerable rote learning, the current curriculum and pedagogy in these fields includes neither a historical account of the changes in scientific and mathematical theory, nor a metaconceptual explanation of what the disciplines are about. Nor are courses in language at the secondary level ever concerned with etymological issues, comparative cultural study of semantic differences, and other topics that might relieve the boredom of rote learning by providing depth of understanding. The broader understanding of science in the modern world—its relation to technology, war and medicine, for example—should surely be integrated into the curriculum; some of these issues appear in the textbooks, but teachers rarely discuss them because they are busy preparing students for the high stakes tests in which knowledge of the social contexts for science, language and math are not included.

I agree with Arendt that education "cannot forgo either authority or tradition". But authority must be earned rather than assumed and the transmission of tradition needs to be critical rather than worshipful. If teachers were allowed to acknowledge student skepticism, incorporated kids' knowledge into the curriculum by making what they know the object of rigorous study, especially popular music and television, they might be treated with greater respect. But there is no point denying the canon; one if the more egregious conditions of subordination is the failure of schools to expose students to its best exemplars, for people who have no cultural capital are thereby condemned to social and political marginality, let alone deprived of some of the pleasures to be derived from encounters with genuine works of art. When the New York City Board of Education (now the department of education) mandates that during every semester high school English classes read a Shakespeare play and one or two works of 19th century English literature, but afford little or no access to the best Russian novels of the 19th century, no opportunities to examine some of the most influential works of western philosophy, beginning with the Milesians through Plato, Aristotle and the major figures of "modern philosophy", and provide no social and historical context for what is learned, tradition is observed in the breach more than in its practice. And when, under budgetary pressures elementary and secondary schools cut music and art from the curriculum, they deprive students of the best sources for cultivating the creative imagination Schools fulfill their responsibility to students and to the communities in which they live when, at every level, they offer a program of systematic, critical learning which, simultaneously, provides students with "access" to the rich traditions of so-called Western thought, history, the arts, including its literature, and opens parallel vistas of Africa, Asia and Latin America. (Aronowitz 2000, chapter 7)

Finally, the schools should relieve themselves of their ties to corporate interests and reconstruct the curriculum along the line of genuine intellectual endeavor. Nor should the schools been seen as career conduits, although this function will be difficult to displace, for among other reasons, that in an era of high economic anxiety many kids and their parents worry about the future and seek some practical purchase on it. It will take some convincing that their best leg up is to be educated. It is unlikely in the present environment, but possible in some places.

One could elaborate these options; this is only an outline.. In order to come close to their fulfillment at least three things are needed. First we require a conversation concerning the nature and scope of education and the limits of schooling as an educational site. Along with this theorists and researchers need to link their knowledge of popular culture, and culture in the anthropological sense, that is, everyday life, with the politics of education. Specifically, we need to examine why in late capitalist societies, the public sphere withers, while the corporatization process penetrates every sphere of life. We need teachers who, by their own education, are intellectuals who respect and want to help children obtain a genuine education, regardless of their social class. For this we need a new regime of teacher education that is founded on the idea that the educator must be educated well. It would surely entail abolishing the current curricula of most education schools, if not the schools themselves. The endless courses on "teaching methods" would be replaced with courses in the natural and social sciences, mathematics, philosophy, history and literature. Some of these would address the relation of education, in all of its forms, to their social and historical context. In effect, the teacher becomes an intellectual, capable of the critical appropriation of world histories and cultures. And we need a movement of parents, students, teachers and the labor movement armed with a political program directed to forcing legislatures to adequately fund schooling at the federal, state and local levels and boards of education to deauthorize high stakes standardized tests that currently drive the curriculum and pedagogy. (Aronowitz and Giroux, 1985)

Having proposed these changes, we need to remain mindful of the limitations of schooling and the likelihood that youth will acquire knowledge that prepares them for life, like sex, the arts, where to find jobs, how to bind with other people, how to fight, how to love and hate, outside of schools. The deinstitutionalization of education does not require abandoning schools. But they should be rendered benign, removed, as much as possible from the tightening grip of the corporate, warfare state. In turn teachers must resist becoming agents of the prison system, of the drug companies, of corporate capital. In the last instance, the best chance for education resides in the communities, in social movements and in the kids themselves.

Online Schooling Grows, Setting off a Debate

—Sam Dillon

Friday, February 1, 2008

MILWAUKEE: Weekday mornings, three of Tracie Weldie's children eat breakfast, make beds and trudge off to public school—in their case, downstairs to their basement in a suburb here, where their mother leads them through math and other lessons outlined by an Internet-based charter school.

Half a million American children take classes online, with a significant group, like the Weldies, getting all their schooling from virtual public schools. The rapid growth of these schools has provoked debates in courtrooms and legislatures over money, as the schools compete with local districts for millions in public dollars, and over issues like whether online learning is appropriate for young children.

One of the sharpest debates has concerned the Weldies' school in Wisconsin, where last week the backers of online education persuaded state lawmakers to keep it and 11 other virtual schools open despite a court ruling against them and the opposition of the teachers union. John Watson, a consultant in Colorado who does an annual survey of education that is based on the Internet, said events in Wisconsin followed the pattern in other states where online schools have proliferated fast.

"Somebody says, 'What's going on, does this make sense?'" Watson said. "And after some inquiry most states have said, 'Yes, we like online learning, but these are such new ways of teaching children that we'll need to change some regulations and get some more oversight.'"

Two models of online schooling predominate. In Florida, Illinois and half a dozen other states, growth has been driven by a state-led, state-financed virtual school that does not give a diploma but offers courses that supplement regular work at a traditional school. Generally, these schools enroll only middle and high school students.

At the Florida Virtual School, the largest Internet public school in the country, more than 50,000 students are taking courses this year. School authorities in Traverse City, Michigan, hope to use online courses provided by the Michigan Virtual School next fall to educate several hundred students in their homes, alleviating a classroom shortage.

The other model is a full-time online charter school like the Wisconsin Virtual Academy. About 90,000 children get their education from one of 185 such schools nationwide. They are publicly financed, mostly elementary and middle schools.

Many parents attracted to online charters have previously home-schooled their children, including Weldie. Her children—Isabel, Harry and Eleanor, all in elementary school—download assignments and communicate intermittently with their certified teachers over the Internet, but they also read story books, write in workbooks and do arithmetic at a table in their basement. Legally, they are considered public school students, not home-schoolers, because their online schools are taxpayer-financed and subject to federal testing requirements.

Despite enthusiastic support from parents, the schools have met with opposition from some educators, who say elementary students may be too young for Internet learning, and from teachers, unions and school boards, partly because they divert state payments from the online student's home district.

Other opposition has arisen because many online charters contract with for-profit companies to provide their courses. The Wisconsin academy, for example, is run by the tiny Northern Ozaukee School District, north of Milwaukee, in close partnership with K12 Inc., which works with similar schools in 17 states.

The district receives annual state payments of $6,050 for each of its 800 students, which it uses to pay teachers and buy its online curriculum from K12.

Saying he suspected "corporate profiteering" in online schooling, State Senator John Lehman, a Democrat who is chairman of the education committee, last month proposed cutting the payments to virtual schools to $3,000 per student. But during legislative negotiations that proposal was dropped.

Jeff Kwitowski, a K12 spokesman, said, "We are a vendor and no different from thousands of other companies that provide products and services to districts and schools."

Pennsylvania has also debated the financing of virtual charter schools. Saying such schools were draining them financially, districts filed suit in 2001, portraying online schools as little more than home schooling at taxpayer expense. The districts lost, but the debate has continued.

Last year, the state auditor found that several online charters had received reimbursements from students' home districts that surpassed actual education costs by more than $1 million. Now legislators are considering a bill that would in part standardize the payments at about $5,900 per child, said Michael Race, a spokesman for the State Department of Education.

The state auditor in Kansas last year raised a different concern, finding that the superintendent of a tiny prairie district running an online school had in recent years given 130 students, and with them $106,000 in per-pupil payments, to neighboring districts that used the students' names to pad enrollment counts. The auditor concluded that the superintendent had carried out the subterfuge to compensate the other districts for not opening their own online schools.

"Virtual education is a growing alternative to traditional schooling," Barbara Hinton, the Kansas auditor, said in a report. Hinton found that virtual education had great potential because students did not have to be physically present in a classroom. "Students can go to school at any time and in any place," she said.

But, she added, "this also creates certain risks to both the quality of the student's education and to the integrity of the public school system."

Rural Americans have been attracted to online schooling because it allows students even on remote ranches to enroll in arcane courses like Chinese.

In Colorado, school districts have lost thousands of students to virtual schools, and, in 2006, a state audit found that one school, run by a rural district, was using four licensed teachers to teach 1,500 students across the state. The legislature responded last year by establishing a new division of the Colorado Department of Education to tighten regulation of online schools.

The Wisconsin Virtual Academy has 20 certified, unionized teachers, and 800 students who communicate with one another over the Internet.

The school has consistently met federal testing requirements, and many parents, including Weldie, expressed satisfaction with the K12 curriculum, which allows her children to move through lessons at their own pace, unlike traditional schools, where teachers often pause to take account of slower students. Isabel Weldie, 5, is in kindergarten, "But in math I'm in first grade," she said during a break in her school day recently.

"That's what I love most about this curriculum," Tracie Weldie said. "There's no reason for Isabel to practice counting if she can already add."

In 2004, the teachers' union filed a lawsuit against the school, challenging the expansive role given to parents, who must spend four to five hours daily leading their children through lesson plans and overseeing their work. Teachers monitor student progress and answer questions in a couple of half-hour telephone conferences per month and in interactive online classes using conferencing software held several times monthly.

A state court dismissed the case, but in December an appeals court said the academy was violating a state law requiring that public school teachers be licensed.

The ruling infuriated parents like Bob Reber, an insurance salesman who lives in Fond du Lac and whose 8-year-old daughter is a student at the academy. "According to this ruling, if I want to teach my daughter to tie her shoes, I'd need a license," Reber said.

Not so, said Mary Bell, the union president: "The court did not say that parents cannot teach their children—it said parents cannot teach their children at taxpayers' expense."

The Weldies and 1,000 other parents and students from online schools rallied in Madison, the state capital, urging lawmakers to save their schools. Last week, legislators announced that they had agreed on a bipartisan bill that would allow the schools to stay open, while requiring online teachers to keep closely in touch with students and increasing state oversight.

Tracking

Tracking is the most commonly used term for ability grouping, the practice of lumping children together according to their talents in the classroom. On the elementary level, the divisions sound harmless enough: Kids are divided into the Bluebirds and Redbirds. But in the secondary schools, the stratification becomes more obvious—some say insidious—as students assume their places in the tracking system.

Opponents of tracking trace the practice to the turn of the century when most children attending public schools were from upper-middle-class families, but large numbers of black and working-class students were starting to enter the schools as the result of compulsory schooling laws and rising immigration. Separate curricula were developed for the relatively small percentage of students destined for higher education and for the masses who went on to menial industrial jobs. Tracking quickly took on the appearance of internal segregation. Today, though the world outside schools has changed, the tracking system remains much the same.

Should schools—as the engine of democracy—provide relatively similar curricula for all students?

Should schools—as the engine of democracy—provide relatively similar curricula for all students? Or should they instead sort students by skill levels and prepare them for their different roles as adults?

Opponents of tracking fear that the labels students are given early on stay with them as they move from grade to grade. And for those on the lower tracks, a steady diet of lower expectations leads to a steadily low level of motivation toward school. In high school, the groups formerly known as the Bluebirds and Redbirds have evolved into new tracks: College Preparatory and Vocational.

A growing number of educators denounce tracking, arguing that the labels students are given early on stay with them as they move from grade to grade. They oppose a system which they say permanently condemns many students—a disproportionate number of whom are minorities—to an inferior education, both in terms of what and how they are taught.

In some cases, a tracked school can literally be unconstitutional. The U.S. Department of Education's Office for Civil Rights has been called upon to work with schools in cases where the effects of tracking students have been a violation of the Civil Rights Act of 1964. This legislation bars racial discrimination in federally financed education programs and prohibits tracking under some circumstances.

The arguments for tracking are more subtle today than they were 90 years ago. Tracking proponents say it is easier to teach relatively homogeneous classes and unrealistic to expect everyone to master the same curriculum. They say students feel more comfortable and learn better when they're grouped with peers of similar abilities. And they say tracking enables teachers to tailor instruction to the needs of respective groups of students. How, after all, can the same English teacher in the same class prepare some students for the Advanced Placement test in literature while others are still struggling with basic grammar?

Many fear that the transition to mixed-ability grouping may hurt gifted and other high-achieving students who have done well in an accelerated program of study. Some parents do not want to see their children's progress slowed down, as they perceive it would be, in order to accommodate slower learners.

Critics of ability grouping are trying to loosen or eliminate the practice, but they often find it's not so easy. Lumping students of all abilities together in one lecture-oriented class won't work; teachers must adopt new methods of instruction and flexible curricula to cope with these more diverse groups of students. As a result, tracking remains the most widely used method for dealing with student diversity, particularly in secondary schools.

Although much of the flap over tracking has been made by factions outside of the schools, teachers find themselves at the center of the issue—and they are far from united. One National Education Association official calls tracking "probably the most professionally divisive issue in the association." Those who teach specialized groups of gifted or learning-disabled students have an extra stake in the grouping process. But for most teachers, the issue boils down to how to give slower students the extra attention they need without shortchanging the more able students who may lose interest.

Should Government Vouchers Be Given to Pay for Private Schools, Even if They're Religious Schools?

In a Nutshell

Yes	No
1. Rich parents have a choice of schools for their kids; poor parents should have the same choice.	1. Since most of the schools in the program are religious, government funding violates the 1st Amendment separation of church and state.
2. Competition between schools is increased, leading to greater efficiency and results in all schools.	2. Vouchers take funds away from already under-funded public schools.
3. Private schools have a better history of getting results in teaching information and values than public schools.	3. Private schools aren't subject to as rigorous of oversight; thus, they may not act responsibly.
4. Those parents who send their kids to private schools must in effect pay twice; i.e. their taxes pay for public schools that their children don't even attend.	4. Public schools must accept everyone regardless of disabilities, test scores, religion, or other characteristics; private schools can show favoritism or discrimination in selecting students.
5. Providing private school access to everyone will increase diversity.	
6. The parent makes the choice between religious or non-religious schooling; thus, the government isn't imposing religion.	

OVERVIEW/BACKGROUND

The first amendment of the Constitution says in part that the U.S. government cannot establish a state religion nor prohibit the free exercise of religion. This clause has been interpreted over the years to mean there should be an impenetrable wall between church and state. As far as the educational system is concerned, it means that government cannot forcibly introduce religion into studies or subsidize its teaching. Many Americans disagree with this interpretation.

The issue has once again come up for debate in George W. Bush's school choice program. This allows parents to choose which school their children attend regardless of religion. Public schools are already fully funded by the government with U.S. tax dollars. If the parents choose a private school in the area, a "voucher" is given to the family which pays the cost of tuition at the private school. The program was developed due to the failure of public schools in many urban areas of the country. These programs have already started up in areas such as Cleveland and Milwaukee.

Yes

1. **Rich parents have a choice of schools for their kids; poor parents should have the same choice.** In all but the smallest areas of the country, parents have a number of options for their child's education. Various religious and non-religious schools are available. Unfortunately, the private schools are not free. They are often very expensive. Rich parents can and do often choose the school which has the best reputation and results. However, poor parents who can't afford the private tuition usually have only one option—óthe public school in their area. That one choice may be a crime-ridden school that fails in all measures of academia. Is it fair that only rich parents can send their children to the best schools?

2. **Competition between schools is increased, leading to greater efficiency and results in all schools.** For too long, public schools have been able to coast along with no level of accountability. When you're the only ones providing a subsidized education, you in effect have a monopoly; thus, you don't have as much of an incentive to improve efficiency. Competition has been the key to success in every area of business. How good would GM cars be if GM didn't have competition from Chrysler, Ford, and for-

Reprinted with permission of Joe Messerli.

eign operations? How good would Dell computers be if Dell didn't have competition from Gateway, IBM, Apple, and others? Competition will force public schools to squeeze out every bit of efficiency and start emphasizing the teaching of values such as hard work, discipline, and respect for others.

3. **Private schools have a better history of getting results in teaching information and values than public schools.** Private schools can cost a significant amount of money. Yet, even with the cost, people with the means will usually choose private over public schools. Why? It's because the reputation and results of private schools are so much better. Measures of both character and academic success are almost always better at the private schools. Private schools have accountability; if they don't do a superior job, they won't have any students (unlike public schools which will have students no matter how bad of a job they do). Private schools are allowed to be more flexible in their teaching methods. Most of all, private schools focus more on teaching lifelong values that are often tied to religion (e.g. respecting your neighbor, not lying or stealing, working hard, etc.).

4. **Those parents who send their kids to private schools must in effect pay twice; i.e. their taxes pay for public schools that their children don't even attend.** Regardless of where their children attend school, parents must pay taxes. These taxes are used to pay for the public school. Because private schools charge tuition, those parents that send their children to private schools are in effect paying twice.

5. **Providing private school access to everyone will increase diversity.** There is little debate that there's an income disparity between whites and other races. The option of expensive private schools often leads to schools that are somewhat segregated. Offering vouchers would introduce more diversity to the all schools since choice would no longer be a factor of income.

6. **The parent makes the choice between religious or non-religious schooling; thus, the government isn't imposing religion.** Each and every parent would have a choice of religious and non-religious school. Thus, the government would in no way be violating the 1st Amendment establishment clause.

No

1. **Since most of the schools in the program are religious, government funding violates the 1st Amendment separation of church and state.** The fact is that over 95 percent of all school vouchers go to religious schools. The Establishment clause of the 1st Amendment was put in specifically by the framers to avoid the abuses that inevitably come about in state-sponsored religious education. Centuries of religious wars in Europe plus the Middle Eastern wahabism serve as painful examples of religious dogma in schools. Religious ideas are invariably based on opinion & centuries-old teaching rather than scientific proof. Thus, they don't belong in the classroom, but in the home. Once government starts funding religious schools, it might start funding other religious institutions. Eventually, we have a religion-dominated society which can lead to discrimination (against gays, women, etc.) and take away individual freedoms (such as pornography, alcohol, etc.).

2. **Vouchers take funds away from already underfunded public schools.** One of the biggest reasons public schools are failing is that they can't keep up with the ever increasing cost of books, teachers, computers, security, etc. If we start subsidizing private schools, much-needed funds will be diverted from the public schools. This will only make bad schools worse.

3. **Private schools aren't subject to as rigorous of oversight; thus, they may not act responsibly.** Public schools are subject to government oversight and more rules & regulation. Thus, tighter control is placed on the teaching methods and system of education. With little or no oversight, we don't know how well private schools will perform.

4. **Public schools must accept everyone regardless of disabilities, test scores, religion, or other characteristics; private schools can show favoritism or discrimination in selecting students.** Private schools can establish any criteria they want for selecting or rejecting students. Thus, they can discriminate or make eligibility standards much more difficult for poorer students. Public schools on the other hand must accommodate all types of students regardless of what challenges they present. Government funds should be kept with the public schools that take on these challenges rather than private schools that may discriminate.

Part 4

Psychology of Education

Introduction to Psychology of Education

Approaching a half century ago, I first became interested—in an academic way—in why people did the things they did, that is, in what motivated human behavior. At the time, it seemed to me, schools of psychology in America were determined to prove that what they were about could be viewed as "true science." Laboratory experiments with rats and controlled studies isolating all the variables were the coins of the realm. Those approaches actually held less "juice" for me than reading the views of Freud and Jung and then in the mid-1960s discovering Maslow, Rogers, Perls, and, finally, Frankl. It was the intuitive speculation as to human motivation, that is, armchair theorizing, that caught my passions.

It seemed that the psychology of education of the time was about creating learning machines based on Skinnerian stimulus-response theory and developing ever more sophisticated testing of children in order to label the ways they differed from the norm. That, too, paled in interest for me compared to thinking about the outer bounds of human functioning.

This section on the psychology of education reflects more my bias toward the "psychology of human potential" and its insights for American education. Here you will find out about inviting children to learn rather than motivating them to do so. You will read an argument against praising children's work through stickers and stars and treats and the ubiquitous "good job." You will see a focus on health versus disease—a focus away from the medical model of diagnosis of malady toward a model of recognizing all the amazingly different ways that we think and function in our worlds. These differences don't make us odd or crazy or dysfunctional, they just make us different.

Five Reasons to Stop Saying "Good Job!"

—Alfie Kohn

Hang out at a playground, visit a school, or show up at a child's birthday party, and there's one phrase you can count on hearing repeatedly: "Good job!" Even tiny infants are praised for smacking their hands together ("Good clapping!"). Many of us blurt out these judgments of our children to the point that it has become almost a verbal tic.

Plenty of books and articles advise us against relying on punishment, from spanking to forcible isolation ("time out"). Occasionally someone will even ask us to rethink the practice of bribing children with stickers or food. But you'll have to look awfully hard to find a discouraging word about what is euphemistically called positive reinforcement.

Lest there be any misunderstanding, the point here is not to call into question the importance of supporting and encouraging children, the need to love them and hug them and help them feel good about themselves. Praise, however, is a different story entirely. Here's why.

1. **Manipulating children.** Suppose you offer a verbal reward to reinforce the behavior of a two-year-old who eats without spilling, or a five-year-old who cleans up her art supplies. Who benefits from this? Is it possible that telling kids they've done a good job may have less to do with their emotional needs than with our convenience?

   Rheta DeVries, a professor of education at the University of Northern Iowa, refers to this as "sugar-coated control." Very much like tangible rewards—or, for that matter, punishments—it's a way of doing something to children to get them to comply with our wishes. It may be effective at producing this result (at least for a while), but it's very different from working *with* kids—for example, by engaging them in conversation about what makes a classroom (or family) function smoothly, or how other people are affected by what we have done—or failed to do. The latter approach is not only more respectful but more likely to help kids become thoughtful people.

   The reason praise can work in the short run is that young children are hungry for our approval. But we have a responsibility not to exploit that dependence for our own convenience. A "Good job!" to reinforce something that makes our lives a little easier can be an example of taking advantage of children's dependence. Kids may also come to feel manipulated by this, even if they can't quite explain why.

2. **Creating praise junkies.** To be sure, not every use of praise is a calculated tactic to control children's behavior. Sometimes we compliment kids just because we're genuinely pleased by what they've done. Even then, however, it's worth looking more closely. Rather than bolstering a child's self-esteem, praise may increase kids' dependence on us. The more we say, "I like the way you. . . ." or "Good_____ing," the more kids come to rely on *our* evaluations, *our* decisions about what's good and bad, rather than learning to form their own judgments. It leads them to measure their worth in terms of what will lead *us* to smile and dole out some more approval.

   Mary Budd Rowe, a researcher at the University of Florida, discovered that students who were praised lavishly by their teachers were more tentative in their responses, more apt to answer in a questioning tone of voice ("Um, seven?"). They tended to back off from an idea they had proposed as soon as an adult disagreed with them. And they were less likely to persist with difficult tasks or share their ideas with other students.

   In short, "Good job!" doesn't reassure children; ultimately, it makes them feel less secure. It may even create a vicious circle such that the more we slather on the praise, the more kids seem to need it, so we praise them some more. Sadly, some of these kids will grow into adults who continue to need someone else to pat them on the head and tell them whether what they did was OK. Surely this is not what we want for our daughters and sons.

3. **Stealing a child's pleasure.** Apart from the issue of dependence, a child deserves to take delight in her accomplishments, to feel pride in what she's learned how to do. She also deserves to decide when to feel that way. Every time we say, "Good job!", though, we're telling a child how to feel.

   To be sure, there are times when our evaluations are appropriate and our guidance is necessary—especially with toddlers and preschoolers. But a constant stream of value judgments is neither necessary nor useful for children's development. Unfortunately, we may not have realized that "Good job!" is just as much an evaluation as "Bad job!" The most notable feature of a positive judgment isn't that it's positive, but that it's a judgment. And people, including kids, don't like being judged.

   I cherish the occasions when my daughter manages to do something for the first time, or does something better than she's ever done it before. But I try to resist the knee-jerk tendency to say, "Good job!" because I don't want to dilute her joy. I want her to share her pleasure with me, not look to me for a verdict. I want her to exclaim, "I did it!" (which she often does) instead of asking me uncertainly, "Was that good?"

4. **Losing interest.** "Good painting!" may get children to keep painting for as long as we keep watching and praising. But, warns Lilian Katz, one of the country's leading authorities on early childhood education, "once attention is withdrawn, many kids won't touch the activity again." Indeed, an impressive body of scientific research has shown that the more we reward people for doing something, the more they tend to lose interest in whatever they had to do to get the reward. Now the point isn't to draw, to read, to think, to create—the point is to get the goody, whether it's an ice cream, a sticker, or a "Good job!"

   In a troubling study conducted by Joan Grusec at the University of Toronto, young children who were frequently praised for displays of generosity tended to be slightly less generous on an everyday basis than other children were. Every time they had heard "Good sharing!" or "I'm so proud of you for helping," they became a little less interested in sharing or helping. Those actions came to be seen not as something valuable in their own right but as something they had to do to get that reaction again from an adult. Generosity became a means to an end.

   Does praise motivate kids? Sure. It motivates kids to get praise. Alas, that's often at the expense of commitment to whatever they were doing that prompted the praise.

5. **Reducing achievement.** As if it weren't bad enough that "Good job!" can undermine independence, pleasure, and interest, it can also interfere with how good a job children actually do. Researchers keep finding that kids who are praised for doing well at a creative task tend to stumble at the next task—and they don't do as well as children who weren't praised to begin with.

   Why does this happen? Partly because the praise creates pressure to "keep up the good work" that gets in the way of doing so. Partly because their *interest* in what they're doing may have declined. Partly because they become less likely to take risks—a prerequisite for creativity—once they start thinking about how to keep those positive comments coming.

   More generally, "Good job!" is a remnant of an approach to psychology that reduces all of human life to behaviors that can be seen and measured. Unfortunately, this ignores the thoughts, feelings, and values that lie behind behaviors. For example, a child may share a snack with a friend as a way of attracting praise, or as a way of making sure the other child has enough to eat. Praise for sharing ignores these different motives. Worse, it actually promotes the less desirable motive by making children more likely to fish for praise in the future.

Once you start to see praise for what it is—and what it does—these constant little evaluative eruptions from adults start to produce the same effect as fingernails being dragged down a blackboard. You begin to root for a child to give his teachers or parents a taste of their own treacle by turning around to them and saying (in the same saccharine tone of voice), "Good praising!"

Still, it's not an easy habit to break. It can seem strange, at least at first, to stop praising; it can feel as though you're being chilly or withholding something. But that, it soon becomes clear, suggests that *we praise more because we need to say it than because children need to hear it*. Whenever that's true, it's time to rethink what we're doing.

What kids do need is unconditional support, love with no strings attached. That's not just different from praise—it's the *opposite* of praise. "Good job!" is conditional. It means we're offering attention and acknowledgement and approval for jumping through our hoops, for doing things that please us.

This point, you'll notice, is very different from a criticism that some people offer to the effect that we give kids too much approval, or give it too easily. They recommend that we become more miserly with our praise and demand that kids "earn" it. But the real problem isn't that children expect to be praised for everything they do these days. It's that *we're* tempted to take shortcuts, to manipulate kids with rewards instead of explaining and helping them to develop needed skills and good values.

So what's the alternative? That depends on the situation, but whatever we decide to say instead has to be offered in the context of genuine affection and love for who kids are rather than for what they've done. When unconditional support is present, "Good job!" isn't necessary; when it's absent, "Good job!" won't help.

If we're praising positive actions as a way of discouraging misbehavior, this is unlikely to be effective for long. Even when it works, we can't really say the child is now "behaving himself"; it would be more accurate to say the praise is behaving him. The alternative is to work *with* the child, to figure out the reasons he's acting that way. We may have to reconsider our own requests rather than just looking for a way to get kids to obey. (Instead of using "Good job!" to get a four-year-old to sit quietly through a long class meeting or family dinner, perhaps we should ask whether it's reasonable to expect a child to do so.)

We also need to bring kids in on the process of making decisions. If a child is doing something that disturbs others, then sitting down with her later and asking, "What do you think we can do to solve this problem?" will likely be more effective than bribes or threats. It also helps a child learn how to solve problems and teaches that her ideas and feelings are important. Of course, this process takes time and talent, care and courage. Tossing off a "Good job!" when the child acts in the way we deem appropriate takes none of those things, which helps to explain why "doing to" strategies are a lot more popular than "working with" strategies.

And what can we say when kids just do something impressive? Consider three possible responses:

- **Say nothing.** Some people insist a helpful act must be "reinforced" because, secretly or unconsciously, they believe it was a fluke. If children are basically evil, then they have to be given an artificial reason for being nice (namely, to get a verbal reward). But if that cynicism is unfounded—and a lot of research suggests that it is—then praise may not be necessary.

- **Say what you saw.** A simple, evaluation-free statement ("You put your shoes on by yourself" or even just "You did it") tells your child that you noticed. It also lets her take pride in what she did. In other cases, a more elaborate description may make sense. If your child draws a picture, you might provide feedback—not judgment—about what you noticed: "This mountain is huge!" "Boy, you sure used a lot of purple today!"

  If a child does something caring or generous, you might gently draw his attention to the effect of his action *on the other person*: "Look at Abigail's face! She seems pretty happy now that you gave her some of your snack." This is completely different from praise, where the emphasis is on how *you* feel about her sharing

- **Talk less, ask more.** Even better than descriptions are questions. Why tell him what part of his drawing impressed you when *you* can ask him what *he* likes best about it? Asking "What was the hardest part to draw?" or "How did you figure out how to make the feet the right size?" is likely to nourish his interest in drawing. Saying "Good job!", as we've seen, may have exactly the opposite effect.

This doesn't mean that all compliments, all thank-you's, all expressions of delight are harmful. We need to consider our *motives* for what we say (a genuine expression of enthusiasm is better than a desire to manipulate the child's future behavior) as well as the actual *effects* of doing so. Are our reactions helping the child to feel a sense of control over her life—or to constantly look to us for approval? Are they helping her to become more excited about what she's doing in its own right—or turning it into something she just wants to get through in order to receive a pat on the head

It's not a matter of memorizing a new script, but of keeping in mind our long-term goals for our children and watching for the effects of what we say. The bad news is that the use of positive reinforcement really isn't so positive. The good news is that you don't have to evaluate in order to encourage.

Part 5

Some Contemporary Issues

Introduction to Some Contemporary Issues

The last section of this text introduces you to the writings of four of my colleagues and their current research. It is foundational in the sense that it gives you a snapshot of the work being conducted in a department of education of a midsize university at the end of the first decade of the twenty-first century.

It is philosophical when Julie Williams explores the moral dimensions of assessment. It is psychological when Dan Glisczinski introduces you to transformational learning. It is historical when Gerry Nierengarten traces for you some of the history of special needs students in America's schools. And it is sociological when Chris Johnson autobiographically travels through the development of literacy in contemporary society.

Special Needs Students

—*Gerry Nierengarten, Ed.D.*

He is dressed in a manner that personified his attitude toward school and life in general: black baggy pants, black T-shirt, black tennis shoes, and chains everywhere. The heaviness of his attire, in combination with his small ninth-grade stature, diminishes him even more. His hair is spiked with gel and there are many piercings. He walks with great labor as if he were carrying a heavy load. There is no interaction between him and the other students in the class. He slouches at his desk, surrendering to one more hour of torture, anonymity and extreme passive-aggressive resignation. With 30 students in this English class, many with special needs (he being one of them), it is an exercise of endurance more than one of learning. He has found creative ways to pass the time without drawing attention to himself—playing with his chains out of sight of the teacher, laying his head on the desk, blankly staring into space. He is a master at hiding because he has been practicing for years. As long as he doesn't disrupt the classroom maybe he will be left alone. He is not at all prepared for class—no paper, pencil, book, or will to engage in the learning process. He is not in school by choice but by law. Chances are pretty good that he didn't have breakfast or even see an adult before he left for school. It doesn't matter—adults only make life more difficult.

As the teacher begins, he resorts to his own world. You can force his attendance but you cannot force his learning. He might as well be a million miles away. This is the way that he copes with school. Ever since elementary school, he has developed coping skills that have served him well. As long as he plays invisible and helpless, he will be left alone. By ninth grade he is a master. On the rare occasion that he is called on or a task is required of him, he simply shrugs and recedes even further, and the teacher just does not have the time or the energy to spend on encouraging him to become involved. There are other students in the class that are ready and willing to engage in the discussion and the teacher has curriculum and standards to fulfill. He can play this game for a very long time.

Each day plays out as the one before. Assignments are incomplete and tests are disastrous. Reading and comprehension have always been difficult. Early in elementary school there was some help and support but that has diminished over the years to where it is nonexistent. He is so far behind that any effort on his part is wasted. Why even try? The downward spiral of failure continues with no end or success in sight. He cannot wait to be out of school.

(Actual observation, ninth-grade English)

This scenario could be repeated thousands if not millions of times in classrooms across America. Students with disabilities who have been placed in the general education classroom find the challenge overwhelming, yet this is considered the least restrictive environment for them. How did it come about that some of the most challenged students find their way into the general education classroom? Are schools equipped to meet the needs of these students? How can teachers achieve some level of success for all the students that enter the classroom?

INTRODUCTION

Since the passage of Public Law 94-142, Education of All Handicapped Children's Act of 1975, and the subsequent reauthorizations through the Individuals with Disabilities Education Act (IDEA 1990, 1997) and Individuals with Disabilities Education Improvement Act (IDEA 2004), public schools continue to strive for the successful inclusion of students with disabilities into the general education classroom. No Child Left Behind (NCLB 2001) has not only increased the pressure on public schools to include students with disabilities in the general education classroom, but has also established a form of yearly progress accountability to which schools must adhere. Clearly, legislation has demanded that students with disabilities be included in every aspect of the general education experience. This experience must include high academic standards that will encourage student success.

In high schools across the United States, special education teachers, parents, and administrators are working hard to find the most appropriate educational delivery model for students with special needs. Efforts are being made to reduce labeling and placement of students in separate special education classes by developing interventions to meet the needs of all students within the regular education classroom (Stainback and Stainback 1992).

When employing the practice of inclusion, students with disabilities are educated with their nondisabled peers, with additional special education supports and services provided as needed (Vaughn, Bos, and Schumm 2007). During 1984 and 1985, only 25 percent of the students aged 6 through 21 with disabilities spent more than 80 percent of their school day in a regular class. By 2002, that figure had risen to 48.2 percent (U.S. Department of Education 2006). Each year there are increased efforts to create an environment within the general education classroom in which all students are provided with the academic, social, and emotional support necessary to achieve success.

Inclusion, in a way, provides a normalized educational experience for all children with disabilities (Scheffel, Kallam, Smith, and Hoernicke 1996). Some of the benefits of inclusion as noted in the research are: strong graduation rates for students with disabilities (Aguilar et al. 2006; Luster and Durrett 2003), improved feelings of self-esteem and self-confidence (Walther-Thomas 1997), improved social skills and positive peer relations (Walther-Thomas, Bryant, and Land 1996), improved academic and behavioral performance (Trent et al. 2003), and a small to moderate beneficial effect on the academic and social outcomes of students with special needs (Baker, Wang, and Walberg 1994).

BRIEF HISTORY OF SPECIAL EDUCATION

There have always been exceptional learners, but there have not always been special educational services to address their needs (Hallahan and Kauffman 2006). In the pre-Revolutionary era, the most society had offered children with disabilities was protection—asylum from a cruel world into which they did not fit and in which they could not survive with dignity, if they could survive at all (Hallahan and Kauffman 2006).

The primary originators of the field of special education were European physicians, Jean-Marc Gaspard Itard and Éduard Séguin. They further advanced practices in the areas of the deaf and so-called idiotic children. Samuel Gridley Howe, Thomas Hopkins Gallaudet, and Dorothea Dix, were among the prominent U.S. thinkers who promoted the practice of special education for students who were deaf and blind (Hallahan and Kauffman 2006). In the years following World War II, such pioneers as Grace Fernald, Marianne Frostig, and Heinz Werner conducted research, developed programs, and gave new impetus to the field of special education (Sadker and Sadker 2003). Over the years, the professionals who worked and advanced the area of special education saw hope and potential for individuals with special needs. Their revolutionary ideas formed the groundwork for present-day practices in special education.

The emergence of psychology and sociology and, especially, the beginning of the widespread use of mental tests in early years of the twentieth century had enormous implications for the growth of special education. With the further advancement of the education profession and mandatory attendance laws, there was a growing realization among teachers and school administrators that a number of students must be given something beyond the ordinary classroom experience (Hallahan and Kauffman 2006). Through the work of Elizabeth Farrell, a teacher in New York City in the twentieth century, students who were being poorly served or excluded from public schools were recognized and afforded an appropriate education for optimum learning. She and the New York City superintendent of schools attempted to use information about child development, social work, mental testing and instruction to address the needs of children and youths who were being ill served in or excluded from regular classes and schools (Hallahan and Kauffman). The use of these multiple sources of information resulted in students with disabilities receiving an appropriate education and related health and social services necessary for the best possible learning (Hendrick and MacMillan1989).

Litigation and legislation have played a major role in the history of special education. In fact, much of the progress in meeting the educational needs of children and youths with disabilities is attributable to the litigation (lawsuits or court decisions) and subsequent laws requiring states and localities to include students with special needs in the public education system (Hallahan and Kauffman).

In the 1950s and 1960s, there emerged an increased recognition and respect for the human dignity of all citizens regardless of their individual differences. There was a powerful momentum away from more segregated options for the education of minority students. In the landmark case of 1954, Brown v. Board of Education, the Supreme Court ruled that separate is not equal, which had an almost immediate impact in breaking down the exclusionary policies toward blacks and other racial and ethnic minorities (Stainback, Stainback, and Forest 1989; Vaughn, Bos, and Schumm 2007). This court decision also paved the way for a closer look at the exclusionary policies in regards to students with disabilities. This court case was the point at which disability rights were launched.

This decade also saw parents of children with disabilities organize and initiate advocacy activities and an increase in federal government–funded legislation supporting increased education for students considered disadvantaged, low income and/or handicapped (Jung, 1998; Stainback, Stainback, and Forest, 1989). During this time in history, the educational support and resources for students with disabilities was experiencing considerable growth and attention. The Elementary and Secondary Education Act (ESEA) passed in 1965 initiated the role of the federal government in protecting and providing for students from disadvantaged backgrounds so that they would have equal access to the public education system. A critical component of ESEA for individuals with disabilities was the grant program that encouraged states to create and improve on programs for students with disabilities (Vaughn, Bos, and Schumm 2007). For those concerned about the education of students with disabilities, their segregation was being viewed as abnormal, inappropriate, and harmful. Greater attention and advocacy was being directed toward including students with disabilities in the general education classroom as opposed to keeping them segregated in institutions, private schools, and special classes.

An additional piece of legislation that affected the definition and delivery of educational services to students with disabilities was Section 504 of the Vocational Rehabilitation Act (P.L. 93-112) of 1973. Section 504 was considered to be the first piece of civil rights legislation specifically providing guarantees of rights to persons with disabilities (Murdick, Gartin, and Crabtree 2002). This section requires that institutions make architectural modifications to increase physical accessibility of buildings and those new structures be accessible to persons with disabilities. This law has visibly changed the look and accessibility of public schools (Choate 2004). Although Section 504 applies to individuals of all ages, school age individuals benefited from its application to educational programs and school environments.

Special education–related litigation began to appear in the 1960s. These lawsuits played a prominent role in the development of current legislation. They led to laws that ensured educational services for individuals with disabilities (Colarusso and O'Rourke 2007). Table 1 lists the most notable of these court decisions from 1967 through 1972.

Table 5.1—*Decisions in Court Cases Relevant to Special Education*

Case	Decision
Hobson v. Hansen (1967)	Resulted in the ruling that ability grouping or tracking violated due process and the equal protection clause of the Constitution.
Diana v. State Board of Education (1970)	Required the use of nondiscriminatory assessments and the elimination of unfair test items as well as testing children in their primary language.
Larry P. v. Riles (1972)	Ruled that intelligence tests cannot be the sole basis for placement and that a test must be developed that is not culturally biased.
Mills v. Board of Education (1972)	Ruled that students cannot be excluded from school because of a disability. Created a zero reject policy. Schools could not claim fiscal inability as an excuse for not providing appropriate services.
PARC v. Commonwealth of Pennsylvania (1972)	The Pennsylvania Association of Retarded Citizens (PARC) filed suit to gain the right for students with mental retardation to attend school. Provided the provision for a free, appropriate public education (FAPE).

In 1975, influenced by nearly a decade of litigation, and after holding hearings across the country, Congress enacted the Education of All Handicapped Children Act (EAHCA), Public Law 94-142. The passage of P.L. 94-142 was a milestone in the education of children with disabilities. The act engaged the federal government as a partner with the states in educating children with the specified disabilities (Huefner 2006).

The basic rights that P.L. 94-142 gave to children with disabilities included (a) the right to a free appropriate public education (FAPE), (b) in a setting that to the maximum extent appropriate allowed education with children who did not have disabilities (least restrictive environment, or LRE), (c) governed by a written, individualized education program (IEP) that was (d) based on a thorough evaluation of the child's needs. Along with the basic rights to specialized instruction and related services came procedural safeguards to ensure the involvement of parents at key stages of educational decision making (Huefner 2006). The burden to locate, identify and evaluate all eligible children rested with the public school system. No one was to be denied service.

In 1986, the U.S. Office of Special Education and Rehabilitation Services in the U.S. Department of Education issued the Regular Education Initiative (REI). The purpose was to find ways to serve students classified as having mild and moderate disabilities in regular classrooms by encouraging special education and other special programs to form a partnership with regular education (Stainback, Stainback, and Forest 1989). REI proponents claimed that students, teachers, administrators and parents would benefit from merging special and general education, wherein more students would participate in mainstream education. Advocates further asserted that the REI would lead to minimizing the negative stigma of labels, increasing opportunity for modeling desired social and academic behaviors, learning in situations more representative of the real world, and increasing appreciation of individual differences (Choate 2004).

In 1990 and 1997 Congress amended P.L. 94-142. With the passage of Public Law 101-476 in 1990, the title of the law was changed from the Education of All Handicapped Children's Act to the Individuals with Disabilities Education Act to reflect the use of people-first language. It also expanded to include services to children with disabilities ages 18 through 21.

The most current reauthorization of IDEA came in 2004 and is referred to as the Individuals with Disabilities Education Improvement Act (Public Law 108-446) or IDEA 2004. Some major changes to the provisions of IDEA were made to align it with No Child Left Behind (2001). Special education law has always recognized the importance of the working relationship between the general educator and the special educator as they meet the needs of the student with disabilities. Additionally, the legislation realized the importance of the participation of the student with disabilities in the general education curriculum as well as the classroom. In fact, IDEA 2004 strongly emphasized the presumption that children with disabilities would be educated in the general education setting as well as having access to and advancing in the general education curriculum, with the general educator having the needed curricular expertise (Hyatt 2007).

The foundation of legislation that addresses the needs of individuals with disabilities has always been built on the presumption of inclusion, not exclusion. From 1973 and the Vocational Rehabilitation Act to the present-day Individuals with Disabilities Education Improvement Act of 2004, the language has only grown stronger for the right of individuals with disabilities to be part of all that society has to offer. There have been parts of our social structure that have progressed slowly and painfully toward this model of inclusion—public schools, for example. The structure of the learning environment in high schools, in particular, has been slow to respond to the changing demands of a unique student population. School reform, though, is prompting schools to evaluate how learning/teaching is delivered and the configuration of the typical classroom.

LEARNING ENVIRONMENTS—AMERICA'S SCHOOLS

In an attempt to understand the learning environments in public education, it is important to look briefly at how public education is structured and the dual systems of general education and special education. Doll (1993) refers to this structure as closed and mechanical in nature. With this perspective we are better able to understand the complexity and the resistance to change that plagues public education and possible means of responding to the opposition.

America's schools are a structured and regimented system. Adhering to the modernist view of predication and control (Doll 1993), bells ring and students and teachers respond automatically. Curriculum is constructed with standards and benchmarks established by local, state, and national organizations. Teachers are assigned to classes and students' schedules are printed. This linear, sequential, easily quantifiable ordering system dominates education today (Doll). It is a familiar routine that has been repeated for many years. Change is difficult when it is deeply entrenched in time and routine.

This learning environment has also fostered isolation among teachers. Each professional has been highly trained to complete a specific task within his or her classroom, with the development of collaborative skills between general and special education teachers just now emerging. Collaboration is taking the form of professional development communities, where there is a recognized need for teachers and other professionals to communicate and share on a personal and professional level across all grade and content levels. Through this information exchange, responsibility is assumed for not only our learning, but also the learning of our colleagues and students. As the classroom becomes more diverse and high-stakes testing increasingly ubiquitous, it is imperative for professionals to collaborate to meet all student needs.

School structure

The modernist paradigm to which America's schools and curriculum adhere embraces programmed learning, teacher-proof curriculum, prediction, and control (Doll 1993). Special education also adheres to the modernist view that promotes a scientific and objectivist perspective of professionalism and student learning (Skrtic 1995).

School organizations are managed as machine bureaucracies; as such, the formal structure of schools rationalizes simple work into a series of routine, prescribed tasks accomplished through standardized work processes (Cole 1995). This is accomplished through formalization—detailed job specifications, precise instructions, and rules (Skrtic 1991). Schools adopt the machine bureaucracy structure because it is what the public expects all legitimate organizations to look like (Skrtic).

There are some significant disadvantages to organizing schools as machine bureaucracies. Such organizations, which are considered closed systems, find it very difficult to change and to adapt to new circumstances. In closed systems, stability, centers of balance, and equilibrium are key ingredients (Doll 1993). With respect to school employees, a machine bureaucracy does not encourage questioning and reflection but rather expects the workers to accept the status quo. Educators are not encouraged to be creative or innovative, and new problems are often ignored or approached in a fragmented fashion (Cole 1995).

Schools exemplify bureaucratic practices. They possess the practices that are commonly attributed to bureaucracies: a fixed division of labor with job descriptions and responsibilities, a set of rules and regulations, hierarchy of authority, technical qualifications, isolation, and planning (Bolman and Deal 2003).

Special education also has bureaucratic practices that operate parallel to general education. Although special education is technically a subsystem of general education, Stainback and Stainback (1984) note that, in effect, it is a dual system of education with its own pupils, teachers, supervisory staff, and funding system. Perhaps the largest, most pervasive issue in special education is its relationship to general education. The relationship of special to general education has been controversial since the beginning of universal public schooling ("History of special education" n.d.). However, in the late twentieth and early twenty-first centuries, attempts have been made to reduce the sharp dichotomy between special and regular education, yet the dual system basically remains intact. This two-box system of public education leads to various misconceptions about students with disabilities, which often negatively influences the way people relate to individuals with a disability (Choate 2004) and the professionals that work with them. Longitudinal studies and research findings confirmed the experience of students, parents, and teachers that the separate system was flawed and unequal; this led to many championing a new inclusive design (Stainback, Stainback, and Forest 1989).

There are not two distinct types of students—special and regular. All students differ along continuums of intellectual, physical and psychological characteristics. Individual differences are universal and thus the study of unusual people is really a study of all humankind (Stainback and Stainback 1984). The concept of neurodiversity is emerging and embraces the idea of that atypical neurological wiring is part of the normal spectrum of human differences and is to be tolerated and respected like any other human difference (Armstrong 2005).

At the heart of the debate on inclusion of students with disabilities and the merging of the parallel systems of special education and general education is the personalizing of instruction for each student and accommodation of all students' needs (Cole 1995). Skrtic (1991) contends that an effort to meet all student needs, both regular and special, would require a fundamentally different type of organization than is currently in our schools. The professional bureaucracy, which is how schools are currently managed, is nonadaptable because it is premised on the principle of standardization, which configures it as a performance organization for perfecting standard programs (Skrtic). Skritic proposes a different type of organization and draws on the work of Henry Mitzenberg (1979), who advanced the idea of an adhocracy. According to Mitzenberg, within an adhocracy, individuals are free to coordinate and collaborate by mutual adjustment. In an adhocracy, existing knowledge and skills are merely bases on which new knowledge and skills can be built. In order for new knowledge and skills to evolve, the boundaries of conventional specialization and differentiation must be broken apart. In operation, the adhocracy solves problems and creates new ideas directly on behalf of its clients. A type of adhocracy emerging in public high schools is the collaboration between general and special education teachers as students with disabilities are being included in the general education classroom on a more frequent basis.

Collaborative schools engage in positive partnerships and interactive team activities to achieve a shared goal of promoting effective instruction for all students (Goor 1994). They embrace a composite of beliefs and practices that support educational improvement through staff harmony, promote mutual respect between teachers and administrators, as well as provide a professional working environment (Goor). Educational improvements and instructional effectiveness are results of a school climate that embraces this new mode of operation.

Educational inclusion of students with disabilities has been widely promoted in recent years, resulting in ever-increasing numbers of students with disabilities receiving all or nearly all of their services in general education classrooms (Mastropieri and Scruggs 2001). In each of the age groups, 6–11, 12–17 and 18–21, the largest proportion of students with disabilities were educated in a regular education classroom for most of the school day; that is, they were outside the regular classroom less than 21 percent of the school day (U.S. Department of Education, 2006). This means that the teachers that serve the students with disabilities, both general and special educators, must work collaboratively to meet the educational and behavioral needs of those students.

CONCLUSION

Students with special needs are first and foremost students. Without a doubt, they bring challenges into the classroom. But they also expose the flaws of the current systems that work to educate them. These systems, university preparatory programs and K–12 public education structures, must quickly move beyond business as usual and recognize that the walls of segregation came down many years ago.

REFERENCES

Aguilar, C. M., Morocco, C. C., Parker, C. E., and Zigmond, N. 2006. Middletown High School: Equal opportunity for academic achievement. *Learning Disabilities Research and Practice* 21, no, 3:159–171.

Armstrong, T. 2005. Special education and the concept of neurodiverstiy. *New Horizons for Learning Online Journal 11*(3). Retrieved February 26, 2009, from http://www.newhorizons.org/spneeds/inclusion/information/armstrong.htm.

Baker, E. T., Wang, M. C., and Walberg, H. J. 1994. The effects of inclusion on learning. *Educational Leadership*, 33–35.

Bolman, L. G., and Deal, T. E. 2003. *Reframing organizations: Artistry, choice and leadership*, 3rd ed. San Francisco: Jossey-Bass.

Choate, J. S. 2004. *Successful inclusive teaching: Proven ways to detect and correct special needs*, 4th ed. Boston: Allyn and Bacon.

Colarusso, R. P., and O'Rourke, C. M. 2007. *Special education for all teachers*. Dubuque, Iowa: Kendall Hunt Publishing.

Cole, C. M. 1995. A contextualized understanding of the teachers' practice, their collaborative relationships, and the inclusion of students with disabilities. Unpublished doctoral dissertation, Indiana University, Bloomington, Indiana.

Doll, W. E. 1993. *A post-modern perspective on curriculum.* New York: Teachers College Press.

Goor, M. B. 1994. Collaboration enhances education for all students. In *Advances in Special Education,* Vol. 8. JAI Press: 33–51.

Hallahan, D. P., and Kauffman, J. M. 2006. *Exceptional learners: An introduction to special education,* 10th ed. Boston: Allyn and Bacon.

Hendrick, I. G., and MacMillan, D. L. 1989. Selecting children for special education in New York City: William Maxwell, Elizabeth Farrell, and the development of ungraded classes, 1900–1920. *Journal of Special Education* 22, 4:395–417.

History of special education. n.d. Retrieved February 20, 2009, from http://www.answers.com/topic/history-of-special-education.

Huefner, D. S. 2006. *Getting comfortable with special education law,* 2nd ed. Norwood MA: Christopher-Gordon Publishers.

Hyatt, K. J. 2007. The new IDEA: Changes, concerns, and questions. Intervention in *School and Clinic* 42, no 3:131–136.

Jung, B. 1998. Mainstreaming and fixing things: Secondary teachers and inclusion. *The Educational Forum* 62:131–138.

Luster, J. N., and Durrett, J. 2003. Does educational placement matter in the performance of students with disabilities? Paper presented at the Annual Meeting of the Mid-South Educational Research Association. Retrieved January 2006 from http://eric.ed.gov/ERICWebPortal/contentdelivery/servlet/ERICServlet?accno=ED482518.

Mastropieri, M. A., and Scruggs, T. E. 2001. Promoting inclusion in secondary classrooms. *Learning Disabilities Quarterly* 24, no. 4:265–274.

Mintzberg, H. 1979. *The structuring of organizations.* Englewood Cliffs, NJ: Prentice Hall.

Murdick, N., Gartin, B., and Crabtree, T. 2002. *Special education law.* Upper Saddle River, NJ: Prentice Hall.

Sadker, M. P., and Sadker, D. M. 2003. *Teachers, school, and society,* 6 ed. Boston: McGraw-Hill.

Scheffel, D. L., Kallam, M., Smith, K. N., and Hoernicke, P. A. 1996. Inclusion: What it is and how it works best. Fort Hays State University, Kansas. (ERIC Document Reproduction Service No. ED412663).

Skrtic, T. M. 1991. *Behind special education: A critical analysis of professional culture and school organization.* Denver, CO: Love Publishing.

Skrtic, T. M. 1995. *Disability and democracy: Reconstructing (special) education for postmodernity.* New York: Teachers College Press.

Stainback, S., and Stainback, W. 1984. A rationale for the merger of special and regular education. *Exceptional Children* 51, no. 2:102–111.

Stainback, S., and Stainback, W. 1992. Including students with severe disabilities in the regular education classroom. Preventing School Failure, 26–30.

Stainback, S., Stainback, W., and Forest, M. 1989. *Educating all students in the mainstream of regular education.* Baltimore: Paul H. Brookes Publishing Co.

Trent, S. C., Driver, B. L., Wood, M. H., Parrott, P. S., Martin, T. F., and Smith, W. G. 2003. Creating and sustaining a special education/general education partnership: A story of change and uncertainty. *Teaching and Teacher Education* 19:203–219.

U.S. Department of Education. 2006. *Twenty-sixth annual report to congress on the implementation of the Individuals with Disabilities Education Act.* Washington, DC: Author.

Vaughn, S., Bos, C. S., and Schumm, J. S. 2007. *Teaching students who are exceptional, diverse and at risk in the general education classroom,* 4th ed. Boston: Allyn and Bacon.

Walther-Thomas, C. S. 1997. Co-teaching experiences: The benefits and problems that teachers and principals report over time. *Journal of Learning Disabilities* 30, no. 4:395–407.

Walther-Thomas, C. S., Bryant, M., and Land, S. 1996. Planning for effective co-teaching: The key to successful inclusion. *Remedial and Special Education* 17:255–265.

Transformational Learning

—Dan Glisczinski, Ed.D.

> *"Is the primary purpose of education to impart information, construct knowledge, or initiate change?" asks Ettling (2006, 61). I trace my visceral investment in this question back to finding myself lost as a disoriented new teacher in a distant education wilderness, seeking to understand education's primary purpose.*

GRINGO PERDIDO

Weeks after graduating from college, I was wrapping up a summer as a wilderness camp counselor and packing my bicycle saddlebags for a volunteer teaching year in Central America. The prior four years of school had made me more informed, resourceful, and engaged in intentional living than I had earlier hoped to be. I learned these things from more skillful teachers than I knew existed. And these lessons transpired in classrooms, courtyards, and cottages on both sides of the Atlantic. And so I felt prepared to sojourn to a distant rainforest school to impart information, construct knowledge, and initiate change in a second-chance secondary school for students ready to improve their lives.

But upon arrival at the humid edge of the Belizean rainforest, I began to sweat the impending reality of teaching. My early idealism faded in the face of concrete complexity. Self-doubt clouded my consciousness, as I began to realize that teaching for change—which once seemed so tidy in the abstract—now revealed itself as contextually complicated. I questioned whether I had anything meaningful to teach, let alone fostering discovery of transforming truths. I wondered whether my early optimism was perhaps founded in folly.

I spent an anxious yet alluring welcome week splitting my time between mapping curriculum and scouting the Maya Mountain range for lessons to be learned. While I envisioned for my students a far-reaching journey of academics and extracurriculars, my very own education in perspective would commence shortly thereafter—as soon as I found myself lost right in the middle of town.

My suspicions of folly were confirmed one morning on my walk to school in the early hours of that sophomoric week. Rapt by the lushness of the scarlet hibiscus hedges, I followed the beauty of the long road to school that morning. The new day was fresh, and the macaws held forth from their verdant perches in the surrounding hills.

Then, in my ears came pointed words through the flowering bush; *"Gringo! Ch!ngada Gringo!"* came a child's voice with borrowed bravado.

"Gringo! Ch!ngada Gringo!" the voice insisted again through the now-thorny hedge. While the small Kriol voice found its way through the bush, his boyish body stayed mostly hidden. My large *gringo* frame, in contrast, was whiter than the bleached clay road on which I stood, scorned and disoriented.

Speechless, I tightened my backpack straps and quickened my pace to school. As I fled, I stole uneasy glances at the hiding hedge, where I saw my juvenile accuser in his brown uniform shorts and yellow collared school shirt scurrying back to the thatched-roof hut where his mother slapped the day's *maize* tortillas over a breakfast fire.

Although I had easily enough escaped the scene, I had a harder time ditching my disorientation. Had I really just been called out as an @*&#!$% imposter by a child? Where did he learn to talk such smack? How did I become a *ch!ngada gringo*—an epithet generally reserved for the disdained white soldiers who sped recklessly atop tanks through the Maya Mountain villages? Neither a soldier nor speeding, I contrived a self-preserving litany of silent objections to the characterization.

Didn't my accuser know I was there as a teacher? That I was there to impart knowledge rather than to perpetuate ignorance? There to construct understanding rather than to fabricate fear? To initiate changes that would improve the courses of our collective existence? Didn't this neighborhood know that I was a *voluntario*, teaching for a year for free? Didn't everyone know that people deserve to be judged on the merits of their own behavior rather than by the deeds of those whom they resemble?

I'm certain that he neither knew nor cared.

So, alas, I said nothing—as nothing I could have said on that white-hot road would have changed much of anything.

WHITE-HOT AND HOLLOW

Feeling disoriented and spurned, I skipped breakfast and fumbled through a doubly self-conscious day playing school. I saw myself standing as a hollow *gringo perdido*—or lost whitey—in the trusting presence of my Mestizo, Kriol, Mayan, Garifuna, Aztec, Caribe, and Arawak students. That morning I traded suspicion for fact. I learned that not only was I the new and untested teacher, I was also the new and unwanted intruder. I heard it straight from the mouth of a child.

As that white-hot and hollow day turned to evening and then to night, I returned to my stilted house where I pined for peace and sleep. Finding neither, I grew weary of my self and my sojourn.

The next day, I took the short cut to school, and then continued to do so for weeks. I was all too willing to forgo the allure of the hibiscus and macaws in order to arrive at school with my self-image moderately intact—rather than mostly unraveled.

Thereafter, for weeks into months, the child's chiding voice echoed in my head on most any road I traveled. As it echoed, I began to recognize in it some perspectives that were not entirely off base. After all, I was pretty much the whitest guy around. I was oddly white, compared to my neighbors and students. I supposed I looked at times like an off-duty soldier who was willing to get lost on most any road that invited travel. Alas, seeing myself through the eyes of my neighborhood, I reluctantly saw in myself the unwitting *gringo perdido*.

THE POISON GIFT OF TRANSFORMATION

Looking back, I recognize that the disorienting events of that poignant morning served as a gift to my development. These events initiated a transformation of my perspective of the roles of teachers, students, and individuals in the context of the larger world. This poison gift of perspective transformation enabled me to simultaneously make space for equal and opposite realities. I discovered myself increasingly able to acknowledge and release my forgivably flawed and culturally inherited beliefs and behaviors in favor of increasingly accurate and justified understandings. I came to realize that gaining valuable information, constructing meaningful knowledge, and initiating sustainable change would demand personal transformation.

TRANSFORMATIVE LEARNING THEORY

Broadly speaking, transformative learning theory, according to Daloz (1990), describes a process of enabling proactive thinking, incorporating multiple perspectives, and encouraging dialogue and construction of knowledge. More specifically, Mezirow (2000) explains that transformative learning is a process through which learners experience a deep shift in perspective—becoming "more inclusive, differentiating, open to other viewpoints, critically reflective of assumptions, emotionally capable of change, and integrative of experience" (pp. 7–8). Brookfield (2000) suggests that through critical reflection, erroneous frames of reference—or inaccurate assumptions and points of view—become apparent. Once such inaccuracies are identified, they may be replaced by more accurate and critically aware frames of reference.

ESSENCE OF PERSPECTIVE TRANSFORMATION

Although the rational and extra-rational dynamics of transformation are the subject of passionate debate among scholars, research conducted by Herbers (1998) has distilled the cognitive essence of transformation into four foundational phases that include: (a) disorienting dilemmas, (b) critical reflection, (c) rational dialogue, and (d) action.

In order to more clearly see these phases, let's return to my own transformative education in perspective that took place in Central America some years ago, viewing the events through these progressive phases.

DISORIENTATION

Perspective transformation—whether gradual and incremental or sudden and epochal—is often triggered by disorienting events that create cognitive dissonance, explains Cranton (2006). Disorientation, in my own experience, came from being called out as a *ch!ngada gringo* in my Belizean host village. Whereas I had anticipated a relationship of mutual regard, in reality, I found myself the subject of scorn. I had operated under the assumption that my own self-favorable interpretation was the primary and logical frame of reference through which to interpret my work and my existence as a volunteer teacher. Disorientation, however, asserted a contrasting interpretation.

In the hours and days thereafter, in the classroom, on the road, and out in the ancient hills, I began to catch glimpses of myself as the lost fool who had allowed a self-aggrandized interpretation of his new existence to cover a deceiving myopic view of reality. I had planned to be regarded as the trusted hermano. In contrast, I came to learn that I was in fact reviled as the ch!ngada gringo—or the current filthy vestige of cultural hegemony.

CRITICAL REFLECTION

In the weeks that followed my disorientating discovery that I was considered a *gringo perdido*, I experienced a shift in perspective from which I could not return. My view of myself was transformed from forgivably flawed to self-aware and increasingly informed. I discovered that my new reality demanded that I acknowledge equal and opposite truths from those I had known in other contexts. Over time, I grew to trust that I could seek what Mezirow (2000) describes as more accurate, permeable, and differentiating perspectives without losing my history, my identity, or myself.

According to Brookfield (2000) the process that enables disorienting dilemmas to foster perspective transformation is called "critical self reflection on assumptions" in order to understand the "culturally contingent . . . tacit, and unproblematized" thoughts and expectations that are "socially created and learned" (pp. 131–33). Critical self reflection on my own assumptions as a teacher and a traveler revealed that although I was aware of multiple and conflicting perspectives, through my own limited frames of reference I uncritically validated some while tacitly discounting others.

Reflecting on my folly, I grew to understand myself as existing in the midst of conflicting yet valid realities. Critical reflection suggested that I attempt to understand contrasting views and practices through both emic— or inside—perspectives as well as from etic—or outside—perspectives. In short, I developed my capacity to be at variance with myself, and to be enriched by multiple and conflicting interpretations.

Disorientation, followed by committed critique of my assumptions, revealed that my previously held and unexamined beliefs about imparting information, constructing knowledge, and initiating change were, in fact, an insufficient match for my new reality. As a result of this perspective transformation, I got to retain a good deal of whom I was. But I also got to release a bunch of ignorance and inauthenticity—in the form of unexamined assumptions. In doing so, I gained an emerging ability to simultaneously acknowledge and critique my culturally bound habits of mind.

RATIONAL DIALOGUE

In the months thereafter, my *gringo* existence became purposively problematized, and foundational questions about whom I was and what I was doing became more frequent. I learned to meet answers with questions that sought not cleverness but instead clarity. My teachers—who ranged from my insightful peers to community sages—helped me acknowledge and become unbeholden to the beliefs that had formerly dictated my thought and behavior.

Rational dialogues with my teachers allowed me to recognize my folly. I was interpreting unfamiliar experiences through familiar frames of reference.

Through dialogue, I learned that part of the folly lay in assuming that imperfect strangers would share accurate and complementary notions of each other's existence. I realized it was folly to assume that the kid who labeled me the *ch!ngada gringo* and I would share the same lily-white assessment of my foreign presence in his neighborhood.

Another part of my folly, I learned through rational dialogue, was failing to acknowledge the varying and often thorny associations that different individuals have with school. Does it exist to impose or impart information? To contradict or construct meaningful knowledge? To obstruct or initiate constructive change? For whom? And to what extent are these experiences universal?

A further dimension of the folly was my mistaken assumption that conflict in community building was, by nature, unconstructive. And so I was operating in a demanding environment under the naive assumption that right intention would bring right effort. I had not learned the noble truth that with striving comes suffering, and so my suffering brought disillusionment instead of right view.

In the weeks, months, and years thereafter, rational dialogue taught me to view disorientation and conflict from a different set of perspectives—namely, that conflict and adversity could be as constructive as I chose these to be. What mattered most was what I chose to do with the complexity.

ACTION

In the semesters that followed, I learned to learn from disorientation. Although my mistakes certainly did not cease, my process for making sense of these mistakes changed fundamentally. Following the lead of my teachers, I learned to process cognitive dissonance through critical reflection, and in doing so I found opportunities for perspective critique that allowed me to survive—and, in some cases, thrive—in the midst of the complexities that are as predictable as they are difficult throughout education and life.

Over the course of those formative semesters, I continued to find myself revealed as a *gringo perdido*. Yet in contrast to that sophomoric week, I learned that I could step outside of myself and laugh about the feelings of embarrassment and self-loathing that come with being called out as lost. It's not that I blew off my mistakes, but instead I chose to critique my own unwarranted expectations to perform flawlessly in the midst of uncertainty.

I learned to meet the cognitive dissonance of disorienting dilemmas with critical reflection. I learned lessons in rational dialogue from my teachers who guided me toward greater clarity in thought and action. I learned to value—while imperfectly practicing—listening with suspended judgment, which may require a lifetime of practice.

In the end, perspective transformation taught me how to grow authentically as an acknowledged *gringo perdido* in that Maya Mountain village. Perspective transformation led me to appreciate and value the insights I gained from seeing myself and the world through the eyes—as well as the conflicting value systems of many—including the trash-talking, hedge-whisperer on the long road to school.

Had perspective transformation not taught me how to learn, I'd have taken off, checked out, or gone through the motions—playing school until my time was up. In doing so, I would have been hiding from myself and from the demands of my future. These demands would surely include skillful negotiation of disorienting dilemmas, critical reflection on the tacit assumptions hidden in conflicting perspectives, rational dialogue on boundless opportunities, and conscientious action. In short, I'd have been hiding from—rather than transformed by—life.

BLESSED BEYOND REASON (NOT THE SHARPEST TOOL)

In the decades since being called out as an unwitting *gringo*, I've been blessed beyond reason in the form of my family and the larger community in which I live and work. And now, when in my memory I hear the echo of my Kriol teacher giving me an education in perspective calling me a *gringo*, I'm happy to nod and acknowledge my young teacher's lesson.

Yet the lessons of a transformed perspective remain to direct me in negotiating the current complexities of life. Finn (2006) refers to these complexities as the crushing and colossal expectations of authentic living in mind, body, and soul in a culturally complex world. In relationship to these expectations, the ability to meet disorienting dilemmas with critical reflection, rational dialogue, and informed action may just be the difference between surviving and thriving.

And as my wise, loving grandmother has reminded me (on multiple occasions, in the presence of my children) that out of all her grandchildren, I'm certainly not the sharpest tool in the shed. So, consider this observation from my grandmother: If this *gringo perdido* can learn how to learn, who then cannot find his or her way through a transforming education in perspective?

PERSPECTIVES ON TRANSFORMATION

For individuals of my generation, effectively negotiating life's disorientating dilemmas may be perceived as a blessing or a desired qualification for success. Yet effective negotiation of cognitive and relational dissonance will be an essential qualification and a required skill for current and future generations of students, teachers, and citizens living in what Friedman (2007) asserts is a flattened and super-connected world.

Marx (2002) underscores this reality in noting, "Major global, demographic, technological, assessment and cultural trends are shaking the foundations of society as we have known it. Nowhere will these seismic shifts have greater impact than in our schools." (p. 1). Achieving an integrated and transformative education is not only possible, but it is necessary for effective and engaged citizenship, through what the American Association of Colleges and Universities calls "Integrated learning, including synthesis and advanced accomplishment across general and specialized studies demonstrated through the application of knowledge, skills, and responsibilities to new settings and complex problems" (2008, 3). In these contexts, Ettling's (2006) question "Is the primary purpose of education to impart information, construct knowledge, or initiate change?" might well be met with an affirmative response to all the above.

FOSTERING PERSPECTIVE TRANSFORMATION

If education is to impart, inform, and initiate change, it might well scaffold the research-based conditions that support transformative learning. These conditions according to Daloz (2000) include: (a) the presence of others who embody difference, (b) reflective discourse regarding the differing assumptions of each, (c) a community of mentorship, and (d) opportunities for committed action.

Cranton (2006) has identified study of self, others, relationships, context, and leading a critical life as key factors in transformative classrooms. "Although transformative learning is stimulated by any event or experience that calls into question our habitual expectations about ourselves and the world around us," explains Cranton, "when a person is engaged in a serous dialogue with someone she knows, likes, and trusts, the potential for examination of previously uncritically absorbed values and assumptions, is I suggest, much greater" (p. 12).

At what age are students understood to be capable of the cognitive demands of critical reflection? Kegan (2000) identified adulthood as the precipitous age for perspective transformation, as individuals are in adulthood equipped with experience and metacognitive abilities to scrutinize uncritically assumed perspectives about the world. Kegan explains that in adulthood, one goes from being psychologically "written by" the socializing process to "writing upon it," a shift from a socialized self to a self authoring epistemology, in the lingo of constructive-developmental theory (p. 59).

Moreover, Perry (1970) advanced understanding of transformative andragogy—or adult education—through his stage theory about the nature of learning among college students. Perry's four main stages include dualism, multiplicity, relativism, and commitment. Dualism means thinking in either-or terms, which can be developed by engaging learners in the search for multiple valid choices. Multiplicity means viewing knowledge in subjective terms, which can be developed by asking learners to differentiate between well-supported and weakly supported ideas. Relativism means constructing knowledge from a variety of perspectives, and can be developed by asking learners to engage in mindfully evaluating the consequences of ideas and choices. Commitment means accepting an ongoing role of journeying toward understanding of complex ideas and perspectives. In this stage, the learner accepts responsibility for the dynamic contexts, interpretations, and consequences in a pluralistic world.

While transformative learning experiences have indeed been identified as taking place in intercultural travel experiences such as my own Central American teaching experience, my research with contemporary college students suggests that students are experiencing perspective transformation in higher education through classroom interactions, campus events, and field experiences (Glisczinski 2005). Although these experiences are divergent in terms of sources of cognitive dissonance, they converge in being fostered by environments that provide students with the perception of a golden mean of genuine support and hospitable dissonance (Glisczinski 2008). Transformation is thus supported by inviting individuals to engage in responsible risk-taking in environments that scaffold critical analysis, constructive dialogue, and committed action.

CONCLUSION: EDUCATION IN PERSPECTIVE

So that is my story. A decade and a half ago, I set out to work as a new teacher in a distant rainforest village intent to impart information, construct knowledge, and initiate change on behalf of my students. What I experienced, however, was a transforming personal change. The education in perspective was mine.

I offer this story to you as a student, teacher, or stakeholder in education for your reflection. If, upon further consideration, you reason that the principles of transformative learning explained herein might well serve students and society, I encourage you to further read and discuss these opportunities for authentic learning.

I encourage you as students and teachers—cognizant of the demands the world will surely place on its citizens—to answer for yourselves Ettling's (2006) ponderous question "Is the primary purpose of education to impart information, construct knowledge, or initiate change?" (p.61.)

However we each answer this question, there are a few things that we think we collectively know. We know that if information is to be imparted, this information must be informed by multiple, divergent realities. In its absence, we're studying only part of the story. We know that if knowledge is to be constructed, this knowledge must be critically examined, lest our perspectives be inaccurate. And we know that if education is to initiate change, the change must invest in each individual's authentic transformation.

Anything less may be an education in need of perspective.

REFERENCES

Association of American Colleges and Universities. 2008. *College Learning for the New Global Century*. Washington DC: AACU.

Brookfield, S. D. 2000. Transformative Learning As Ideology Critique. In *Learning as Transformation: Critical Perspectives on a Theory in Progress*, ed. J. Mezirow. San Francisco: Jossey-Bass.

Cranton, P. 2006a. Fostering Authentic Relationships in the Transformative Classroom. In *Teaching for Change: Fostering Transformative Learning In the Classroom*, ed. E. W. Taylor. San Francisco: Jossey-Bass.

Cranton, P. 2006b. *Understanding and Promoting Transformative Learning: A Guide for Educators of Adults*. San Francisco: Jossey-Bass.

Daloz, L. A. 2000. Transformative Learning for the Common Good. In *Learning as Transformation: Critical Perspectives on a Theory in Progress*, ed. J. Mezirow. San Francisco: Jossey-Bass.

Daloz, L. A. 1990. Slouching Toward Bethlehem. *Journal of Higher Education* 38, no. 1:2–9.

Ettling 2006. Ethical Demands of Transformative Learning. In. *Teaching for Change: Fostering Transformative Learning In the Classroom*, ed. E. W. Taylor. San Francisco: Jossey-Bass.

Finn, C. 2006. Stuck Between Stations. *Boys and Girls in America*. Santa Monica: Vagrant.

Friedman 2007. *The World Is Flat*. New York: Farrar, Straus, and Giroux.

Herbers, M. S. 1998. *Perspective Transformation in Preservice Teachers*. Unpublished doctoral dissertation, University of Memphis.

Kegan, R. 2000. What "Form" Transforms? A Constructive-Developmental Approach To Transformative Learning. In *Learning as Transformation: Critical Perspectives on a Theory in Progress*, ed. J. Mezirow. San Francisco: Jossey-Bass.

Marx, G. 2002. Ten Trends: Educating Children for Tomorrow's World. *Journal of School Improvement* 3(1).

Mezirow, J. 2000. Learning to Think Like an Adult. In *Learning as Transformation: Critical Perspectives on a Theory in Progress*, ed. J. Mezirow. San Francisco: Jossey-Bass.

Perry, W. G. 1970. *College Student Intellectual Development*. Retrieved February 13, 2009, from http://www.utdallas.edu/dept/ugraddean/theory.html.

Getting Testy: Assessment, Evaluation, and Two Weeks in Kindergarten

—Julia Williams, Ph.D.

Click, click, click, you tap a #2 pencil nervously on the polished desk. You sigh and shuffle your feet on the dusty floor. You listen to coughs, sputters, groans, and the occasional smacks of hands on foreheads that accompany the tick-tick-tick of the big clock on the wall. The unsmiling proctor walks the aisles of aligned desks. Her passing creates the only airflow in the room as she places the test in front of you. You, with your nose down, dart your eyes around, and you wonder whether you studied the right stuff the right way. Will you get enough of the answers right? Will the results of this test reveal competence and potential or incompetence and lack of potential? Will this test tell a positive story, or will it tell a condemning tale? You breathe hard and begin.

We all have tests. As we look at the bigger picture of our lives, we can look back and most likely find a lot of them. In schools, the tests we have taken have perhaps placed us in learning groups and in social groups. School tests have supposedly provided information to us, our teachers, and our schools about what we know, can do, and understand. They have been the basis for grades on our report cards. The tests we have passed or failed have helped to establish our personalities, including our individual ideas about justice and fairness, and they have helped to form our inner pictures about who we are and what we can accomplish. Sometimes the information provided by tests has been accurate and helpful, and sometimes that information has been just plain wrong. What would a collection of all of the tests you have taken in schools tell others about you? What has that collection told you about yourself?

There is power in tests. Tests results in schools are often used to determine who is or who is not on honor roles, admitted to classes, awarded certain privileges, assigned higher or lower grades, or even allowed to enter some schools. Test results are used to decide where money goes for scholarships, rewards, and for support. Tests, in U.S. schools, have traditionally been used to document reasons to favor, discipline, or dissolve. That's a lot of power. Do you believe that the results of tests are a good basis for making decisions about students? Do all students have the same chance to do well on every test?

THE POWER IN ASSESSMENT

If we acknowledge power in the uses of tests, we must also acknowledge the responsibility of the test maker to think carefully in order to make sure that tests can accurately reflect what is learned. The test maker's work should include consideration of the *interpretation* of a score earned. The truth is that the power of tests never really has rested in the test questions or even in the test itself at all. Instead, the real power to decide who is rewarded and who is punished rests in *what we say the scores mean*. It rests in the **inferences** made (Popham 2008). Inferences include the consequences that accompany a score.

Inferences are constructed meanings. For instance, a score of 80 percent could mean that a learner is brilliant in a subject. It could also mean that the learner is below average. That same score on a selected test could allow a learner to enter a particular university, or it could deny entrance. In some classrooms, a score on one test will decide a grade; yet in others, the grade is based on a collection of assessments. In some classrooms, scores on tests have labeled groups of students as "bright and promising" and other groups as "not so bright and promising."

How many times do you think you have been affected by inferences made due to test scores? Have you ever taken a test that did not show your teacher what you did know?

ASSESSMENT, TESTS, AND EVALUATION

Assessment is a word that is often used synonymously for test, which is unfortunate. The word assessment actually comes from the Greek word "assidere," which means "to sit beside" (Wiggins and McTighe 2001, 337). When we choose to look at assessment as a means of conversation with a teacher *sitting beside* a student, we can see that assessment certainly does not need to be a multiple-choice type of test—or even a test at all. In fact, if we see assessment as being a means of communicating understanding and knowledge between teacher and students, assessment can be seen as the answers to the teacher's question, What have you learned? rather than a stamp of approval or displeasure. Assessment, as seen through the frame of a conversation, can become part of the learning/instruction process, as opposed to only being used to judge and to label students.

Assessment and evaluation indeed are, by definition, separate entities. *Assessment* is a measurement of learning. E*valuation* is a judgment, and it assigns a value to the student's performance. Assessment and evaluation, however are rarely far removed from one another in many schools, it seems. I once asked a veteran kindergarten teacher if she could tell which of her little ones were going to excel all the way through school. She told me that her predictions were about 100 percent accurate. I asked her how many months she needed to interact with her precious charges before she could make accurate predictions. She told me that it usually took her about two weeks (Personal communication E. Koski 2005; Williams 2008). How long do you believe it takes for a child to see in the mirror what a kindergarten teacher sees in two weeks? How many classroom tests happen before a child labels himself or herself as a loser or a winner in school?

It is important that we take seriously the classroom teacher's responsibility to separate the tasks of assessment and evaluation in order to give learning a chance to happen before a label is assigned. Teachers, parents, administrators, and students should know that there are many ways to measure student understanding in classrooms and that there are many ways that students can demonstrate what they have learned, starting in kindergarten. It is also important that all of us consider what it is we believe we are communicating when we are using assessment as a means of communication in classrooms, and when it is used to evaluate students and assign a grade to their work.

CLASSROOM-LEVEL ASSESSMENT

Classrooms can provide us with some of the very best possibilities of knowing the most about what each student has come to know in schools. It is in the classroom that the learners, the teachers, and the topics are most directly connected and communicating.

Classroom assessment is the means by which we can measure an individual learner's mastery. It should also let the teacher see whether, what, and to what degree the class as a whole has learned. Quality assessment in classrooms can be seen as dances between what it is that the teacher hopes to have taught and how to best measure that learning—keeping in mind that evaluation need not be always attached to good assessment.

Richard Stiggins (2002) separates the measurements teachers use into two categories: assessments *for* learning and assessments *of* learning. When teachers assess to see whether the class is ready to move on, they are employing assessment *for* learning. Teachers and schools (and governments) that measure in order to make a judgment are employing assessment *of* learning—evaluation. Assessment, when viewed through Stiggins' lens, is the conversation between learner, teacher and the system. Stiggins tells us that if students know where they are expected to go and where they are currently, learning increases more dramatically than with any other factor. If students know what is expected, and how far to go to get there, Stiggins says they can and do arrive. Good classroom assessment provides clear targets and accurately informs the learners how close to that target they stand.

Researchers Wiggins and McTighe (2001) and Stiggins et al. (2004) tell us that our first work as teachers in using assessment effectively is to name the target clearly so that it is visible to all students. The second is to match the named target to forms of measurement that can actually and accurately measure that target best. A third challenge is to decide which of the many conversations (assessments) will be used to pass a judgment, or evaluate a student's performance and assign a grade.

Think for a minute. What was the best test you have ever taken? Have you taken tests that really did a great job of measuring your mastery of a concept or a skill?

That first challenge: to match a clear learning target to an assessment, is more easily done with some targets than with others (Stiggins et al. 2004; Wiggins 1998; Wiggins and McTighe 2001). In a classroom where quality assessment takes place, there is a seamless line between assessment and learning. In other words, learning doesn't stop when assessment happens. Assessment and learning talk to each other, inform one another, and change one another. An "assessment-savvy" instructor learns to dance with at least six forms of measurement and chooses the right partner in order best to measure different types of learning. In classrooms, where the assessment conversation is between teachers and learners, a teacher can and should be able to choose from a menu of appropriate assessment formats to match the best assessment tool with the target learning.

SIX FORMS OF ASSESSMENT

Six forms of assessment from which a classroom teacher may choose might all be familiar to you, and yet you may not have been aware that your teacher was using some of them to measure your understanding. Let's look at these six forms of measurement—selected response, extended response, performance assessment, personal communication, longitudinal measurement, and affective measurement—and see whether you remember how you have been assessed in school, and what forms of assessment best fit your own ways of learning (Chatterji 2003; Gronlund and Waugh 2009; Musial et. al. 2009; Oosterholm 2003; Payne 2003; Popham 2008; Stiggins et al. 2004).

Selected response is only one of many possible assessment tools, yet it certainly is most often used in schools. This type of assessment asks the learner to identify or *select* a correct answer from several provided options, by *matching*, stating whether something is *true or false*, or by completing a statement by choosing the most correct response from *multiple choices*. This type of assessment is very efficient, and it is effective in measuring whether a learner has mastered vocabulary and factual knowledge. If multiple choice, matching, or true/false questions are created carefully, selected-response assessments can also measure types of reasoning skills.

Extended-response assessments can be used to communicate about a learner's capacities to express, compose, solve, organize, analyze, interpret, and combine ideas and concepts. This type of assessment can be restricted, as when you are asked to make a list or fill in a blank. Extended-response assessments can also be open, with no limits on how long the answers should be or how much time they should take to complete. Extended-response assessments, when written skillfully, can provide a teacher with solid insights regarding a student's thinking processes, and abilities to integrate and apply what has been learned.

Personal communication (Stiggins et al. 2004) used as assessment may feel informal to some students, but it is a very powerful assessment for learning. It often takes the form of class discussions, but it also appears as blogs, journals, interviews, conferences, and oral examinations. Personal communications as assessments are effective at revealing misconceptions, rich and personal applications and interpretations of information, and students' unique approaches and points of view regarding concepts presented, and they often provide a chance for one-on-one teaching opportunities.

Longitudinal assessment uses the element of time. Often, it takes the form of a portfolio or a folder, which includes a collection of items and the learner's analysis of those items. Depending upon what the portfolio hopes to measure, artifacts entered in a longitudinal assessment could include tests, journals, pictures, reflections, samples of compositions, products, performances, critiques, evaluations—the list could go on and on. Determining what to place in an electronic or hard-copy portfolio should result from the teacher's target measurement. For instance, if the teacher is using a longitudinal assessment to measure growth over time, the items in the portfolio would be selected to demonstrate that growth. If the teacher is using the portfolio to help a student identify achievement of a standard, the items chosen should be the student's best work. If the purpose of the portfolio is to provide communication to parents about a student's strengths and needs or to document a student's abilities to work in groups, items should reflect those assessment purposes. There are many uses for longitudinal assessment, including measurement of growth, achievement, self-knowledge, project completion, task management, goal setting, and communication. The collection in the portfolio, therefore, should always match the reason for creating it, and the collection itself should only be part of the story. The "assessment" part of a well-constructed portfolio is in the reflection or student narration surrounding the artifacts. Can the student accurately describe the growth, achievement, or skills demonstrated through the collected items?

Performance assessment requires that the learner create a product or a performance. Popham (2008) argues that all types of assessment except selected response could be included in this category if we think about it a bit. However, for our consideration, we will define performance assessment as containing two crucial ingredients: a task and a set of criteria for the product or performance created by the student. Performance assessments could include speeches, musical solos, sculpture, dance, original histories, poetry, and fiction. These assessments could require a learner to create new, more efficient shipping routes, solar energy receptacles, antibiotic protocols, or machines that manufacture better cheese products or other widgets. Performance assessment is valuable in measuring complex outcomes and skills, and it often is motivating in itself, providing relevance and authentic use for the work of the learners.

Affective assessment measures areas of learning that could make a great deal of difference to the teacher when planning instruction and should not be overlooked as part of the conversation between the teacher and the learner. Affective assessment includes measurement of attitudes, interest, orientation, values, beliefs, and desire to learn. Affective assessment, however, should always be anonymous in order to reduce intimidation (Popham 2008), and it is effective when used as pre- and postinstruction assessment to measure changes due to what was taught and learned (Chatterji 2003; Gronlund and Waugh 2009; Musial et. al. 2009; Oosterholm 2003; Popham 2008; Stiggin, et al. 2004).

Which of these forms of assessment are unfamiliar to you? Which forms do you feel best measure your own understandings? Are there some forms that intimidate you?

CLASSROOM EVALUATION AND GRADES

Skilled classroom teachers match a course's learning goals to assessment forms that have the capacities to yield the most valid inferences. For instance, a teacher could choose a portfolio format to reflect growth in student skills at drawing or a portfolio assessment requiring a display of mastery of various drawing techniques. Another teacher could choose to use affective measures to provide insight into students' attitudes toward responsibilities of citizens before and after a unit on voters' rights. In order to provide a rich basis for teachers' decisions, skillful classroom teachers combine various forms of measurement that act as continuous conversations between the teacher and the learners, saying, Here's what I believe that I have taught you, and Here's what I think I have learned.

As teachers, we begin the conversation by naming our targets—What should students know or be able to do after instruction? Then, we can match those targets to the most appropriate forms of measurement in order to make good inferences from the results. As learners, we need to be willing to bring our best efforts and concentration to the assessment conversation.

As our nation moves forward in this global economy, we are going to need all our learners, all the time, leaving no one behind from kindergarten onward. One test, of course, should never be able to tell the whole story of a whole class's experience. We should not even try to define success in school by success at taking narrowly structured selected response tests. We cannot afford to tie our futures only to those individuals who can fill in the right blanks! Ideally, classroom-level assessment should provide the classroom teacher with information from all the learners, and it should also provide the teacher with sets of information to use to communicate levels of achievement to others, including parents, employers, policymakers, other educators, and to the students themselves.

A course grade should always be based on inferences carefully made from strategically selected assessments that represent the student's achievement. The course grade should, ideally, be a valid and meaningful communication about a student's mastery of a course's content (Musial et al. 2009). Have you ever received a grade that did not match your mastery of the course's work? Can you say with certainty what a grade of B in any course can tell you about what a student knows or is able to do?

Determining grades that communicate effectively is a complicated process, asking the teacher to conscientiously make several decisions before the course even begins (Chatterji 2003; Gronlund and Waugh 2009; Musial et. al. 2009; Oosterholm 2003; Payne 2003; Popham 2008; Siggins et al. 2004). Knowing that grades can be used to provide feedback and communication as well as forms of accountability, teachers do need to consider what, exactly, their course grades should reflect. Knowing, also, that grades are sometimes used to sort and label learners, grades should never be assigned without justification.

Stiggins et al. (2004, 308–311) tell us that there are three principles of grading:

1. The purpose of grades is to communicate.

2. Grades communicate about achievement.

3. Grades reflect current levels of achievement.

Musial et al. (2009) tie communication about achievement directly to identified standards, "Grades that reflect valid data based on students' academic achievement related to standards provide an accurate picture for students, parents, and others" (p. 268). Clearly naming the performance, content, and process standards that will be used to assign grades is the first step toward making sure that course grades communicate effectively.

Once standards are identified, teachers should make several more decisions about what will constitute a letter grade. One of those decisions is whether the grades will be criterion-referenced or norm-referenced. If a course grade is *criterion-referenced*, then a performance standard is set before the course begins. If a student attains the standard, the corresponding grade is assigned. In a criterion-referenced course, it is entirely possible that all students could receive As, and it is entirely possible that no students could receive As. A *norm-referenced* course does not set a performance standard. Instead, a norm-referenced course grade depends on a student's performance *relative* to other students' performances. Points or percentages are determined by distribution on a curve. There will always be As, Bs, Cs, Ds, and Fs or other types of even distributions in a strictly norm-referenced course.

Before a course begins, teachers should also consider whether the grade will be holistic or based on separate and distinct criteria. In other words, will the grade be a reflection of a student's mastery of each skill individually, or will it be based on the student's ability to "pull it all together," toward the end of the course? A teacher will also need to determine whether the course grade will be a communication about achievement or if it should also communicate whether the student was compliant in the course. *Compliance* grading includes items such as attendance, tardiness, homework submitted, participation, extra credit, conduct, and whatever the teacher may determine to be attitude or effort exerted. If compliance is included in grade determination, then learning is not the sole criteria for assigning a grade. If compliance is included in the grade, to be clear, the weight and criteria should be communicated to the learner and to all those who would be informed by that grade, including other educators, administrators and would-be employers (Gronlund 2003; Stiggins et al. 2004.).

Once grading criteria has been determined, teachers should make additional decisions in order to choose the most accurate evidence. If the course assessments are well matched to the learning outcomes, teachers will still need to choose which assessments will provide the best information for evaluation. Questions for teachers include whether evaluation should be based on all the assessments over the entire course or on only selected assessments that reveal mastery of the course content at the end of the grading period. Teachers should also consider whether grades should be based on averages, group work, and/or improvement and whether grades should have anything to do with the student's ability to learn.

Gronlund and Waugh's (2009) advice to teachers regarding grades includes making sure that the teacher communicates grading procedures before beginning and that the teacher bases grades only on achievement and on a wide variety of data. Others advise that grades should provide as accurate a picture of learning as possible and that grading procedures should provide means by which students can improve. Still others warn us that grades should first do no harm (Chatterji 2003; Gronlund and Waugh 2009; Musial et. al. 2009; Oosterholm 2003; Payne 2003; Popham 2008; Stiggins et al. 2004).

What do you think about grades that include compliance as well as performance? What about extra credit? What grading procedures have you encountered that were not helpful to your learning? Have you been graded in situations that were harmful or biased?

SOMETHING TO THINK ABOUT

Making good assessments and giving valid grades should never be easy. Grades, scores, and the power they carry to communicate, sort, and label should not rest easily on the shoulders of educators. There is no scientific, empirical, and bulletproof means by which totally objective assessments can be created or by which grades can be assigned. The power and responsibility to judge and evaluate student achievement lie with the creator of the assessments, the interpreters of the scores, and the ones who decide which measurements count and how much they count. Who are those people in your world?

How does it happen, do you think, in schools that serve a nation where all things are possible, that an experienced kindergarten teacher can accurately predict which of her little ones are going to do well and which are going to do poorly for the next twelve years? What does that tell us about how we use assessment and evaluation in our classrooms and in our school systems? What do you think could or should happen differently in the way we assess and evaluate so that all kindergarten predictions do not necessarily need to come to pass for your students or for the next generation of school children? Grant Wiggins (1998) tells us that, "Assessment reform is essentially a moral act" (p.17). Do you agree?

REFERENCES

Chatterji, Madhabi. 2003. *Designing and using tools for educational assessment.* Boston: Allyn & Bacon.

Gronlund, N.E. 2003. *Assessment of student achievement,* 7th ed. Boston: Allyn & Bacon.

Gronlund, N.E., and Waugh, C.K. (2009). *Assessment of student achievement,* 9th ed. Upper Saddle River, NJ; Pearson.

Marzano, R. J. 2003. *What works in schools: Translating research into action.* Alexandria, VA: Association for Supervision and Curriculum Development.

Musial, D., Neiminen, G., Thomas, J., Burke, K. (2009. *Foundations of meaningful educational assessment.* Boston: McGraw-Hill Higher Education.

Oosterhoff, A. 2003. *Developing and using classroom assessments,* 3rd ed. Upper Saddle River, NJ; Merrill Prentice Hall.

Payne, D.A. 2003. *Applied educational assessment,* 2nd ed. Belmont, CA: Wadsworth Thompson.

Popham, W. James. 2008. *Classroom Assessment: What teachers need to know.* Boston: Allyn and Bacon

Stiggins, R. J., Arter, J. A., Chappuis, J., and Chappuis, S. (2004). *Classroom assessment for student learning.* Portland, OR; Assessment Training Institute.

Wiggins, G. 1998. *Educative assessment: Designing assessments to inform and improve student performance.* San Francisco: Jossey-Bass.

Wiggens, G., and McTighe. 2001. *Understanding by design.* Upper Saddle River, NJ: Merrill Prentice Hall.

Williams, J. M. 2008. *Jules on schools: Teaching, learning, and everything in-between.* Duluth, MN: Clover Valley Press.

Literacy Education

—C. W. Johnson

"[T]he reader's own disposition will never disappear totally; it will tend instead to form the background to and a frame of reference for the act of grasping and comprehending. If it [the reader] were to disappear totally, we should simply forget all the experiences that we are bringing into play as we read—experiences which are responsible for the many different ways in which people fulfill the reader's role set out by the text"(Iser 1978).

I enjoy the texture of books. From my childhood, I can recall the shelves of books in my parents' home, the spines and cloth coverings of history books in the living room, the patchwork kaleidoscope of children's books on the varnished pine shelves in the boys' bedroom, and the metal shelves of books atop glass flooring in the old Carnegie library in my hometown. My love of reading, and even my competence as a reader, is in many ways contingent on the knowledge that readers bring to text before they read. As Iser (1978) argued in *The Act of Reading,* no theory of literacy—the process of reading and writing texts—can proceed without attention to the ways that readers use their prior knowledge. What readers know before they attempt to construct meaning from texts is crucial, so in this sense literacy is a deeply autobiographical process, one built on many complex, nuanced, and even messy interactions, skills, and understandings.

Those who teach for literacy must always remember the crucial role of prior knowledge in determining the reader's dispositions toward reading. Academic research in reading and cognition since the 1970s has emphasized the role that prior knowledge plays in reading comprehension (Dole et al. 1991; Stahl 1998). This role, and the correlated roles of reader questions, activation of knowledge, and readers' use of schema, represents a dramatic shift from previous paradigms of learning from text. Bruner (2004) instructs us that in the 1920s, E. L. Thorndike popularized the practice and repetition mode of teaching for modern educators, where students would learn content by rote, "as you would were you memorizing non-sense syllables" (2004, 17). The practice dates largely from the twenty-five years between 1875 and 1900, when associationist psychologists sought to reduce learning to elemental associative correspondences between the empirical world and knowledge in the brain. In this period, learning exercises frequently became lengthy lists of words to be associated, but there was little room for learner construction of understanding (Bruner 2004, 15). The Cognitive Revolution brought down learning theory (behaviorism) in the 1960s (Bruner 2004; Flavell 1999), offering a different paradigm of knowledge acquisition. This early cognitive paradigm used the model of computer science to suggest how information (inputs) was processed by brains (computers) to produce outputs (knowledge).

This computer science model, while useful, was gradually replaced by cognitive models stemming from the work of Piaget and Vygotsky, models that invoked biology to a greater degree than information processing paradigms (Flavell 1999). With this new conception of learning came a greater emphasis on learner's active construction of knowledge. Within the cognitive revolution we can see the roots of reading research interest in the relevance of prior knowledge to reading comprehension. Grisham and Wolsey (2008) cite Bartlett (1932) and Smith (2004) as reading theoreticians who argued for the fundamental role of prior knowledge in reading comprehension. Prior knowledge is crucial to a cognitive model of constructing meaning from text; indeed, rich background knowledge provides for rich comprehension (Santa, Havens, and Harrison 2008).

I've loved words and language for as long as I can remember, so it is no surprise that I've made literacy—the process of reading and writing texts—the centerpiece of my lifework. I remember writing my name with parent prompting at age four, and I remember my parents' reading to me rapidly segueing into an early fascination with reading and books. Experts on reading suggest that print and texts must be present in the formative years of children, the years so instrumental to the acquisition of literacy, for the fullest fruition of reading development. Because of my intense early interaction with texts of all kinds, it is true today that my senses are alive to every possible texture, shape, color, and pattern of books, and the words of the pages are inexorably linked in my mind with all this sensory information. This was true for me, but it is also true for all would-be readers. Affective and sensory information play a critical role in the interactions between caregivers and children. According to Piagetian theory this sensorimotor stage is the foundation for all later learning. Although some call this stage of development preliteracy, one need only see the rapt attention of a child listening to *Goodnight Moon* or interacting with *Pat the Bunny* to understand how important the twin roles of sensory input and positive affective feedback are in beginning the journey of literacy.

Emergent literacy is the next stage for learners acquiring the ability to read and write. Learners gain a new awareness and a new cognitive map or schema—one that more explicitly links the sounds of a language with the existence of words on a page. This is alphabetic awareness and skill, a stage where learners develop recognition of the names and sounds of letters, as well as their representation on a page, what we might call orthographic skill. As learners gain a sense of the correspondence between sounds as heard in the language and letters and word parts as represented on a page, they are acquiring phonological awareness, the awareness that sounds in a language correspond with letters, word parts, and whole words in printed texts.

Phonics, a systematic pedagogy for instruction in phonetic patterns, is what many people associate with the process of learning to read. Phonics as a gateway to reading provokes a complicated and ambivalent response from me. I learned to read early, and I quickly immersed myself in a variety of texts at home and in school; fortunately, both places were print-rich environments that motivated and rewarded my reading. Like other readers, I experienced the acquisition of phonological awareness, but I did not need the instrumental approach to it that is the staple of some reading programs. Not surprisingly, I remember being bored and frustrated by instruction in phonics in first and second grade. I did not appreciate basal readers (in my day, Dick and Jane books) and I resented the fact that much of our reading class focus became the sounding out of words, which constituted essential practice for readers less skilled than I was. I also remember being among the first U.S. students exposed to phonics instruction via *Sesame Street* and *The Electric Company*, and I preferred to go to the library rather than watching television "about how to read."

Faltering steps in the phonological process create problems for readers it seems, as the wiring that sets up the ear-eye correspondence between what is heard in language and what print does is a halting and labor-intensive process. Decoding, something that we all do at one time or another (who has not had to sound out a word?) is built on this complex set of skills. Science suggests that not all readers will succeed in this stage at the same rate, so, of course, the arbitrariness of grade-level reading expectations in the first years of school can play havoc with readers whose phonological development happens slowly.

Shanahan (2005) argues that the importance of phonics might be greater for language learners in grades K–2 and much less effective for later learners. From this perspective, comprehension becomes the goal and concern of grades 4–12 in our schools, a stage or "reading to learn the new" (Chall 1983). I concur with this emphasis on the proper role of phonics, as far as developmental progression goes, but for different reasons than the one Shanahan offers. Shanahan says that this "falling off" in phonics effectiveness has to do with the structure of English and the nature of texts. I offer this alternative possibility—that phonics instruction is most effective as the culmination of Piaget's sensorimotor stage in young learners and an effective transition to the concrete learning stage. There is brain-based research evidence that seems to confirm this view; that is, the period of myelinization of neural sheaths, synaptic proliferation, and increased integration of the 4- to 6-year-old brain modules all lend themselves to phonics instruction being effective for a significant (but brief) developmental period. In my interpretation, systematic phonics instruction makes sense as a good match for a particular biological period of developmental period. Wolf (2007) makes this point in *Proust and the Squid: The Story and Science of the Reading Brain*. She points out that phonics fits into the developing brains of learners who have been introduced to the social and emotional richness of a text-rich environment.

Effective teachers of this age group need a sound understanding of how phonics instruction can be integrated into the whole learning experience of acquiring literacy in the early grades. Wilson et al. (2004) argue for this kind of judicious and integrated approach, pointing out that exclusive use of phonics methodology may not encourage learning of comprehension of "whole texts." I sympathize with this, as someone who learned from whole texts rather early. Even so, I would not argue that phonics is unnecessary merely because I skipped through the decoding quickly during my own acquisition of literacy.

Later, learners acquire the building blocks of literacy, the thousands of words that allow successful interactions with literate conventions—signs, picture books, storybooks, fairy tales, and informational books. Here, the social discourse and the realities of economic life can have a gritty and difficult effect on the less fortunate within society. A study at the University of Kansas revealed the critical role of early experiences in prompting a literate trajectory.

I guess it is no surprise that I became a student of literature, a 7–12 language arts teacher, and, now, a literacy educator. At the same time, I am cognizant that word recognition, while easy for me, is not similarly easy for other learners and readers. At this point in my life and career, word recognition is not phonics, but it is *morphological*; that is, my knowledge of word origins, word parts, denotation, and connotation provides a toolbox of approaches for comprehending words and reading a variety of challenging texts.

The conventions of print, as well as the assumptions of sociocultural discourse, represent ways readers rely upon prior knowledge to negotiate texts. According to the Rand Reading Study Group, the physical or organizational elements of a text have a large impact on readers' success with negotiating the text with comprehension (2002, in Robinson and McKenna 2008). Anderson cites Armbruster (1984) in reminding us that writers must consider the prior knowledge of their readers as they determine the focus of a text intended for a particular audience. In this respect, decisions about audience by writers and decisions about text selection by teachers include a critical element of prior knowledge assessment. For teachers, using prereading strategies such as the K-W-L chart designed by Ogle or the anticipation guides advocated by Beers (2003) are ways of establishing the appropriate match between readers and texts. Some texts may be considered more or less considerate in terms of prior knowledge; for instance, an "inconsiderate" text may fail to account for the real interests, skills, or knowledge schemata of readers (Armbruster 1984, in Alexander and Jetton 2000, 289). When a teacher plans for the appropriate level of skill building and scaffolding to provide readers, instruction with texts will include consideration of the physical features of the text, including genre, manuscript format, technical vocabulary, and graphic representation.

Furthermore, educators must assess the source and nature of student motivation—how motivated a learner is to make sense of a new text can depend on discourse specific or sociocultural factors that include prior knowledge. Gardner (1991) argues that the intellectual assumptions of a discipline may often be implicit, and readers will not see or know the relevant prior knowledge within an academic domain. What are implicit skills for an expert may be completely hidden for novice readers within a particular domain or discourse. Gee (2001) shows how students misread the texts of secondary discourses as they come to an unfamiliar discourse with different implicit assumptions about text. Classroom teachers can alleviate this prior-knowledge "trap" by successfully invoking, and explicitly teaching, the skills or strategies that connect readers' prior knowledge to the implicit demands of a new text (Alexander and Jetton 2000). Such practice effectively creates scaffolding from readers own knowledge to *knowledge to be learned*, a pedagogical aim consistent with Vygotskyan theory (1978) and the work of Bruner (1991).

Some challenges for adolescent readers can be ascribed to sociocognitive factors. Chief among these is the issue of relevance, authenticity, affect, and motivation. Adolescent readers often encounter a struggle caused by texts that strike them as irrelevant or only poorly connected to their lives. Next, many teen readers confront too many tasks related to texts and comprehension that are inauthentic tasks; that is, the things they are asked to do with texts lack 'real-world' purpose, and adolescent learners resist committing themselves to these unrealistic purposes. Next, many adolescent readers need teachers to engage them in emotional and social issues that involve the readers' emotional affect and motivation for finding meaning. For example, some teens may no doubt be able to read *King Lear,* but the problems of the play may be less relevant for teens than the existential angst of Salinger's *A Catcher in the Rye,* or Wiesel's *Night.* Without this connection of relevance, challenging reading may be lost on teens when they are not engaged emotionally. Finally, many teen readers have had aversive experiences with texts, and may see themselves as inveterate failures as readers. Given the great premium that teens place on competency among peers (and even among adults, although they'll rarely admit it!) this aspect of struggling with reading can crush student motivation, and perpetuate an aversive affect to the reading experience.

A second layer of challenges for adolescent readers may stem from challenges related to prior knowledge. As we've discussed elsewhere, the cognitive work of reading comprehension is made vastly easier when readers have relevant prior knowledge. Cognitive load theory suggests that readers who still struggle with fluency may not readily do the work of comprehension—there aren't enough free circuits, if you will, for the brain to do this work readily. The work of inference and prediction is lost on readers who are not skilled or fluent with these explicit tasks of comprehension. Successful readers may do these tasks implicitly, of course, but this prior knowledge/schemata effect is invisible to the struggling reader, and too few classrooms successfully address this by teaching careful reading comprehension strategies. Finally, many adolescents struggle with the leap from storybook, narrative, of fiction genre work in the primary grades to demanding expository prose in the middle and upper grades. The conventions of print, the vocabulary challenges, and the internal organization of expository prose effectively conspire to thwart readers' progress. Without skillful teaching, this problem creates its own vicious circle, and students continue to struggle, with the result that the sociocognitive factors discussed earlier get activated yet again, and readers lose motivation and interest in texts.

A traditional model of adolescent pedagogy is transmissive in nature; that is, students come to the teacher to "receive" texts, which are taught to them. Moreover, school curricula, for a variety of reasons, many of them good ones, employ classic or traditional texts that reflect the narrative of the canon in Western civilization. This model has its place, but it is not sufficient for authentic engagement with a variety of texts in a diverse world.

At a foundational level, the teacher of a diverse classroom must understand that various psycholinguistic factors will affect learners' work with texts in English. A student's L1 language will have phonological and syntactical factors that affect work in English, and, of course, family culture and heritage may affect student interest and engagement with texts that describe unfamiliar sociocultural realities. A caring classroom teacher of adolescents has to approach the multicultural nature of texts, literacy, and society in a very thoughtful way. Teachers can offer students exercises where cultural contrasts are graphically represented with work in one or more languages (Cummins et al.). I think this is a place where good teachers do some metacognitive modeling, where they teach different texts, whether *Macbeth* or *The Way to Rainy Mountain*, as discussed in our text (Glazier and A-Seo 2005) in ways that include active discussion of what it means to view life and stories through the lenses of one cultural perspective or another. Ideally, students are given authentic, meaningful opportunities to demonstrate and explore their own cultural heritage and assumptions, and opportunities to connect this part of their prior knowledge to the work of reading diverse texts. Teachers need to create models of the variety of perspectives within literature and must be careful to discourage the objectification of multicultural literature in ways that keeps the texts *outside* the experience of the learners.

Teachers who use multicultural texts and who teach diverse learners, as most do today, must engage the social and cultural realities of all learners. As Cummins et al. (2005) assert, a teacher who embraces the identities of diverse students will be more effective and will likely find ways to connect the teaching of texts to learners' real lives. By teaching about cultural constructions of knowledge and understanding, teachers can help students make sense of diverse texts. Even better, good teachers find ways to help students activate their own schema, knowledge, and cultural inheritance in ways that enrich the reading and comprehension of new texts.

A reader's readiness to tackle the work of comprehension depends on prior knowledge and will predict the reader's ability to organize and systematically store knowledge, a vital factor in recall. We have mental representations of the world, which we activate to tell what's going to happen next. The more such representations that we have and the more flexibility we have in manipulating those representations, the more success we will have in accommodating new understandings or making successful inferences. In a 2002 review of reading comprehension research, Snow et al. argue for instructor sensitivity to the factors that combine to create text comprehension specifically, and understanding, generally: "Appropriate instruction will foster reading comprehension, which is defined two ways–the comprehension of the text under current consideration and comprehension capacities more generally" (Robinson and McKenna, 2008, 67). This comprehension work—the business of asking questions, sorting patterns, and adjusting schmemas, all involving prior knowledge—probably represents a reading stage beyond the skill set of decoding and phonological awareness. McKenna and Robinson write that according to Paris and colleagues, ". . .[A] certain threshold of decoding and memory would need to be exceeded before strategies such as skimming, rereading, using context, planning, paraphrasing, and summarizing could "play [a significant role in children's reading comprehension" (Robinson and

McKenna 2008, 74). This is analogous with research into the notion of cognitive load; that is, readers who are juggling the work of word-sound correspondence or decoding will have relatively few cognitive resources left for deep processing of comprehension tasks. Readers who have these skills, but who have few skills or strategies for the cognitive work of comprehension, will tend to have superficial understandings. This is akin to the transmission model of reading described by Schraw and Bruning (1996).

Ideally, readers learn ways to use prior knowledge, a relevant and meaningful text, and new understandings that they gain from that text to create an integrated system of new knowledge. Ivey and Fisher argue that in this sense, part of the relevant work of incorporating prior knowledge theory in instruction is choice of texts that connect to students actual sense of the world: "If we want students to comprehend what they read, we must begin by letting them experience texts that make sense to them" (Robinson and McKenna 2008, 101).

In the case of a specific discipline such as science, prior knowledge might make all the difference in a student's ability to organize and synthesize text. In science, background knowledge is vital, because science courses often demand of students that they "... survey an entire field of knowledge" (Santa, Havens, and Harrison 2008, 240). It is crucial that teachers in technical fields such as science invoke strategies that help students utilize prior knowledge so that the demanding informational content of courses is not lost on uncomprehending readers. Santa, Havens, and Harrison pose four questions that all teachers of science reading might well utilize:

1. How can I help students figure out what they know or don't know about a topic?

2. How can I help students assess the accuracy of their background knowledge?

3. What knowledge do my students need before they read? Or what misconceptions need to change before students read?

4. What do I want students to focus on during the assignment? (p. 240).

Questions and hypothesis-making strategies are crucial to the integration of prior knowledge in reading comprehension. Pressley (1992) has been instrumental in attempting a comprehensive research project into the relationship of prior knowledge to strategies of questioning by student readers and teachers. He states, "Generating answers to thought-provoking questions may promote learning by activating relevant prior knowledge" (1992, 101; Pressley 2006). Pressley argues that the amount by which questions help learning is a function of how consistent questions are with prior knowledge and new material to be read and learned (1992, 102; Pressley 2006). In his review of empirical work in this area, Pressley notes that questions that are answered with elaborated and justified answers do a better job of improving learning from text. This is consistent with theory—the more readers fully integrate their answers about text with what they already know about the world, the deeper the learning result we might expect to see.

Specific prior knowledge strategies such as textual conventions, organizational schemata, and active questioning are all related to an overarching theme in comprehension instruction. All effective instruction with prior knowledge in mind is a matter of making reader knowledge explicit._ Cunningham and Shagoury (2005) identify specific strategies for improving reading comprehension that relate strongly to prior knowledge theory. Instructional plans should afford opportunities for *making connections between the texts and the readers' lives.* Students and teachers should frequently engage in *asking questions* to transact with the text in meaningful ways. Students need explicit instruction in *determining importance*, which may be understood as an active process of relating prior knowledge to what is important to acquire as new knowledge. Finally, like Smith (2004), Cunningham and Shagoury emphasize the importance of *inferring*, or making a connection between what is known and what is likely to happen next in the text. Deep comprehension may be understood as *synthesis*, or using what is known by a reader prior to reading and extending it to a new comprehensive understanding (Robinson and McKenna 2008, 96).

By contrast to the constructivist inclinations of many researchers into prior knowledge and reading comprehension, some reading researchers are confident that the instrumental, rote-skills models of explicit phonics instruction are what work at elementary levels; for these practitioners, all reading instruction must be explicit and guided, downplaying comprehension strategies in favor of "specific guidance" (Williams 2006, 139).

Williams's intensely structural and instrumental model of instruction might be understood as an example of "reading first" pedagogy, which in 2001 became the official reading policy of the U.S. Department of Education, so, of course, it is very relevant to practicing teachers. Only future research will be able to show whether or not this emphasis on teacher-directed instruction will improve literacy, given its caveats about independent reading and student-generated interactions with texts.

By contrast, other researchers into cognition and reading offer a more constructed notion of human learning, one more amenable to prior knowledge theory. Steven Pinker (1997) is an advocate of phonics instruction and a psycholinguist whose rules-based models of cognition help to define our understanding of language and brains today. This vision would seem to fly in the face of holistic visions of literacy, yet it comes down on the side of a more integrated approach to reading, one that offers language that is congruent with a prior knowledge theory: "The goal of education should be to provide students with new cognitive tools for grasping the world" (p. 29). Stahl (1998) argues against the pure "theory" of whole language advocates but makes the following case for balanced, and even eclectic, approaches: ". . . an effective teacher of reading has to understand how reading develops, in all of its manifestations. This involves deeper understanding of the development of automatic word recognition, comprehension, and motivation and appreciation and skill in weaving these various goals into a coherent program" (p. 61).

Allington (2005) reiterates this point of view from the perspective of a reading pedagogy specialist who has actively protested the pedagogy of highly scripted and instrumental reading pedagogy: "Good teaching, effective teaching, is not just about using whatever science says 'usually' works best. It is all about finding out what works best for the individual child and group of children in front of you" (p. 462). Rich models of the mind, and of the development of literacy through the active engagement with altering and building knowledge, are vastly preferable because they emphasize the constructive nature of knowledge. Lee (1997) argues:

> *This approach to conceptualizing knowledge and learning differs dramatically form traditional accounts that take learning to be a matter of accumulating discrete items of knowledge—as though knowledge comes in concrete pieces that can be sorted, counted, stored in mental boxes or filing cabinets, valued or audited in quantitative terms. . . . or even given by one person to another Beck and Olah 2001, 99).*

Prior-knowledge theory is among best practices for teachers (Daniels and Zemelman 2004), but it also represents good science in the context of what we now understand about the human brain, the evolution of language, and the ways we are probably "wired" to learn. Pinker, the psycholinguist who has revolutionized interest in the evolution of language and the brain, is careful to show how vital context, intention, and meaning are to understanding language: "Cognitive neuroscientists must get the whole person to behave, and any bit of language behaviour must recruit many abilities at once: words, grammar, meaning and knowledge, intentions to speak or believe what is spoken. . . ." (1997, 548). Zull (2001) develops a model of student instruction based on holistic models of the brain and cognition, models that call the senses, emotions, reflection, and action into play. Instead of being antiscientific, this holistic model is actually based on brain biology.

And finally, all reading is a matter of making sense of new text in terms of what we already know about the world and about the ways that texts relate to our prior knowledge. Bruner cites Krech as emphasizing that human learning "is hypothesis driven, not just passive registration" (2004, 18). This is consistent with the prior-knowledge reading research of Pressley, who is deeply interested in empirical investigation of student questioning and hypothesizing about text. Pressley et al. stress how often postreading strategies emphasize superficial aspects of learning and do not force students to do the "deep processing" that relates prior knowledge to new learning (1992, 92) "What a reader knows prior to approaching a text is a key factor in whether that reader will be able to understand and transform the concepts found in text to new crystallized knowledge or learning" (Grisham and Wolsey 2008, 388).

Reading is messy meaning-making that draws upon the rich cognitive resources of human brains. Books and texts cannot be reduced to simple formulaic algorithms. Books are messy. I filled my college dorm rooms with them, and they collected dust and took up too much space until I had to send them home. I spent college beer money sending books around the U.S., and I never stopped shaping a collection of ideas and texts.

Apartment after apartment and home after home—each place was the sensory and physical chaos of boxing and unpacking and shelving and unshelving hundreds of books. Messy, perhaps, but messy in a way that is the epitome for me of meaning. We can tell our life stories through our literacy generally and our libraries specifically. For me, each book I read, each book I collect, is a piece of a larger narrative that is my journey for understanding. I like to think of understanding as a collection of chaotically juxtaposed ideas and images, and my books are my handhold on this messy system of relationships. The places where one book touches another are real to me, as are the spaces between books, the failed connections where one text falls short of meeting another. Like the literacy theorist David Barton (2007), I can think of my books and my reading as interdependent practices and artifacts within an ecological system. In such a system, all the skills, all the practices of reading, and all the texts function in complex ways to create a whole system where no single factor functions alone. In this system, prior knowledge is the key to better literacy because it is the essential habitat for healthy reading development.

As Iser enjoined us to do, we now understand that readers do not approach texts as black boxes receiving inputs. Because of this, prior-knowledge theory and research should play a vital role in our approach to pedagogy for reading comprehension. Any attention to helping readers learn to read is a good thing, but formulaic or mechanical approaches to literacy rarely match the authentic literacy narratives of actual readers. Books are alive and messy, as is life itself, and so is the process of becoming a more fluent, agile, and comprehending reader.

REFERENCES

Alexander, P. and Jetton, T. 2000, Learning from text, A multidimensional and developmental perspective. In *Handbook of reading research*, 4th ed., ed. D. Pearson. Mahwah, NJ: Lawrence Erlbaum.

Alexander, P.; Schallert, D. and Hare, V. 1991. Coming to terms: How researchers in learning and literacy talk about knowledge. *Review of Educational Research* 6, no. 3:315–343.

Barton, D. 2007. *Literacy: An Introduction to the ecology of language.* Malden, MA: Blackwell.

Beers, K. 2003. *When kids can't read: What teachers can do.* Portsmouth, NH: Heinemann.

Bruner, J. 1991. The narrative construction of reality. *Critical Inquiry* 18, no. 1:1–21.

Bruner, J. 2004. A Short history of psychological theories of learning. *Daedalus* (Winter, 2004).

Chall, J. 1983. *Stages of reading development.* New York: McGraw-Hill.

Daniels, H., and Zemelman, S. 2004. *Subjects matter: Every teacher's guide to content-area reading.* Portsmouth, NH: Heinemann.

Dole, J.; Duffy, G.; Roehler, L. and Pearson, D. 1991. Moving from the old to the new: Research on reading research comprehension. *Review of Educational Research* 61 no 2:239–264.

Flavell, J. 1999. Cognitive development: Children's knowledge about the mind. *Annual Review of Psychology* 50:21–45.

Gardner, H. 1991. *The Unschooled mind: How children think and how schools should teach.* New York: Basic Books.

Gee, J. 2001. Reading as situated language: A Sociocultural perspective. *Journal of Adolescent and Adult Literacy* 44, no. 8:714–725.

Grisham, D., and Wolsey, T. 2008. Literacy and technology integration in the content areas. In *Content area reading: Instructional strategies* 3rd ed., ed. D. Lapp, J. Flood, and N. Farnan 237–256. Mahwah, NJ: Lawrence Erlbaum Associates.

Iser, W. 1978. *The Act of reading: A Theory of aesthetic response.* Baltimore: Johns Hopkins University Press.

Lee P. 2001. Language in thinking and learning: Pedagogy and the New Whorfian Framework. In *Perspectives on language and literacy*, ed. S. Beck, and L. Olah. Cambridge, MA: Harvard University Press.

Pinker, S. (1997) Words and rules in the human brain. *Nature* 387 (June 5,1997): 547–548.

Pressley, M. (2000). What should comprehension instruction be the instruction of? In *Handbook of reading research, ed. Kamil et al.* Mahwah, NJ : Lawrence Erlbaum.

Pressley, M. 2006. *Reading instruction that works: The Case for balanced teaching.* New York: Guilford.

Pressley, M.; Wood, E.; Woloshyn, V.; Martin, V.; King, A. & Menke, D. 1992. Encouraging mindful use of prior knowledge: Attempting to construct explanatory answers facilitates learning. *Educational Psychologist* 27, no. 1:91–109.

Robinson, R. and McKenna, M. 2008. *Issues and trends in literacy education.* Boston: Pearson.

Santa, C., Havens, L., and Harrison, S. 2008. Teaching secondary science through reading, writing, studying, and problem solving. In *Content area reading and learning: Instructional strategies,* 3rd ed., ed. D. Lapp, J. Flood, and N, Farnan. 237–256). Mahwah, NJ: Lawrence Erlbaum Associates.

Schraw, G., and Bruning, R. 1996. Readers' implicit models of reading. *Reading Research Quarterly* 31, no. 3:290–305.

Smith, F., and Goodman, K. 1971. On the Psycholinguistic method of teaching reading. *The Elementary School Journal* 71:177–181.

Stahl, S. 1998. Understanding Shifts in Reading and Its Instruction. *Peabody Journal of Education* 73 3/4,:31–67.

Williams, J. 2006. "Stories, Studies, and Suggestions About Reading." *Scientific Studies of Reading* 10, no. 2:121–142.

Zull, 2001. *The Art of changing the brain.* Sterling, VA: Stylus.